AFRICA'S
Great Wild Places

AFRICA'S
Great Wild Places

CHRIS AND TILDE STUART

SOUTHERN
BOOK PUBLISHERS

Title page: A maze of necks and legs – lesser flamingos at Lake Bogoria. PHOTO: NIGEL DENNIS.
Above: A Hyperolius *reed frog male doing its best to attract a mate in the Kibale Forest, Uganda.*
Opposite: Elephants have suffered considerable declines over much of their African range but they still survive in substantial numbers in some of the great wild places. PHOTO: GERALD HINDE.
Contents page: The Kalahari Gemsbok National Park is one of the few places on earth that gives one that feeling of aloneness and unspoilt wilderness. PHOTO: AFRICA WILDLIFE FILMS.

ISBN 1 86812 670 6

First edition, first impression 1998

Published by
Southern Book Publishers (Pty) Ltd
PO Box 3103, Halfway House, 1685

Cover design by	Alix Gracie
Cover photograph by	Martin Harvey, ABPL
Maps by	CartoCom, Pretoria
Designed and typeset by	Alix Gracie
Set in	10/12pt Bembo
Reproduction by	Hirt & Carter Repro, Cape Town
Printed and bound by	National Book Printers,
	Drukkery Street, Goodwood,
	Western Cape

For our parents ...

A C K N O W L E D G E M E N T S

Firstly, thanks must go to Louise Grantham of Southern Books for
suggesting this title, and to Kate Rogan for seeing the manuscript through its various stages.
Marina Pearson is thanked for editing the manuscript. But the biggest thanks of all must go to
the African continent, with its immense diversity, those still intact wild places
and the greatest influence in our lives.

CONTENTS

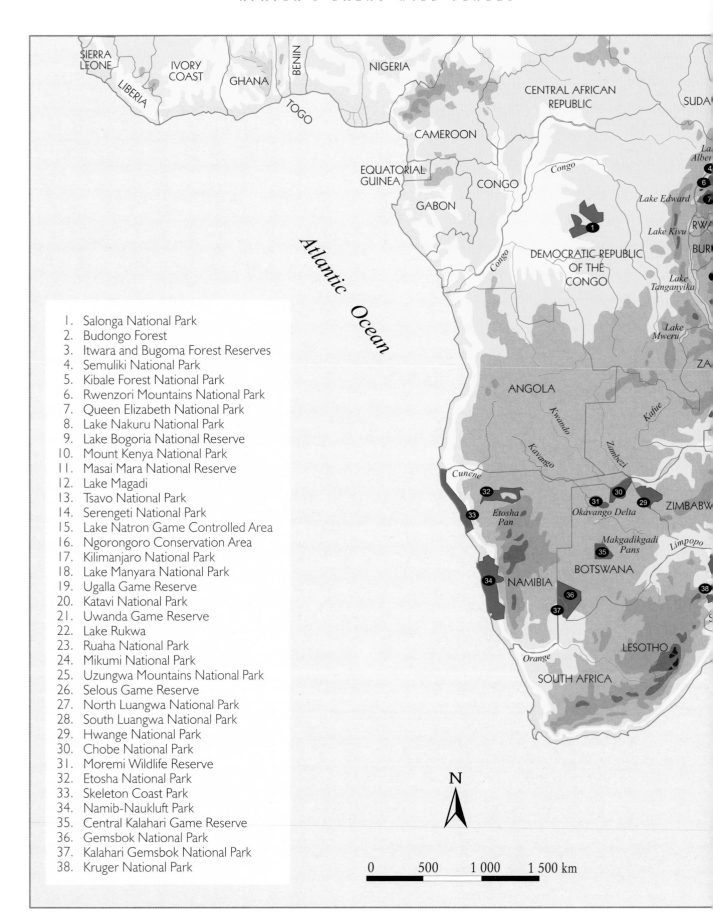

1. Salonga National Park
2. Budongo Forest
3. Itwara and Bugoma Forest Reserves
4. Semuliki National Park
5. Kibale Forest National Park
6. Rwenzori Mountains National Park
7. Queen Elizabeth National Park
8. Lake Nakuru National Park
9. Lake Bogoria National Reserve
10. Mount Kenya National Park
11. Masai Mara National Reserve
12. Lake Magadi
13. Tsavo National Park
14. Serengeti National Park
15. Lake Natron Game Controlled Area
16. Ngorongoro Conservation Area
17. Kilimanjaro National Park
18. Lake Manyara National Park
19. Ugalla Game Reserve
20. Katavi National Park
21. Uwanda Game Reserve
22. Lake Rukwa
23. Ruaha National Park
24. Mikumi National Park
25. Uzungwa Mountains National Park
26. Selous Game Reserve
27. North Luangwa National Park
28. South Luangwa National Park
29. Hwange National Park
30. Chobe National Park
31. Moremi Wildlife Reserve
32. Etosha National Park
33. Skeleton Coast Park
34. Namib-Naukluft Park
35. Central Kalahari Game Reserve
36. Gemsbok National Park
37. Kalahari Gemsbok National Park
38. Kruger National Park

N

0   500   1 000   1 500 km

ETHIOPIA

SOMALIA

Lake Turkana

KENYA

Jubba

Shebele

Tana

9

10

8

11

12

15

17

13

16

18

ZANIA

24

25

26

e
awi

Ruvuma

ZAMBIQUE

Indian Ocean

MADAGASCAR

0 - 200 m
200 - 400 m
400 - 1 000 m
1 000 - 1 500 m
1 500 - 2 000 m
2 000 - 3 000 m
over 3 000 m

River
Lake
Conservation Area
International Boundary

INTRODUCTION

All experience is an arch wherethro'
Gleams that untravelled world, whose margin fades
For ever and for ever when I move.

Alfred Tennyson, *Ulysses*

We had to ponder long and hard before finally deciding which "great" game parks and "wild" areas we would include and which we would exclude from this book. The dictionary defines *wild* as uninhabited or desolate but we decided that another definition better suits our ideas – intensely enthusiastic! A *wilderness* is "a wild, uninhabited, uncultivated region", and *great* indicates a place "of larger size or more importance than others". In the end our choice became very personal, although we admit to having included some places with reluctance: Kruger National Park by definition is a great game reserve but it has become, in our eyes, a bit of a circus. Although it contains areas away from the tourist pressures, nevertheless the park is highly managed. Sadly, in future the only conservation areas in Africa that are likely to survive the onslaughts of humans are those that are managed, controlled and adequately financed.

More than 400 conservation areas on the continent can be considered to be of major importance, with the total area receiving real or paper protection reaching almost 990 000 km². However, those parks and reserves in West Africa and through the Sahel belt, which separates the Sahara Desert from the rest of Africa, have almost without exception been abused or threatened to a greater or lesser degree. The

Manovo-Gounda-St Floris National Park in the Central African Republic has lost most of its elephant population and all its black rhinos, and nomads from Sudan and Chad have moved large numbers of cattle across its unfenced boundaries. Tai Forest National Park in south-western Ivory Coast has been invaded by thousands of refugees from neighbouring Liberia, hunting and timber extraction are rife and also illegal mining flourishes. The same problems, and worse, exist in the Mount Nimba Strict Nature Reserve on the border of Ivory Coast and Guinea. The Nigerian parks are all but written off by the international conservation community as many have been settled by agriculturalists and pastoralists and very little remains of that country's once prolific wildlife. Even its national bird, the black crowned crane, probably no longer breeds within the national boundaries, with only a few now entering the extreme north in passage. The Sahel and its wildlife have been dealt a series of blows from which they are unlikely to recover – severe drought aggravated by removal of the once extensive woodlands, and uncontrolled hunting through easy access to firearms both outside and inside conservation areas. Within West Africa and the Sahel many species, including a broad spectrum of antelope, are on the brink of extinction. Some unfortunates number in the low hundreds. With few exceptions, the circumstances that exist in the parks in this region are unlikely to improve; if anything conditions will worsen as the human population continues to explode and make greater demands on natural resources. We could cite similar problems in parks in Sudan, Congo, Gabon and many other countries, but instead we will focus on some of Africa's finest conservation areas and wild places. However, we should never lose sight of the fact that what is wild and great today could be facing the same problems in the future.

It is not always the direct activities of people within the parks and reserves that encourage their slide into the abyss but also actions that take place outside. Even such a highly managed park as South Africa's Kruger has seen once perennial rivers stop flowing during the dry season as a result of water extraction for agricultural and industrial use. The Djouj National Park in Senegal and Ichkeul in Tunisia have suffered irreversibly from the changing of natural water regimes. With the erection of the veterinary cordon fences that stretch over hundreds of kilometres in Botswana, tens of thousands of head of game died as they were no longer able to travel their traditional migration routes to new grazing grounds and water. A number of parks, mainly in southern Africa, are now completely fenced. They include Kruger and Etosha. Apart from severing seasonal migration routes, fencing causes populations of some species to increase to unsustainable levels and culling is frequently the only reasonable option.

Within the East African tourist circuit an additional problem is the impact that large numbers of visitors have on many parks. Two of our least favourite parks lie in Kenya: they are Masai Mara and Amboseli – we can already hear the howls of protest! The migration of white-bearded wildebeest and plains zebra as they enter Masai Mara from Tanzania's Serengeti is a natural event of the top order but the hordes of safari vehicles harassing the animals at the already hazardous Mara River crossings are sickening. Here and in Amboseli the drivers go where they will with a total disregard for the vegetation and wildlife. These in our eyes are no longer great game parks, nor can they be given the labels of wild places. Neither is likely to see us again. We had reservations about including Masai Mara in this book but the park cannot be divorced from the Serengeti ecosystem, so here it is. Likewise with the Ngorongoro Crater, but again it is a small part of a much bigger conservation area that is truly a great game reserve and a wild place.

Below: Once widespread in sub-Saharan Africa, the lion is increasingly restricted to large conservation areas.
Bottom: Many plant species occur on the slopes of the equatorial snow peaks, with diversity decreasing with altitude.

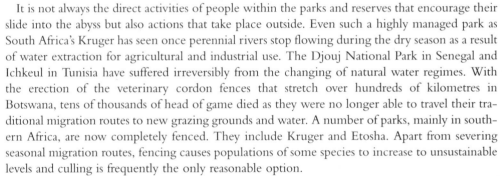

Readers may find it strange that we have included the necklace of soda lakes that lie in the bed of the Great Rift Valley. These constitute some of the most hostile habitats known, but a select few thrive here, including the greater and lesser flamingos – exclusive "masters of the primordial soup". One vast area that probably has the right to the title of a truly wild place is the Sahara Desert, but we had a number of reasons for leaving it out. How does one decide on which areas to select for coverage? To tackle the Sahara as a whole would require several volumes with many more pages than this book has. There is the Aïr Massif in Niger, sometimes called the "Alps of the Sahara", a mountain range that covers 80 000 km² and rises to 2 300 m above sea-level. But this shrinks into insignificance when compared to the Ahaggar Mountains of southern Algeria, which extend over a staggering 550 000 km² and have never been fully explored. There is the massive Tibesti range in northern

Chad and the Tassili N'Ajjer to the north of the Ahaggar. The volcanic massif of Emi Kussi, rising to 3 415 m, is the Sahara's highest point. Then there are the great sand dune "oceans", or ergs, such as the Grand Erg de Bilma which reaches from the northern shore of Lake Chad to the southern fringes of the Tibesti Massif, and the Western Great Erg which smothers 45 000 km². Another reason for our deciding not to include any Saharan wild places is that its once amazingly prolific wildlife is virtually no more. The great herds of scimitar-horned oryx, addax and gazelles have been decimated by a combination of drought, competition for food with increasing numbers of camels, sheep and goats, and most seriously uncontrolled hunting by heavily armed and vehicle-equipped nomads. Where game could once be counted in the tens of thousands, today there are fewer than 500 each of oryx, addax and at least two gazelle species. The Barbary sheep, a denizen of the Saharan mountains and hills, was once abun-

dant, yet despite the harshness and difficult terrain of their chosen habitat they have also been greatly reduced by hunting. Just a few thousand years ago the Sahara received more bountiful rains than it does today and early humans recorded in rock paintings an array of wild beasts that they hunted across what is today desert. Here were elephants, giraffes, rhinos and hippos!

We know that not all readers will agree with our choice but this was a personal journey to a few of our favourite areas, not just for the wildlife but also because these are places where humans rarely intrude. What is a wilderness experience to some is but a journey to the fringes of civilisation to others. A person from London, Cape Town or New York may regard a visit to Kruger National Park as a visit to wildest Africa and the thought of journeying to a paradise (in our eyes) such as Uwanda or Ugalla in Tanzania as horrific. This is the beauty of many truly wild places: few make the journey. Unfortunately, many of these wild places are also paradise to such "human-unfriendlies" as the disease-carrying tsetse fly and mosquito and even big beasties such as crocodiles, lions, buffalo and elephant that might eat or squash the unwary. Long may they all remain, with guardian tsetse watching over all and keeping Africa's great cattle herds at bay!

The lists of species to watch for are based on "a good place to see them as there are plenty about", or the only really "ease of access" place to see them, or they are rare but you have a fair chance of spotting them. Our idea of "specials" may not concur with lists of others, but they constitute a personal choice.

Above: It is hard to define a truly wild place, as it means different things to different people. To us, perhaps a large shady tree overlooking a floodplain, game and birds, and no people for days on end.

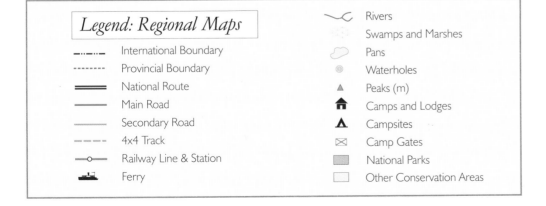

Legend: Regional Maps

▬ ▪ ▬ ▪ ▬ International Boundary	∿ Rivers
------- Provincial Boundary	Swamps and Marshes
═══ National Route	Pans
——— Main Road	⊚ Waterholes
——— Secondary Road	▲ Peaks (m)
- - - 4x4 Track	🏠 Camps and Lodges
—o— Railway Line & Station	▲ Campsites
🚢 Ferry	⊠ Camp Gates
	▦ National Parks
	▢ Other Conservation Areas

Chapter 1

KRUGER NATIONAL PARK

THE PRESSURES OF POPULARITY

Because I see these mountains they are brought low,
Because I drink these waters they are bitter,
Because I tread these black rocks they are barren,
Because I have found these islands they are lost;
Upon seal and seabird dreaming their innocent world
My shadow has fallen.

Kathleen Raine

The savanna baboon troop was foraging along the south bank of the Shingwedzi River, pulling out small clumps of grass and carefully wiping off the earth against their forearms before biting off the roots, plucking small dark berries from low bushes and scratching in the soil – possibly for seeds or small insects. Apart from the occasional contact mutter, the only sounds were from the birds and a lone cicada – suddenly this peace was shattered by a high-pitched scream, loud barks from two males threatening each other. Was this just a disagreement, or was there more involved? One of the males suddenly dashed across the road and in one hand he clutched a still feebly flut-

tering Swainson's francolin, the other big fellow in hot pursuit. The pursued male had no chance to outdistance the opposition and dropped the bird, which was immediately snatched up by what turned out to be the troop leader. He walked a short distance, sat on his haunches in the shade of a fig tree and proceeded to tear the francolin apart, eating the flesh with gusto.

Our feelings about the world famous Kruger National Park are ambiguous: on the one hand we are awed by its diversity of species, on the other we are depressed by the pressures people are placing upon it! It is indeed a great game reserve in the truest sense

and it is without doubt one of the most frequently visited conservation areas in Africa but with its commercial airfield, network of tourist "villages" and the interlinking web of roads, supermarkets, restaurants and traffic police it is no longer our idea of wild Africa. However, this is the price that has to be paid for its very survival. It faces pressures from a burgeoning peasant-farming population on its western border, the serious effect of commercial agriculture on river-flow, increases in river and airborne pollution, and the spread of alien pest-plant species. There are demands for the restitution of land rights in some parts, opening up the park for grazing and firewood col-

Above: Although Kruger is bisected by several important west-east flowing rivers, a number that previously carried water throughout the year no longer flow during the dry season. This change in water regime has resulted from the extraction of water by upstream farmers and industrialists before the rivers enter the park.

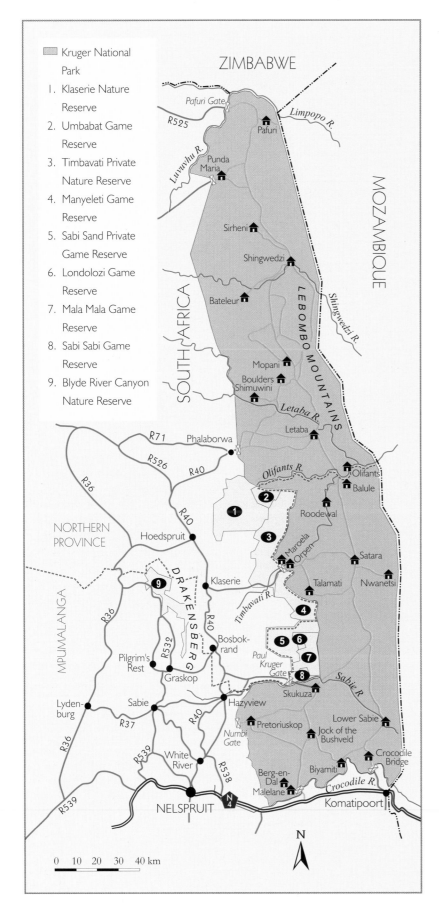

Kruger National Park

1. Klaserie Nature Reserve
2. Umbabat Game Reserve
3. Timbavati Private Nature Reserve
4. Manyeleti Game Reserve
5. Sabi Sand Private Game Reserve
6. Londolozi Game Reserve
7. Mala Mala Game Reserve
8. Sabi Sabi Game Reserve
9. Blyde River Canyon Nature Reserve

lection and increasing tourist developments on its fringes. Only in very recent years have management practices such as elephant culling, necessitated by the park's being completely fenced, been drawn into the public forum. We reason that perhaps it is good to have a few parks such as Kruger, Masai Mara and Amboseli drawing the big crowds, in order that the pressures are eased on other conservation areas.

Prehistory

It is only relatively recently that real interest has been shown in the prehistory of the Lowveld area now encompassed by the Kruger National Park, and quite a history it is! The earliest Stone Age inhabitants are believed to have lived and hunted in this area at least as far back as half a million years before present, to be followed by Late Stone Age and Iron Age peoples. Evidence of their passing remains in rock paintings that have been ascribed to the San and are of relatively recent origin, and the more than 300 Iron Age sites, some of which date back at least 1 500 years before present. Some of the more recent Iron Age sites, with their hilltop locations, extensive stone walling and stone-built structures, are believed to belong to what has come to be known as the Zimbabwe Culture. A number of these sites, including Thula Mela, Matjigwili and Makahane, have been extensively studied. Apart from evidence of iron smelting, it has been discovered that at Thula Mela, occupied between the 7th century AD and the early 17th century, the inhabitants were smelting and moulding gold. This represents the first evidence of indigenous gold production and working in South Africa. Iron smelting was undertaken as late as the 19th century by the baPhalaborwa people near the park's western boundary. Activities such as gold and iron production in the area have been, in part, ascribed to the fact that the local people were unable to keep cattle because of the abundance of the tsetse fly and the dreaded disease *nagana* which it transmits.

History

A Dutch East India Company expedition led by Francois de Kuiper in 1725 is believed to have been the first European incursion into the area we now know as the Kruger National

Far left: A young square-lipped rhinoceros attended by a yellow-billed oxpecker. Kruger now has the largest number of these once endangered rhinos, even exceeding that of Hluhluwe/Umfolozi in KwaZulu-Natal.

Left: Male tree agamas during the breeding season are brightly coloured but at other times they resemble the greenish-brown, black marbled females. Although most of their time is spent in trees they will readily descend to the ground to feed.

Below: The smallest and one of the commonest of Kruger's seven species of hornbill, the red-billed hornbill occurs throughout but reaches its highest densities where game numbers are highest, where it seeks food among droppings and heavily grazed vegetation.

Park. The purpose of this exploratory journey was to investigate trading possibilities and trade routes that might link the Mozambique coastline with the interior. But at Gomondwane the expedition found themselves in a skirmish with a hostile tribe and they hotfooted it back to the coast.

Chronology and details on early explorations of the area prior to 1725 are not accurately known but it is probable that undocumented expeditions by Portuguese and possibly even Arab traders did take place. The next documented white-led expedition involved two parties of *Voortrekkers* – Dutch-speaking settlers seeking their own land away from British domination – who crossed the central park area, following the Shilowa and Mbhatsi gorges into Mozambique.

With the discovery of gold in 1869, to the west of the present-day park boundary, there was a major influx of Europeans, including farmers from the interior who exploited the abundant winter grazing, and an array of adventurers, hunters and traders. From an abundance of game at the time of the "discovery" of that pernicious metal (remember indigenous people had been working gold and living in the area for centuries), within but a few years game numbers dwindled dramatically. The area was generally unsuitable at that time for permanent settlement or year-round

pastoralism, because of malaria, sleeping sickness, *nagana* and African horse sickness; traders in passage and hunters were transients.

President S.J.P. Kruger of the *Zuid-Afrikaansche Republiek*, who had hunted in the Lowveld in his youth and as a young man, became alarmed by the dwindling game numbers in his former stamping grounds and in 1884 he proposed the establishment of a game sanctuary in the Lowveld. But at that time he was very much a lone voice in the wilderness and it was only on 26 March 1898 that his vision became a reality with the proclamation of the land lying between the Sabie and Crocodile rivers as a game sanctuary.

The 4 600 km² of the Sabie Game Reserve and the smaller Shingwedzi Reserve were the forerunners of what was to become the almost 20 000 km² Kruger National Park. Two game rangers were appointed in the short period leading up to the second Anglo-Boer War, but during that bloody chapter in South Africa's history the new reserve was nowhere near the top of the priority list. Fortunately the new British authority reproclaimed the reserve and appointed Major (later promoted to Colonel) James Stevenson-Hamilton as its first warden. He was to remain in his post for more than 40 years and he nursed the reserve through many serious teething problems; in fact, without his diligence, perseverance and strong will it is

questionable whether Kruger National Park would have survived to the present day. When Stevenson-Hamilton took up his post some species had been greatly reduced in numbers through hunting, including buffalo, giraffe, hippopotamus and rhino, with elephant only occasionally visiting from neighbouring Mozambique. By 1904, a scant two years later, he had wrested control from the hunters and poachers and the time of recovery had begun. However, his efforts were not appreciated in many circles and it was only on 31 May 1926 that the game reserve was given upgraded status as a national park, and assigned the name of Kruger National Park in honour of its instigator, "Oom Paul" – President Kruger. This new park incorporated the Sabie and Shingwedzi game reserves and the 70 privately owned farms that separated them. The pri-

mary problem faced by the park's first warden was to seek out a reason for the conservation area's existence, other than conservation for conservation's sake, and this he was to find in its tourist potential. During the year 1936 some 26 000 visitors made use of the growing road network and rustic restcamps. Today well over half a million visitors per year make the pilgrimage to Kruger.

Geography

Kruger National Park, the largest conservation area in South Africa, runs for approximately 350 km from north to south, and averages 60 km in width. Its eastern boundary is shared with Mozambique and for much of this distance follows the low hill range of the Lebombos. In the north the park is separated from Zimbabwe by the Limpopo River and in the south the Crocodile River is the barrier between it and commercial farmland. The western boundary abuts communal land and extensive private game reserves, whose eastern boundary fences have been removed to allow free movement of game to and from the park.

Much of the park consists of flat to slightly undulating plains, bisected by a number of perennial rivers that drain from west to east and end their journey in the Indian Ocean. These include the Luvuvhu, Letaba, Sabie and Olifants. There are also numerous annually flowing rivers, of which some eight carry significant quantities of water during good rain

Below: Cattle egrets at ease on a plains zebra. These egrets frequently forage for insects disturbed by game animals, such as elephant, buffalo and antelope, as they feed. The ungulates benefit by having alert avian eyes warning them of the proximity of predators.

Above right: With the onset of the rains, there is a proliferation of mating and breeding activity in the insect world, and some of the most prominent are the larvae of the many species of butterfly and moth that occur in the park.

Below right: Many species of grasshopper are known to occur in Kruger, including members of the bush locust group; here a mating pair showing the considerable disparity in size of male and female.

years. Altitudes range from 122 m above sea-level to 839 m at Khandizwe in the south: no great mountains here. Apart from the Lebombos there are rocky outcrops scattered throughout the park.

In its broadest sense the geology of the park can be divided into two principal units, with granitic rocks dominating the west of the park and basalts to the east. These differences greatly influence the vegetation structures as the basaltic zone produces dark soils with a high clay content and the granites erode into sandy, light-coloured substrates. Rainfall also has a strong influence on the vegetation, with the highest falls occurring in the south-west and averaging 760 mm per year, decreasing by as much as 200 mm on the central plains but again rising to some 640 mm in the north-west. The lowest falls are recorded in the extreme north as one enters the Limpopo River basin and in dry years may barely scrape over 200 mm.

Flora

In the east of the park, and running much of its length, is a belt of varying width consisting mainly of open grassland and different open woodland communities. To the south lies a variety of woodland types, each with its own dominant tree species. In the west, in the vicinity of the Olifants River and northwards, the mopane *Colophospermum mopane* dominates. Only in the north can the great gnarl-barked baobabs be seen. This is one of Africa's most distinctive and unusual trees; the many holes and crannies in its lava-like bark and fibrous trunk offer safe havens to many animal species. Fruit bats are among its principal pollinators and several insectivorous bat species are recorded as using this tree as a roost. It is also a popular sleeping venue for the bushbaby and a number of owl species, with Böhm's and mottled spinetails frequently building their nests in these noble patriarchs.

The major watercourses are lined by riverine woodland which includes many large wild fig trees. In swampy or water-logged soils the tall yellow-barked acacia, or fever tree, occurs in loose woodland stands. This tree with its yellow-green bark takes its alternative name from the belief of early travellers and explorers that they caught the dreaded malaria from this plant, little knowing that it was the wet, swampy ground in which it grew that provided ideal breeding grounds for the *Anopheles* mosquito,

Above: *The Olifants River, one of the park's most important watercourses, traverses the centre of the park and is a focal point for many species, particularly during the dry season.*
Below: *Crested barbets are common and widespread in the park but are largely absent from the extensive tracts of mopane woodland in the north.*
PHOTO: JOHN CARLYON

S P E C I E S   T O   W A T C H   F O R

M A M M A L S

Elephant	*Loxodonta africana*	Nyala	*Tragelaphus angasi*
Hippopotamus	*Hippopotamus amphibius*	Common reedbuck	*Redunca arundinum*
Square-lipped (white) rhinoceros	*Ceratotherium simum*	Sharpe's grysbok	*Raphicerus sharpei*
		Lion	*Panthera leo*
Hook-lipped (black) rhinoceros	*Diceros bicornis*	Leopard	*Panthera pardus*
		Cheetah	*Acinonyx jubatus*
Plains zebra	*Equus burchellii*	Spotted hyaena	*Crocuta crocuta*
Giraffe	*Giraffa camelopardalis giraffa*	Wild dog	*Lycaon pictus*
Buffalo	*Syncerus caffer*	Black-backed jackal	*Canis mesomelas*
Impala	*Aepyceros melampus*	Dwarf mongoose	*Helogale parvula*
Tsessebe	*Damaliscus lunatus lunatus*	Banded mongoose	*Mungos mungo*
Lichtenstein's hartebeest	*Sigmoceros (Alcelaphus) lichtensteini*	Slender mongoose	*Galerella sanguinea*
Common waterbuck	*Kobus ellipsiprymnus ellipsiprymnus*	Peters's epauletted fruit-bat	*Epomophorus crypturus*
Greater kudu	*Tragelaphus strepsiceros*	Four-toed elephant shrew	*Petrodromus tetradactylus*

B I R D S

Ostrich	*Struthio camelus*	Palm swift	*Cypsiurus parvus*
Goliath heron	*Ardea goliath*	Giant kingfisher	*Ceryle maxima*
Woolly-necked stork	*Ciconia episcopus*	Brown-hooded kingfisher	*Halcyon albiventris*
Saddle-billed stork	*Ephippiorhynchus senegalensis*	Southern carmine bee-eater	*Merops nubicoides*
Marabou	*Leptoptilos crumeniferus*	Little bee-eater	*Merops pusillus*
Knob-billed duck	*Sarkidiornis melanotos*	Lilac-breasted roller	*Coracias caudata*
White-backed vulture	*Gyps africanus*	Trumpeter hornbill	*Bycanistes bucinator*
Lappet-faced vulture	*Aegypius tracheliotus*	Southern ground hornbill	*Bucorvus leadbeateri*
African hawk-eagle	*Aquila fasciata*	Crested barbet	*Trachyphonus vaillantii*
Martial eagle	*Polemaetus bellicosus*	Arrow-marked babbler	*Turdoides jardineii*
Bateleur	*Terathopius ecaudatus*	Heuglin's robin	*Cossypha heuglini*
Black sparrowhawk	*Accipiter melanoleucus*	Yellow-breasted apalis	*Apalis flavida*
Little banded goshawk	*Accipiter badius*	Barred warbler	*Camaroptera fasciolata*
Dark chanting goshawk	*Melierax metabates*	Fan-tailed flycatcher	*Myioparus plumbeus*
Double-banded sandgrouse	*Pterocles bicinctus*	Wattle-eyed flycatcher	*Platysteira peltata*
Green pigeon	*Treron australis*	Gorgeous bush-shrike	*Malaconotus quadricolor*
Brown-headed parrot	*Poicephalus cryptoxanthus*	Long-tailed shrike	*Corvinella melanoleuca*
Purple-crested turaco	*Tauraco porphyreolophus*	Red-billed helmet-shrike	*Prionops retzii*
White-browed coucal	*Centropus superciliosus*	White-bellied sunbird	*Nectarinia talatala*
Scops owl	*Otus senegalensis*	Red-headed weaver	*Malimbus rubriceps*
Pearl-spotted owl	*Glaucidium perlatum*	Cut-throat finch	*Amadina fasciata*
Giant eagle-owl	*Bubo lacteus*	Golden-breasted bunting	*Emberiza flaviventris*

Right: *The impala lily with its fleshy stem and branches, resembles the much larger baobab tree. Although in Kruger they seldom exceed 1 m in height as a result of grazing by herbivores, elsewhere through their extensive African and southern Arabian range they may reach 3 m.*

the carrier of malaria! Of the 2 000 or so species of plant recorded in the park, more than 200 are true trees and there are some 235 species of grass.

Fauna

The diversity of the fauna of the Kruger National Park is great indeed and is known to include some 148 mammal species, 114 reptiles, 33 amphibians and more than 520 species of bird. This park is probably the most intensively surveyed and collected large conservation area in Africa. There is little of its soils and rocks, rivers and swamps that have not felt the hands and feet of scientists and naturalists recording and documenting its biota. It is certain that if such poorly known conservation areas as Selous and Ruaha in Tanzania or Garamba and Salonga in Democratic Republic of Congo received such dedicated attention, similar, if not greater, totals would be realised. Be that as it may, there is no doubt that Kruger is well endowed with fauna!

Culling

Because the park is entirely fenced, although not resistant to a determined elephant looking for greener pastures, it has been policy until recently to maintain the numbers of elephant and buffalo at what was believed to be optimum for the carrying capacity of the vegetation and for balancing the interests of all species. The policy of culling in the park dates back to 1903. From that time to 1958 large predators, in particular lion, wild dog and spotted hyaena, were targeted in the belief that this would give a chance of recovery to the grazers and browsers. Between 1903 and 1958 a total of 2 486 lions were killed, and in a controversial culling programme in 1975, kept quiet initially by the park authorities, 62 lions and a number of spotted hyaenas were shot in a limited area. It would seem that these cullings had little overall impact on the large predator populations. Today it is estimated that the park holds more than 1 500 lions (one of Africa's largest populations, possibly second only to Serengeti), 2 000 spotted hyaenas, perhaps as many as 900 leopards, 300 cheetahs and approximately 350 wild dogs.

But the culling of elephants has raised the ire of a whole battalion of animal-rights groups both locally and internationally. It is an indication of the fickle and strange nature of the human animal *Homo sapiens* that outcries for the banning of any elephant culling in Kruger rang loud and clear throughout the world but the poor old buffalo, of which substantial numbers are killed each year to maintain a population of about 25 000, cow-like as it is, receives not a dot of sympathy!

Managers try to maintain the elephant population close to 7 500 individuals. This necessitates the culling of the equivalent of the annual growth rate, which lies between 300 and 560 individuals. Animal-rights advocates offer the alternative solution of capturing surplus animals and translocating them to other parks and game farms, but in southern Africa the options are severely limited. In any case,

when small numbers have been translocated to reserves and farms, what happens when they increase to the point of overpopulation? Another non-lethal solution being investigated is the development and use of contraceptives for elephants, but as far as we are aware not a great deal of progress has been made in this potentially expensive direction.

The worldwide ban on the sale of elephant ivory, put in place largely because of the inability of the East African authorities to

curb illegal hunting, means that a once important source of income for the park is no longer available, and the outcry for culling alternatives places a further financial burden on the authorities. Weep for the buffalo!

Burning

Despite its size the Kruger National Park is probably the most intensively managed large park in Africa. Its staff undertake burning as it is argued, and probably correctly, that this is necessary in order to sustain substantial game numbers. Fire maximises plant productivity and serves to retard woody plant growth, which keeps large tracts of grassland and open woodland available to those ungulates that favour this type of habitat; without burning bush encroachment would take place and be detrimental to the survival of many "tourist-visible" species.

Above left: *A "creche" of impala fawns avoiding the midday heat. The impala is the most abundant antelope occurring in the park, with well over 100 000 animals. They form an important component of the diet of many predators.*
Above: *Leopards occur throughout the park but are not often seen by visitors; this can be attributed to their secretive nature, superb camouflage and solitary habit. It is not known exactly how many leopards roam here but it could be as high as almost 1 000 individuals.*

The entire park is divided into 300 blocks for burning and about one third of the park is put to flame each year, although some sensitive vegetation types and habitats are excluded. This high level of management ensures excellent game and bird viewing.

Birds

With more than 520 bird species recorded in Kruger, of which more than 100 are considered to be vulnerable in the rest of South Africa, this is one of the subcontinent's premier "twitchers' meccas".

Those tourists who "hunt" the big five, the "dreaded dust-dashers", are unlikely to see much of the abundant bird life (nor likely to be interested in it). Those who bide their time at waterholes or wander the camps and picnic sites are generally rewarded. A typical exchange as you are sitting peacefully watching a pair of saddle-billed storks feeding near one of the river fords, when a saloon car screams to a halt next to you in a cloud of dust, with radio blaring (goodbye storks!), is: "Where are the lions?" "There are none, we were watching two storks." "Is that all!" Windows wound up, flying gravel and gone!

The future

In recent years there has been increasing talk of the "superpark" concept, which would involve the linking of conservation areas. Kruger has been a forerunner in these discussions. The idea is to link Kruger with Gonarezhou in Zimbabwe, and proclaim a vast tract of adjacent land in Mozambique and add it to the conservation real estate. This would enable the authorities to remove the eastern boundary fence, allowing free movement of species such as elephant, and would obviate, at least for a while, the need to cull surplus animals or dally with putting the pachyderm cows on the pill. Even the poor old buffalo could disperse and halt the need to can its (delicious!) meat and turn its hide into fancy shoes and briefcases!

Kruger National Park faces numerous problems, some that may even involve its long-term survival in its present form: its rivers are drying up and it accommodates more and ever more tourists, making it difficult to justify the statement that the environment and its various components come before people. To some it has become a glorified zoo, to others a wilderness experience; we lean towards the former!

Below right: The crested guineafowl, with its curly crest and bright red eye, skulks among riverine vegetation in smaller flocks than its helmeted cousin.
Bottom: Buffaloes and elephants feeding in open woodland. The buffalo are predominantly grazers but elephant eat a wide range of plant foods, with large quantities of grass being consumed seasonally.
Far right: The visitor to Kruger seldom sees a snake, but they are common and most, like this rhombic egg-eater, are harmless to man. As their name implies they live on bird eggs, which are swallowed and then crushed in the throat, the shell being regurgitated after the content has been swallowed.

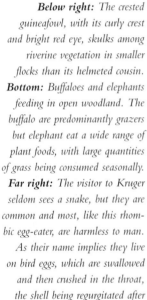

KRUGER NATIONAL PARK

Travel and access: Kruger National Park has eight public entrance gates. From north to south they are:

PAFURI: From Louis Trichardt take the N1 northwards, and after about 60 km turn right onto the R525 towards Tshipise; continue past the Aventura Tshipise Resort to the Pafuri gate, which is approximately 130 km from the N1. The nearest camp, Punda Maria, is about 60 km further on.

PUNDA MARIA: From Louis Trichardt take the R524 eastwards, through Thohoyandou, to reach the gate after about 140 km. Punda Maria Camp is 8 km further on.

PHALABORWA: From Pietersburg follow the R71 eastwards for 214 km, passing through Tzaneen and the town of Phalaborwa before reaching the gate. The nearest camp is Letaba, 50 km further on.

ORPEN: From Tzaneen in the north or Nelspruit in the south follow the R40 to Klaserie, then take the clearly signposted turn-off to Orpen and continue for 45 km to the gate. Orpen Camp is situated near the gate.

PAUL KRUGER: From the R40 turn onto the R536 near Hazyview and continue for about 45 km to the gate. Skukuza is located 13 km further on.

NUMBI: From Nelspruit take the R40 to White River, then follow the R538 for approximately 25 km before turning right onto the R569; continue for 7 km along this road to Numbi gate. Pretoriuskop lies 8 km further on.

MALELANE: From Nelspruit follow the N4 towards Komatipoort and after about 70 km take the clearly signposted left turn to the gate, which is 3 km further on. The nearest major camp is Berg-en-Dal, 12 km away.

CROCODILE BRIDGE: From Nelspruit follow the N4 towards Komatipoort for about 110 km before turning left to Crocodile Bridge gate, which is about 10 km further on. The camp of the same name is a short distance from the gate.

SKUKUZA has an airfield which is served by regular commercial flights to and from Johannesburg.

Mobility: There is an extensive network of game-viewing roads. The main roads between camps are tarred; other roads are gravel but well maintained and suitable for all types of cars. A few of the low-lying gravel roads may be flooded in summer. Some gravel roads are not accessible to cars towing caravans, but these are clearly signposted.

Accommodation: Kruger National Park has 24 restcamps, ranging from huge to small and private. Available are 6-bed family cottages, 2- and 3-bed huts, with bathroom or with communal facilities, and caravan and campsites with communal cooking facilities and ablution blocks. Almost all camps have electricity. Many cottages and huts have airconditioning.

Skukuza is the largest camp and houses the park's headquarters. It is almost a small town with restaurants, shop, bank, post office, conference facilities, a library, information centre, resident doctor and garage with workshop.

Satara, Shingwedzi, Pretoriuskop, Olifants, Mopanie, Lower Sabie, Letaba and *Berg-en-Dal* are medium to large camps providing different types of accommodation and almost everything a traveller might need.

Orpen is a small and quieter camp close to Orpen gate, *Punda Maria* is a small camp in the far north. *Balule*, a small camp on the Olifants River, has 3-bed huts with no refrigerator or electricity. There is an ablution block and a caravan and camping site, but no shop and no fuel.

Boulders, Jock of the Bushveld, Malelane, Nwanetsi and *Roodewal* are fully equipped private camps. Each must be booked as a unit by one group.

Maroela campsite, overlooking the Timbavati River near Orpen, accommodates 20 caravans and is administered by Orpen Camp.

Bushveld camps are slightly larger than private camps and offer accommodation in fully equipped, serviced huts; these huts may be reserved individually. Supplies and fuel must be purchased in the nearest large camp. The following camps fall into this category: *Bateleur, Biyamiti, Shimuwini, Sirheni* and *Talamati*.

Other facilities: An extensive network of game-viewing roads; waterholes and dams which make game-viewing particularly rewarding during the dry winter months; picnic sites with hot water for tea or coffee. Six wilderness trails: a maximum of 8 people meet their ranger guide and set out for the 2-day, 3-night trail. Each is based at a bush camp where accommodation, bedding, eating utensils and food are provided, and from which daily walks are undertaken. These trails must be booked in advance.

Climate: The winter months – April to September – are generally dry, with the rains falling during the summer – October to March. Winter days are mild but the nights can be cool to cold, whereas summer days can be very hot and the nights warm.

Best times to visit: The dry season is best for game-viewing, when animals frequent the permanent water points, but the peak time for bird-watching is during the rains when species diversity is boosted by influxes of breeding and non-breeding migrants.

Main attractions: Great species diversity; excellent dry season waterhole watching; most comprehensive infrastructure and facilities of any major African conservation area – if that's what you are after! Ease of access.

Hazards: Malaria; potentially dangerous animals on occasion, although infrequently, enter the fenced camps at night – we have seen lion, leopard and spotted hyaena; large numbers of tourists increasing the risk of car accidents.

For further information: National Parks Board

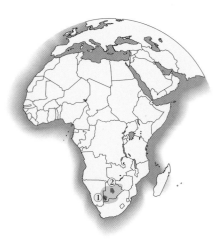

①   *Gemsbok National Park*
②   *Central Kalahari Game Reserve*
●   *Approximate extent of the Kalahari*

Chapter 2

THE KALAHARI

SEA OF RED SAND

You throw the sand against the wind,
And the wind blows it back again.

William Blake, *Mock on, mock on, Voltaire, Rousseau*

Winter mornings can be harsh in the Kalahari, when the cold wind blows across the dunes and along the dry river beds. Lions seek out sheltered sites among the calcrete caps of the riverbanks and the black-backed jackals curl themselves into a ball, burying their snouts in their warm belly fur. The only obvious activity is from the doves and the Namaqua sandgrouse winging in to drink at the overspill from the reservoir. Birds preening and resting in the surrounding trees are also feeling the cold, and those on the ground

have their feathers puffed out, perhaps a little less alert. This is when the female gabar goshawk sees her chance, and it is all over in a blur and a cloud of dove feathers. The gabar carries her prey to the branch of a great old camel thorn, possibly one of her habitual "plucking-blocks", and proceeds to clean her meal. But as she starts to feed, the smaller male gabar suddenly descends from the upper branches intent on getting his share. The female objects. An impressive protective display, with wings partially opened over the

hapless dove, is enough to see her mate off.

It is believed that the name Kgalagadi was derived from the Bakgalagadi tribe who once inhabited the area of the southern Kalahari but withdrew deeper into the territory we now know as Botswana. European explorers and travellers often mangled local African place names, in part to make them easier on the unaccustomed tongue and to avoid misunderstanding the unfamiliar words. Hence we have Kalahari in the place of Kgalagadi. It is possible, but by no means certain, that the

Above: *The southern oryx (Oryx gazella) is arguably the Kalahari's most elegant antelope, with its bold black patterning and rapier-like horns.*

Below: Also known as the striped sandveld lizard, tiger lizards are specialist feeders with the bulk of their prey consisting of scorpions which they dig out of their burrows.

explorer-naturalist Andrew Smith was the first to use the name Kalahari in 1834.

The Kalahari is a special place and there are still locations outside the national parks and game reserves where one can travel and camp for days on end without seeing other people. None of the associated conservation areas have become "Disneyland" parks; tourist loads are minimal, and this is their principal attraction. So if you want bright lights, supermarkets and tar roads head eastwards to Kruger National Park and you will not be disappointed. In the Kalahari you can settle for the company of Namaqua doves and star-spangled skies.

Prehistory

An error that frequently creeps into ecosystem studies is the exclusion of humans and their prehistory and history, their role and impact

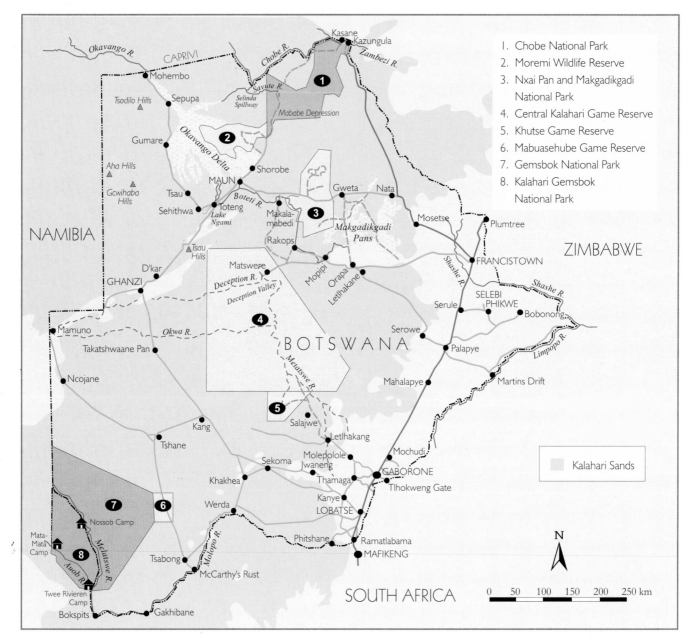

1. Chobe National Park
2. Moremi Wildlife Reserve
3. Nxai Pan and Makgadikgadi National Park
4. Central Kalahari Game Reserve
5. Khutse Game Reserve
6. Mabuasehube Game Reserve
7. Gemsbok National Park
8. Kalahari Gemsbok National Park

on the area or region. In the words of Robert Smith:

> *The ecosystem has historical aspects; the present is related to the past, and the future is related to the present.*

The oldest signs of humans in the Kalahari date back more than 100 000 years to the Early Stone Age. Artefacts have been found in association with existing and extinct river courses but this period of prehistory is poorly known. In the Middle Stone Age – between 20 000 and 100 000 years before present – humans thrived. Water was apparently more abundant than it is today, and the area was

and black tribes and particularly European colonisers, they retreated to the arid interior. Although the San were active and efficient hunters, plant food was extremely important to their diet and ranged from 50% to 90% of their intake. Today there are few, if any, "wild" Bushmen; most now live in fixed settlements but sadly often in squalid conditions, having lost their traditional way of life but not having been able to assimilate to a new culture.

Just over 2 000 years before present the first black pastoralists moved into the Kalahari from the north and they had a much greater impact than did the thousands of years of San occupation.

Below: Blue wildebeest on the move to new pastures. Wildebeest have died by the tens of thousands in recent years along the veterinary cordon fences erected throughout Botswana.

home to large game animals that have long since become extinct, including a giant buffalo *Pelorovis antiquus*, a giant zebra *Equus capensis* and a small form of the present-day springbok *Antidorcas bondi*.

The San (Bushman) people first appear in the record in the Late Stone Age, about 20 000 years before present. They remain, albeit to a greatly decreased degree, part of the Kalahari ecosystem. These diminutive hunter-gatherer people were nomadic and once ranged widely in southern Africa, from high to low rainfall areas and mountains to arid plains, but as conflict increased between them

History

With the arrival of the European hunters and farmers the Kalahari and its wildlife were to be changed for ever. For this account we have mainly limited ourselves to the area that now encompasses the South African Kalahari Gemsbok National Park and the adjoining Gemsbok National Park in Botswana, together totalling 36 200 km². Missionaries, hunters and *trekboers*, or migrant farmers, passed through this area during the 19th

Below: The weevils are the largest of insect families with more than 60 000 individual species. This specimen from the Kalahari had a head and body length of six centimetres.

and early part of the 20th century. After the First World War the area between the Auob and Nossob rivers was occupied by a handful of settlers. In 1914, as a preparation should it be used as an invasion route into German Southwest Africa, a number of boreholes were drilled in the Auob River bed, but as it turned out troops from the Union of South Africa invaded along the Kuruman River.

In the early part of this century, before its proclamation, what is now the conservation area was extensively utilised by meat hunters. Game populations were becoming rapidly depleted. The South African Kalahari Gemsbok National Park was proclaimed on 3 July 1931 and in 1935 additional farms were purchased and added to the holdings, with other areas being added over the next few years. In the early years the park faced numerous problems that were aggravated by a total lack of funds. The first ranger was powerless to stop the ongoing poaching. The illegal slaughter of game escalated after the end of the war because of the sudden abundance of

firearms and ammunition, and a heavy toll was exacted before things could be stabilised.

The Gemsbok National Park of Botswana had its beginnings in 1937 as a small protected area on the border with South Africa. It was expanded to its present size in 1967. Until

Below: The communal nests of the sociable weaver may weigh several hundred kilograms and be in continuous use for many years.
Below right: The ground squirrel is one of the most engaging of Kalahari-dwelling mammals. This rodent lives in small colonies in self-excavated burrows and thrives on a diet of plant roots and seeds.
Bottom right: Wolf spiders are ground hunters that stalk their prey and do not spin webs to ensnare unfortunate insects. The arachnid fauna (spiders, scorpions and mites) of the Kalahari is still poorly known.

recently the Botswana park was managed by the South African national parks authorities and was closed to the public, but this has now changed. Although the western and southern boundaries of the South African park are fenced, the international border remains unfenced to allow game free movement, an essential element that if changed would have catastrophic consequences for the nomadic wildlife. The erection of veterinary cordon fences in the Botswana Kalahari to control the spread of foot and mouth disease and other illnesses that can be passed from game to cattle, often across migration routes, resulted in the death of thousands of head of such species as plains zebra, red hartebeest and in particular blue wildebeest.

For much of the year there is no surface water in the Kalahari, so it was deemed essential to drill boreholes along the Auob and Nossob river beds and the dune road linking the two, to ensure that at least some game stayed within the South African park. It was only from the early 1950s that attention was given to encouraging tourism, with a grand total of 515 people visiting the park in 1954. Even today annual totals do not exceed 18 000.

The Central Kalahari Game Reserve, a vast tract of 51 800 km², is a truly wild area, although it has its problems. It was established in 1961 with the specific aim of providing a refuge where small groups of San (Bushmen) could continue their traditional lifestyle as hunter-gatherers. Although the Botswana government has tried to persuade the San to move to permanent settlements outside the reserve, they have resisted and insist on exercising their rights of domicile. The reserve was closed to tourists until very recently, but limited access is now possible in the north. The south, where most San live, is still a no-go area. Fewer than 1 000 people live within the reserve boundaries, of whom half are true San. It is of interest to note here that in the South African Kalahari Gemsbok National Park, a number of groups of people of mixed descent but claiming San ancestry are fighting in the courts for the right to live and hunt in the park; it could hold important consequences for future management of the park if they are successful.

Other parks and reserves associated with the Kalahari in Botswana are Mabuasehube and Khutse, and on its eastern fringe the Makgadikgadi and Nxai Pan national parks.

Geography

The central Kalahari is a seemingly endless flat plain. Most of it is sand-covered, with the exception of the low rocky outcropping known as Tsau Hill in the north-west. Providing evidence of much wetter times are the fossil river systems, Okwa, Quoxo, Letiahau and Passarge, and many shallow saline pans that hold water only for short periods after good rains.

Over the past few million years the world's climate has see-sawed between dry and wet periods, and cold and warm, with some extremely arid times resulting in the linking of the Kalahari with the Sahara, as well as north-eastwards with the Horn of Africa. Although the Kalahari is referred to as a desert, it is in fact a semi-desert. The definition of a true desert is that it receives less than 100 mm of rain each year. The Kalahari is best described as an arid sandy area with no permanent surface water. Kalahari sands cover large tracts of southern and central Africa, extending as far north as the southern basin of the Congo River and the coastal plain of Mozambique, but it is only in the south that arid conditions prevail. The Kalahari is the largest single area covered by sand on earth, not even exceeded by the mightiest ergs of the Sahara Desert.

The Kalahari is dominated over much of its area by deep (12 m to 60 m) red sands, with extensive but relatively low, parallel sand-dune systems that are mainly orientated in a north-westerly to south-easterly direction. These sands overlay, among others, blue shales of the Dwyka Series, an element of the Karoo System. There are extensive beds of calcrete which are most visible along the banks of the Nossob and Auob rivers beds.

Evidence of extinct river systems and extensive permanent, shallow pans is present throughout the Kalahari. The abundance of fossil diatoms and molluscs in some deposits indicate that there were a number of wet periods over the past few thousand years. There are numerous shallow pans scattered throughout the Kalahari. Many are small but a few, such as the Makgadikgadi, cover hundreds of square kilometres. These pans only hold water for relatively short periods after good rains, as evaporation rates are high, but nevertheless they attract great numbers of waterbirds, including flamingos, avocets and duck species. Of particular importance to many game animals are the deposits of salts and other minerals associated with many of these pans, as the sands are generally low in minerals and so, therefore, are the plants.

The two principal rivers in the south-west, the Auob and Nossob, flow very irregularly and for short periods only; often several years elapse between flooding. This rare flow is, however, enough to keep these two rivers from being overwhelmed by the wind-blown sands and buried – a fate that has befallen many of the Kalahari watercourses.

Top: Good summer rains rapidly transform the drab browns and yellows of the dry season to lush green growth.
Above: *The tsamma melon is an important source of water and food for many animals, including man, throughout the Kalahari.*

Flora

The vegetation of the Kalahari can broadly be described as savanna grassland interspersed with tall shrubs, thickets and scattered large trees, the latter being associated with river courses and areas where the water table is relatively high. The dominant trees throughout are *Acacia* species, most of a size that they can be classified as bushes, but there are some notable exceptions. There are mighty camel thorns *Acacia erioloba*, with their gnarled bark and nutritious grey pods, many of which serve as props for the colossal roofed nests of the sociable weaver birds. The smaller but striking shepherd's tree *Boscia albitrunca* is distinguished by its white bark.

It is hard to imagine at the peak of the dry season that shortly after the onset of good rains vast tracts of the Kalahari will turn green with waving meadows of annual grasses. These rains, however, seldom fall regularly and they are usually patchy: copious showers may fall in some localities and nothing in others. It is because of this uncertainty that the principal game species are nomadic, following the rains which they know will encourage seeds to germinate and push their new leaves through the sand.

Fauna

Even up to the middle of the last century there was permanent surface water in the Kalahari, and game species that must drink frequently were present. But today elephants, black and possibly white rhinos, buffaloes and plains zebras no longer occur in the southern reaches of the Kalahari. Instead the nomadic antelope species, such as oryx (or gemsbok as it is called in southern Africa), eland, red hartebeest and springbok became well established. These species move great distances in search of fresh grazing and although all drink readily when water is available, whether at rain-filled natural pans or the artificial waterholes provid-

Above: *The suricate, a mongoose, is a diurnally active and highly social carnivore that occurs throughout the Kalahari. Although most visitors go in search of the Kalahari lion, we would much rather spend a few hours observing these engaging beasties!*

SPECIES TO WATCH FOR

MAMMALS

Southern oryx (gemsbok)	*Oryx gazella gazella*	Black-backed jackal	*Canis mesomelas*
Red hartebeest	*Alcelaphus buselaphus caama*	Bat-eared fox	*Otocyon megalotis*
Springbok	*Antidorcas marsupialis*	Cape fox	*Vulpes chama*
Steenbok	*Raphicerus campestris*	Honey badger	*Mellivora capensis*
Lion	*Panthera leo*	Yellow mongoose	*Cynictis penicillata*
Leopard	*Panthera pardus*	Suricate	*Suricata suricatta*
African wild cat	*Felis libyca*	Egyptian slit-faced bat	*Nycteris thebaica*
Cheetah	*Acinonyx jubatus*	Ground squirrel	*Xerus inauris*
Brown hyaena	*Hyaena brunnea*	Porcupine	*Hystrix africaeaustralis*
		Brants's whistling rat	*Parotomys brantsii*

BIRDS

Ostrich	*Struthio camelus*	Spotted sandgrouse	*Pterocles burchelli*
Abdim's stork	*Ciconia abdimii*	Double-banded sandgrouse	*Pterocles bicinctus*
Secretary bird	*Sagittarius serpentarius*	Namaqua dove	*Oena capensis*
Lappet-faced vulture	*Torgos tracheliotus*	Scops owl	*Otus senegalensis*
Tawny eagle	*Aquila rapax*	White-faced owl	*Otus leucotis*
Martial eagle	*Polemaetus bellicosus*	Pearl-spotted owl	*Glaucidium perlatum*
Black-breasted snake eagle	*Circaetus gallicus*	Giant eagle-owl	*Bubo lacteus*
Bateleur	*Terathopius ecaudatus*	Swallow-tailed bee-eater	*Merops hirundineus*
Gabar goshawk	*Micronisus gabar*	Monotonous lark	*Mirafra passerina*
Pale chanting goshawk	*Melierax canorus*	Stark's lark	*Alauda starki*
Red-necked falcon	*Falco chicquera*	Black-eared finch-lark	*Eremopterix australis*
Pygmy falcon	*Polihierax semitorquatus*	Pied babbler	*Turdoides bicolor*
Kori bustard	*Ardeotis kori*	Black-chested prinia	*Prinia flavicans*
Black bustard	*Eupodotis afroides*	Crimson-breasted shrike	*Laniarius atrococcineus*
Spotted dikkop	*Burhinus capensis*	White-browed sparrow-weaver	*Plocepasser mahali*
Bronze-winged courser	*Rhinoptilus chalcopterus*	Sociable weaver	*Philetairus socius*
Namaqua sandgrouse	*Pterocles namaqua*	Red-headed finch	*Amadina erythrocephala*

ed in the South African park, it is not essential that they drink every day. Most of the animal species occurring in the Kalahari can survive for long periods without surface water.

Sometimes the usually meagre and widely scattered rains stay away altogether. Since the inception of the Kalahari parks several such dry years have been recorded. Then large herds of antelope stream into the South African sector to the vicinity of the boreholes. In 1979 it is estimated that as many as 180 000 blue wildebeest, 6 000 red hartebeest and 5 000 eland moved into the park. These numbers soon depleted the available grazing and many animals died. A similar mass movement occurred during the drought of 1985.

In the southern Kalahari there is a clear tendency for the nomadic antelope to concentrate in the vicinity of the beds of the Auob and Nossob rivers during the wet season but with the onset of the dry season many disperse east onto the savanna plains and into the sand dunes, where there is little or no surface water available during the dry season. This is in direct contrast to the situation that occurs in better watered parts of Africa.

The oryx occurs in three separate populations, one (the gemsbok) associated with the Kalahari and Namib deserts, and the other two, the beisa and fringe-eared, in East Africa. This is one of several species indicat-

ing that the Kalahari and the East African drylands were once linked, although today they are separated by higher rainfall regions that sustain miombo woodlands.

Although most of the larger species of antelope are to some extent nomadic, the tiny, large-eared steenbok is a solitary and permanent resident of the sands. It avoids the exposed river beds and does not need to drink, meeting its moisture needs from its food. But the steenbok has evolved no other adaptations to dryland living, unlike the oryx.

The oryx has adapted to tolerate high temperatures by a process known as adaptive heterothermy, which enables it to maintain the temperature of its brain at a lower and more constant level than that of the rest of the body. A network of blood vessels lies below the brain and as the oryx pants, blood in the nasal sinuses is cooled, with an exchange of heat taking place between the veins and arteries so that blood entering the brain is several degrees cooler than in the rest of the body.

Above: This male ground agama is taking advantage of the early morning sun before moving off to hunt ants and termites, its principal prey. A common species throughout the Kalahari.
Above right: The small white-faced owl is one of seven species that call the Kalahari home.
PHOTO: JOHN CARLYON
Far right: The Namaqua sand-grouse, in this case a male, often arrives in vast numbers at the limited dry season waterholes.

Sighting lions is usually at the top of many visitors' Kalahari wish-list. Except on a cool day, or in the immediate post-dawn and pre-dusk hours, the most likely sight is of these great tawny cats sprawled in the shade of a camel thorn tree. Movement is usually restricted to the occasional ear-flicking, tail-switching and stretch, or to lazily rising and sauntering into deeper shade. Lions usually do their hunting at night.

In the south-western Kalahari more than 50% of the prey of most lion prides is made up of just two species, oryx and porcupines. Although porcupines – giant, animated pin-cushions – are killed and eaten by lions in other regions, this is a rarity, whereas in the Kalahari they are actively hunted by these cats and form an essential component of their diet. Lions in general have a fairly low hunting success rate but when they pursue porcupines this soars to 85%, therefore the risk of injury to the predator is outweighed by the relative ease with which the food is obtained.

A porcupine's defence against attack is not to run away but to present its sharp-pointed quill armoury to its attacker, giving the lion a chance to seek an opening, flip the rodent on its back and bite the vulnerable, unprotected throat or chest.

The Kalahari leopards also are partial to porcupine flesh. Porcupines comprise 40% of all kills recorded in one study, with other species ranging from 5% to 15% of recorded kills. Both lions and leopards also take considerable numbers of antelope of all the principal species present, but the cheetah takes most of its food from the large springbok population.

An amazing diversity of carnivores occur in the Kalahari, ranging in size from the diminutive white-naped weasel to the lion, but many are nocturnal and are therefore seldom seen by the visitor. Two frequently seen exceptions are the black-backed jackal and the bat-eared fox. We never tire of watching them.

On a recent visit to the southern Kalahari we spent time at a waterhole where a lioness had been killed in a fight. The carcass was being attended by a solitary jackal. This "song dog" would grasp the cat's tail in its mouth and pull and twist it, almost as if saying (we know one shouldn't think these anthropomorphic thoughts!), "I couldn't tease you in this way when you were alive, but ...".

Of the large carnivores the brown hyaena is the most common and widespread over most of the Kalahari, with its ability to survive on small, scattered food items of many different kinds and a social system ideally suited to this arid environment.

Conservation issues

As in all African conservation areas and wild places there are problems. One of the greatest worries is that a fence will be erected along the Nossob River separating the Kalahari Gemsbok National Park of South Africa and the Gemsbok National Park of Botswana. This would cut off essential migration routes of nomadic species and result in overgrazing and other problems, and the need to cull some populations. As it is, the fence separating the western park from Namibia prevents any movement in that direction, except for lions which see this as no barrier and hunt domestic stock on farms in that country. Consequently many lions are shot, which does not bode well for this cat's population.

KALAHARI GEMSBOK NATIONAL PARK

Travel and access: From Upington take the N10 towards Namibia; 10 km outside town turn right onto the tarred R360. This road is tarred for 150 km (early 1997); the untarred section is variable in condition but some stretches can be badly corrugated; be alert for soft sand patches and sharp curves. Nevertheless ordinary saloon cars should experience no difficulty. It is approximately 278 km from Upington to Twee Rivieren, the park's southernmost camp. Fill up with fuel before leaving Upington, the next reliable fuel point is only in the park. There is no longer access to the park from Namibia via the Mata Mata Camp, you have to travel via Keetmanshoop, Aroab, Rietfontein and Andriesvale to Twee Rivieren.

All three camps have a landing strip.

Mobility: There is an extensive network of game-viewing roads. During the rains some sections may be impassable even for 4x4 vehicles for short periods, otherwise mobility is good even for saloon cars.

Accommodation: TWEE RIVIEREN CAMP: 4-bed huts with fully equipped kitchens, showers and toilets; 2- to 4-bed huts each with kitchen and bathroom; this is the only camp with air-conditioned accommodation.

MATA MATA CAMP: 6-bed cottages, each with a fully equipped kitchen, shower and toilet; and 3-bed huts.

NOSSOB CAMP: 6-bed cottages, each with a fully equipped kitchen, shower and toilet; and 3-bed huts.

All accommodation is supplied with bedding. There is a campsite with full ablution facilities at each of the three camps.

Other facilities: Picnic sites, shops selling groceries, fuel supplies; Twee Rivieren Camp has a restaurant and take-away food, as well as a swimming pool.

Climate: Summer temperatures are high – often exceeding 40 °C. It is at this time that the average precipitation of 200 mm falls. The winters are dry, with mild to cool days and cold nights, with temperatures frequently falling below freezing.

Best times to visit: The dry winters ensure excellent game and bird-viewing at waterholes; the summer months are the time when many animals have their young, and it is excellent for bird-watching as many migrant species are present. During the rains some road sections become waterlogged but this is usually of short duration.

Main attractions: Low game diversity but easy viewing; one of southern Africa's best raptor-watching destinations, particularly during the summer months; low tourist densities.

Hazards: There is a rare chance of contracting malaria during the wet season, but prophylaxis is not regarded as necessary for healthy people without predisposing conditions.

For further information: National Parks Board; the Park Warden, Kalahari Gemsbok National Park, Private Bag X5890, Gemsbok Park 8815.

CENTRAL KALAHARI GAME RESERVE

Travel and access: The reserve can be entered from Rakops, Ghanzi or Maun, or from the south from Letlhakeng. From Rakops follow the signposts to Matswere game scout camp (54 km) where permits are issued. From Maun travel on the road to Nata for 50 km, then turn right and proceed to Makalamabedi; turn right at the fence and continue about 90 km to the gate, from there it is a further 18 km to Matswere.

Mobility: A 4x4 vehicle is essential; most routes traverse deep sand.

Accommodation: None; camping is allowed at Deception Valley, Sundays Pan and Piper's Pan. There are no facilities, and no water is available.

Other facilities: Visitors must be totally self-sufficient.

Climate: The meagre rains fall in the summer months and at this time temperatures are usually blistering hot; winter days are warm to hot but nights are bitterly cold and frost is frequent.

Best times to visit: Game-viewing is at its best March to June.

Main attractions: Wide open spaces and few tourists; no infrastructure.

Hazards: Malaria; always carry adequate water and food in case of breakdown.

For further information: Department of Wildlife and National Parks, P.O. Box 131, Gaborone, Botswana; tel. 267 371405.

① Skeleton Coast Park
② Namib Naukluft Park
⬤ Approximate extent of the Namib Desert

Chapter 3

THE NAMIB

A DESERT MIRACLE

Oh! that the Desert were my dwelling place,
With one fair Spirit for my minister,
That I might all forget the human race,
And, hating no one, love but only her!

Lord Byron, *Childe Harold's Pilgrimage*

We have heard them referred to as the "nocturnal Serengeti of the dune slopes" – the predators and their prey, the loners and the socialisers. The only difference is that these are not the lions and the wildebeest, but the geckos and the termites, the spiders and the crickets. To observe the dune slopes on a warm, wind-still night is to see a world that teems with life. The web-footed geckos emerge from their sandy underworld, lick the odd errant sand grain from their eyeballs, and the hunt is on. The golden moles also emerge

from beneath the sand blanket, to bulldoze a seemingly haphazard trail of pathways in their relentless search for termites, beetle larvae and legless lizards. The pair of barn owls that roost and nest on the wind-battered crags of the Anachankirab fly to the dunes to hunt, descending on silent wings to snatch up gerbils, geckos and golden moles. These are the master aerial predators of the Namib night.

"Miles and miles, of miles and miles." We are not sure who originally made this statement, and whether in fact it referred to the Namib Desert, but it suits this arid area well. But within those miles and miles, of miles and miles, there is an immense diversity of landscapes, as well as of animal and plant life, making it probably the "richest" true desert in the world. You will not see great herds of antelope gambolling across the plains but in the sand dunes and along the sandy river beds teeming troops of vegetarian beetles forage. This is the domain of lizards and golden moles that swim through the soft sands, geckos that bark to the moon, chameleons that never climb trees, div-

Above: The isolated hill ranges, or inselbergs, of the Namib offer some of the finest scenery in this desert.

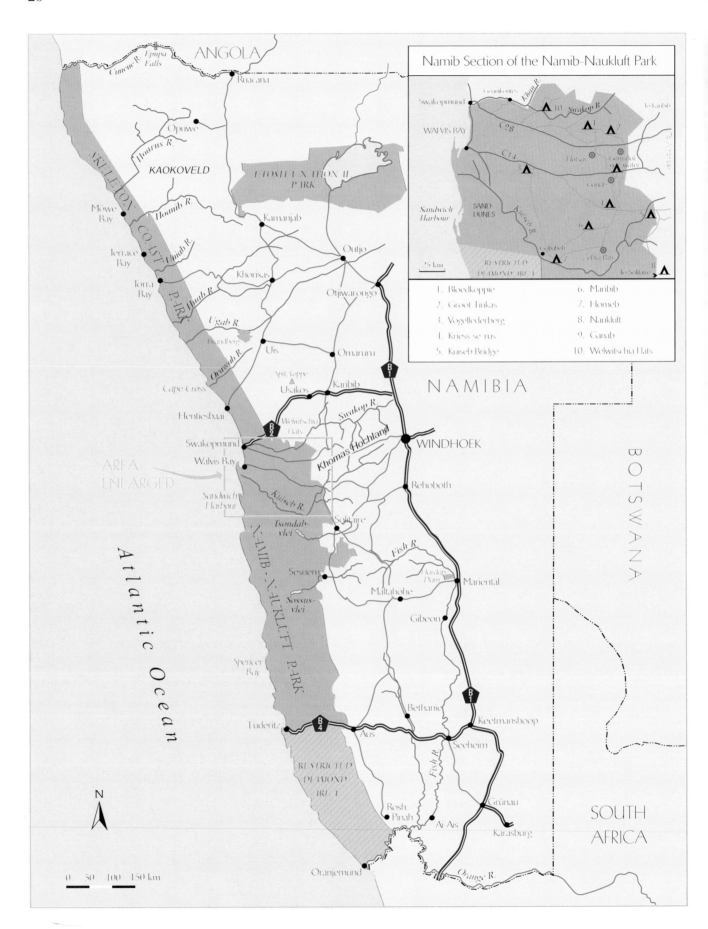

ANGOLA

Cunene R. *Epupa Falls*

Ruacana

Opuwe

Hoarus R.

KAOKOVELD

ETOSHA NATIONAL PARK

Mowe Bay

Hoanib R.

Kamanjab

Terrace Bay

Uniab R.

Outjo

Torra Bay

Huab R.

Khorixas

Otjiwarongo

Ugab R.

Brandberg

Uis

Omaruru

Omaruru R.

Cape Cross

Spitzkoppe

Usakos

Karibib

NAMIBIA

Hentiesbaai

Welwitschia Flats

Swakop R.

SKELETON COAST PARK

Swakopmund

Khomas Hochland

WINDHOEK

Walvis Bay

AREA ENLARGED

Kuiseb R.

Rehoboth

Sandwich Harbour

Tsondab-vlei

Solitaire

Fish R.

Sesriem

Hardap Dam

Sossus-vlei

Maltahöhe

Mariental

BOTSWANA

Atlantic Ocean

NAMIB-NAUKLUFT PARK

Gibeon

Spencer Bay

B1

Bethanie

Keetmanshoop

Lüderitz

Aus

Seeheim

B4

RESTRICTED DIAMOND AREA

Fish R.

Grünau

SOUTH AFRICA

Rosh Pinah

Ai-Ais

Karasburg

N

Oranjemund

Orange R.

0   50   100   150 km

Namib Section of the Namib-Naukluft Park

Swakopmund

Khan R.

Swakop R.

10

To Karibib

WALVIS BAY

C28

C14

Hotsas

Gobabeb Valley

Sandwich Harbour

SAND DUNES

Kuiseb R.

Gobabeb

RESTRICTED DIAMOND AREA

To Solitaire

25 km

1. Bloedkoppie	6. Mirabib
2. Groot Tinkas	7. Homeb
3. Vogelfederberg	8. Naukluft
4. Kriess se rus	9. Ganab
5. Kuiseb Bridge	10. Welwitschia Flats

ing lizards that eat windblown seeds, a primitive conifer that lives for more than 1 000 years and ancient "forests" of lichens that grow on the coastal plain.

Geography

Stretching more than 2 000 km along the south-west African Atlantic Ocean coastline, from San Nicolau in Angola, southwards to the estuary of the Olifants River in South Africa, lies what is reputed to be the world's oldest desert, the Namib. It is believed to have see-sawed between an arid and semi-arid state for at least 80 million years, but there were times when there were more rivers and surface water. Not all of the landscape features that we see today, however, are of a venerable age. They have been modified and changed greatly over the ages by the forces of water, wind, heating and cooling.

The Namib Desert forms a narrow ribbon along the coastal plain, rarely more than 200 km wide and bounded in the west by the cold oceanic waters and in the east by the escarpment known as the Khomas Hochland. The Namib can be divided into a number of distinct units for convenience of description: the vast sand dune oceans, extensive gravel and calcrete plains, hill ranges and massive granitic inselbergs, seasonally flowing rivers, perennial rivers in the north and south, and the coastal plain.

Apart from the Orange River which forms part of the international border between Namibia and South Africa, and the Cunene in the north, separating western Angola and Namibia, all of the other rivers flow only after good rains have fallen in the highlands. A few of these rivers, such as the Kuiseb and Swakop, flow more frequently than others, and in the case of the former this plays a crucial role in preventing the mighty longitudinal sand dunes from relentlessly marching northwards. Many of these rivers have names that evoke something of the mystery of this desert: Hoarusib, Hoanib, Uniab, Huab, Ugab and Orawab. Even though flowing water is a rare and unpredictable phenomenon, many rivers retain pools throughout even the driest years, and the underground water can be substantial.

These river courses allow many non-desert adapted creatures and plants to penetrate what would otherwise be a totally hostile environment for them. If we take one of these rivers, the Kuiseb, as an example, we find around it a great spectrum of both desert-adapted species, as well as those that would perish without this lifeline. This river also prevents the southern sands spilling northwards.

Top: Although frequently referred to as the sand "ocean", the longitudinal sand dunes of the Namib Desert are separated by flat, calcrete covered, inter-dune valleys.
***Above:** The quiver tree is extremely hardy and is able to survive under extremely harsh conditions, as does this specimen in the central Namib.*

Above: The Cape Cross fur seal reserve on the desert coast of Namibia is a breeding refuge for probably half of this species' entire population. This is truly an experience of sound and smell unequalled in the Namib.

Far right: *Scorpions, in this case a* Parabuthus *sp., are abundant in the Namib but as they usually emerge at night they are not commonly seen.*

The Benguela Current

The Namib's most important feature of all is the life-giving, cold Benguela Current. The great diversity and richness of the Namib Desert revolves around the plankton-rich waters of this ocean current which peels off the mighty West Wind Drift in the cold Southern Ocean. The Benguela Current flows northwards along the south-western coastline of Africa, causing deep cold water to be pushed onto the shallower coastal shelf in a process called upwelling. As this nutrient-rich water enters the light zone near the surface it supports unbelievably large populations of minute organisms known collectively as phytoplankton, which serve as bountiful grazing grounds for a host of zooplankton species. This combination of minerals, including phosphorus, and energy-producing sunlight supports these pastures and their predators, which in their turn sustain vast shoals of pelagic fish. These form the principal prey of huge flocks of Cape gannets, Cape cormorants and jackass penguins. Also not to be left out of the equation are the fish-eating Cape fur seals, cetaceans and predatory fish species.

But what really concerns us here is another feature of this cold, productive oceanic current: fog. Rainfall in the Namib, as is to be expected in a true desert, is minimal and rarely exceeds 100 mm each year. It is more likely to be close to 15 mm, particularly along the coastal plain. The cold Benguela Current,

Fauna

In the battle for survival many species have evolved to utilise the Namib's fog, the only regular source of moisture. Most incredible of all are a number of the flightless tenebrionid beetles that have developed unique methods of harvesting the minute water droplets. The "head-standing" species *Onymacris unguicularis* is diurnal, spending the nights under the dune sand, but as the heavier fog rolls in from the cold ocean during the early morning hours these beetles have to make their way laboriously to the top of the dune slipface. Here they turn to face into the fog-laden wind,

Below left: *The Namaqua chameleon, occurring throughout the Namib, is unique in that it spends most of its time foraging on the ground, rarely ascending into bushes.*

Below: *The "halfmens" or half person is one of the Namib's strangest plants, reaching on occasion between four and five metres and covered with an awesome array of flesh-piercing spines. It is restricted to the southern reaches of the desert.*

already fully established some five million years before present, is influenced by the South Atlantic Anticyclone pressure system. Cool water flows close inshore, ensuring the frequent development of fog and maintaining high coastal humidity levels and the steep climatic gradient from the coast to the interior. Great, rolling banks of fog push their way inland from the coast during the darkness of night, not infrequently penetrating more than 50 km from the coast, and reaching their greatest density at altitudes of 300 m to 600 m. The inselbergs, hill ranges and in particular the sand dunes act as fog traps, and it is within these zones that the greatest species diversity is evident. A diversity that equals the riches of Serengeti or Ndoki.

with the hindquarters raised so that the water droplets run down to the mouth.

There are also several species of very flat, rounded beetles of the genus *Lepidochora*, which have developed an even more ingenious method of water collection. These small coleopterans construct narrow trenches on the surface of the sand that run perpendicular to the direction of the fog-bearing wind. The ridges of these trenches absorb more water than the surrounding undisturbed sand surface and the beetles return to extract the water from the sand ridges that they built.

But it is not only the fog that enables the great diversity of animal life to survive in the Namib; there are

SPECIES TO WATCH FOR

MAMMALS

Cape fur seal	*Arctocephalus pusillus*	Black-backed jackal	*Canis mesomelas*
Hook-lipped (black) rhinoceros	*Diceros bicornis*	Bat-eared fox	*Otocyon megalotis*
		Cape fox	*Vulpes chama*
Hartmann's zebra	*Equus zebra hartmannae*	Brown hyaena	*Hyaena brunnea*
Southern oryx (gemsbok)	*Oryx gazella gazella*	Rock hyrax	*Procavia capensis*
Springbok	*Antidorcas marsupialis*	Round-eared elephant shrew	*Macroscelides proboscideus*
Klipspringer	*Oreotragus oreotragus*	Cape hare	*Lepus capensis*
Steenbok	*Raphicerus campestris*	Mountain ground squirrel	*Xerus princeps*
Leopard	*Panthera pardus*	Dassie rat	*Petromus typicus*

BIRDS

Ostrich	*Struthio camelus*	Namaqua sandgrouse	*Pterocles namaqua*
White pelican	*Pelecanus onocrotalus*	Rosy-faced lovebird	*Agapornis roseicollis*
Cape cormorant	*Phalacrocorax capensis*	Monteiro's hornbill	*Tockus monteiri*
Bank cormorant	*Phalacrocorax neglectus*	Sabota lark	*Mirafra sabota*
Crowned cormorant	*Phalacrocorax coronatus*	Dune lark	*Mirafra erythrochlamys*
Lappet-faced vulture	*Torgos tracheliotus*	Stark's lark	*Alauda starki*
Black-breasted snake-eagle	*Circaetus gallicus*	Gray's lark	*Ammomanes grayi*
Pale chanting goshawk	*Melierax canorus*	Short-toed rock thrush	*Monticola brevipes*
Lanner falcon	*Falco biarmicus*	Tractrac chat	*Cercomela tractrac*
Red-necked falcon	*Falco chicquera*	Green eremomela	*Eremomela gregalis*
Ludwig's bustard	*Neotis ludwigii*	Grey-backed cisticola	*Cisticola subruficapilla*
Rüppell's bustard	*Eupodotis rueppellii*	Pale-winged starling	*Onychognathus nabouroup*
African black oystercatcher	*Haematopus moquini*		

Below left: The extensive sand dune network of the Namib Desert is in constant motion, a servant of the winds that blow off the cold Atlantic Ocean and the great plateau of the interior.

Below right: The Cape, or silver, fox occurs at very low densities throughout the eastern Namib Desert. This individual and its mate visited our camp in the hope of sampling the zebra steaks we were grilling!

also large quantities of wind-blown plant and animal detritus that catch in the lee slopes of the sand dunes and provide food for many invertebrates and a few vertebrates. Apart from numerous species of tenebrionid beetle and fishmoths that partake of this wind-delivered feast, there is also a lizard that specialises in feeding on the seeds of one bush, *Trianthema hereroensis*, which have been carried by the winds; this is the shovel-snouted lizard.

Sitting on the crest of a sand dune at between two and five o'clock in the morning, with a cold, moisture-laden wind beating against one's face and clothing doesn't appeal to everyone, but this is when the seemingly barren Namib Desert is at its best. The powder-puff-like golden mole has been moving around on the surface of the lower dune slopes, seeking out beetle larvae and legless lizards. The web-footed gecko and the white lady are also out hunting for insect prey. The web-footed gecko is so named for an obvious reason, and this adaptation allows it to "swim" under the soft surface of the dune sand as well as walk more easily on the surface. The white lady is a large spider that shelters in burrows during the day, emerging in the hours of darkness to stalk its prey on the slopes of the sand dunes, but what is unusual about this desert arachnid is its escape mechanism. When threatened it forms its legs into the shape of a wheel and rolls rapidly down the dune slope.

Although it is the smaller creatures that tend to draw one's attention in the Namib Desert, there are also small numbers of game animals and their predators. During times of good rain oryx penetrate deep into the dune system to feed on the grasses whose seeds may have lain dormant for several years. Springbok also take advantage of this short-lived bounty, moving in small herds along the inter-dune plains, or streets, nibbling the new growth.

As the hot winds blow the land dries out and the oryx and springbok leave the dune

fields to disperse over the gravel plains in the direction of the Khomas Hochland where higher rainfall ensures the availability of grasses for a longer period. It is here that the Hartmann's mountain zebra has its stronghold. This once common species has been hunted so ruthlessly that only a few thousand survive along the Namib fringes.

One of the mammalian wonders of the Namib is the Cape fur seal colony at Cape Cross, but the combination of noise and smell is not for the faint-hearted. Up to 100 000 of these large fur seals may be present on this rocky promontory at certain times of year but in October, when the mature bulls fight for the right to become "beach-masters" and establish harems, things are at their most interesting. From late November to early December the small black pups are born and the bulls assert their right to mate. Black-backed jackals and brown hyaenas patrol the fringes of the colony, feeding on dead or weak seal pups and debris. Kelp gulls also grab any morsel.

Great skeins of Cape cormorants, flying just above the waves, wing north and south along the Namib coastline, moving between the pelagic fishing grounds and their roosting sites.

Flora

It is not only the animals that benefit from the approximately 60 "fog-nights" produced by the cold ocean each year. The Namib is home to one of the world's most extraordinary perennial plants, the *Welwitschia*. Leathery-leaved and with a somewhat octopus-like appearance when mature, it is able to withstand even the most protracted drought. *Welwitschias* thrive along the inner fringe of the coastal plain, taking root in the dry washes that perhaps flow only once in 100 years. With their long tap roots they are able to draw on deep groundwater sources, and their leaves have the ability to absorb water droplets from the fog.

Welwitschias are grouped with the conifers, but to the non-botanist it bears no similarities to a pine tree, except that both male and female plants bear cones. Although it gives the appearance of being multi-leaved, it in fact carries only two large, leathery leaves. These become split and tattered. During periods of good rain – not common in the desert – the leaves may grow by as much as 10 cm in a month, but in dry times that length may only be achieved in 12 months.

The fruits of another plant, the nara *Acanthosicyos horrida*, which grows on the dune-field fringes, are a source of nourishment for many animals, from beetles to oryx, jackals to gerbils. This unusual Namib endemic is a member of the cucumber family but bears little resemblance to the common or garden cucumber. It has an amazingly deep root system. The plant has a covering of very sharp thorns but this does not prevent many of its fruits from being eaten.

Below: The small-spotted genet has succesfully exploited many different habitats, including the riverine and inselberg environments of the Namib, where it feeds on small rodents, birds, invertebrates and wild fruits.

Bottom: The male Cape flat lizard in its breeding finery. This species is restricted to rocky areas in the southern Namib and its eastern fringes along the lower Orange River.

Sights

For us the Namib is so diverse and offers so much that it is difficult to define our favourite locations. Some we will single out here but there are two that we will keep to ourselves. There are some areas we usually avoid, such as the fishing settlements and camps along parts of the coastline and anywhere where there are too many people!

Large tracts of this desert have been set aside as conservation areas, including Iona National Park in south-western Angola, but sadly this has been out of bounds for many years because of civil wars and lack of infrastructure. On a visit to the area in the early 1970s we still recorded black rhino, Hart-

Top: One of the most bizarre of the Namib's endemic plants is the Welwitschia, *with its close relationship to pine trees (it is certainly like no typical conifer we have ever seen!) and the fact that the larger specimens are believed to be well over one thousand years old.*
Above: In the south the Orange River, or Gariep, forms a corridor of lushness flanked by desert.
Right: Surprisingly, several species of frog and a toad occur in the Namib Desert, and in permanent pools in the higher reaches of the Naukluft range the river frog has a toe-hold!

mann's zebra, oryx, springbok and the rare black-faced impala, but unsubstantiated reports indicate that little has survived.

Fortunately this is not the case in the Namibian conservation areas, which include the Skeleton Coast Park, so named for the great number of ships that have foundered on this hostile coastline and left the bleached skeletons of many sailors to be covered and uncovered by the ever-shifting sands.

On the fringe between the Namib and the highland escarpment lies the granite massif of the Brandberg, "fire mountain": appropriate for the searing heat that rises from the hard rock as it bakes in the sun. This giant rock extends over 500 km² and at its highest point, Konigstein, rises to 2 579 m, the highest in all Namibia. Although no longer given formal protection, its very nature serves to prevent its despoliation. The few visitors to the Brandberg arrive primarily to see the magnificent

rock paintings, some believed to date back to 16 000 years before present, including the over-publicised, so-called *white lady*, located at the only really accessible point. However, if you really want to experience solitude and peace explore more deeply, but remember that this is an unforgiving place and should never be underestimated.

Further south lies one of Africa's largest conservation areas, the Namib-Naukluft Park. The original park covered some 23 400 km² but inclusion of two restricted diamond areas has more than doubled its size. These diamond areas, still inaccessible to the general public, are dominated by dune-fields and are still largely unexplored. However, the northern part of the park has several locations that can offer the peace and tranquillity that we are always in search of. Watch a sunset from the ridge of Bloedkoppie and hear the first jackal calls; sit under a rock overhang at Anachankirab, share the evening with a pair of Cape foxes and hear the screeches of the barn owls as a prelude to their hunt for gerbils, geckos and golden moles. Camp at Klein Tinkas and find yourself competing with a colony of barking geckos for conversation rights.

One other location that deserves a special mention is Sandwich Harbour, situated to the south of Walvis Bay, but only those with 4x4 vehicles will reach it. The only industry this shallow lagoon has seen is whaling, with evidence in the form of vast rusted blubber pots and timbers at its southern point. At times the lagoon plays host to large numbers of flamingos and white pelicans, terns in their thousands and large mixed flocks of Palaearctic waders during the northern winter.

In the Namib there are still places where the only other people you may see for days on end are those who accompany you.

NAMIB-NAUKLUFT PARK

Travel and access: From Windhoek take the C28 westwards towards Swakopmund; this road passes through the northern sector of the reserve. The C14 from Walvis Bay also passes through the reserve to the south of the C28. From Mariental in the south, take the C19 westwards to Maltahöhe and continue on the graded gravel westwards, ignoring the turn-off to the right (C14 to Solitaire); after 160 km there is a left turn to Sesriem campsite, and 20 km beyond it a right turn to the Naukluft sector of the park. Permits are not required for any of the above public roads, but are necessary for the internal road network in the north. They can be obtained at Hardap or Sesriem, at tourist offices in Swakopmund, Lüderitz or Windhoek, or during weekends from Charly's Desert Tours or Hans Kriess Service Station in Swakopmund, and from Troost Transport, Namib Ford or CWB service stations in Walvis Bay.

Mobility: Internal roads, while they can be badly corrugated at times, are regarded as suitable for most vehicles. The Walvis Bay to Sandwich Harbour road and the last 4 km of the road to Sossusvlei, however, both necessitate a 4x4 vehicle.

Accommodation: Naukluft campsite has four stands with ablution facilities, water and firewood; groups are only allowed to stay overnight. Sesriem campsite has 18 camping and caravan stands with ablution facilities. There are basic campsites at Kuiseb Bridge, Homeb, Kriess-se-rus, Vogelfederberg, Bloedkoppies, Groot Tinkas, Ganab and Mirabib in the north, with minimal facilities; take all water and supplies. Swakopmund and Walvis Bay have a number of hotels, holiday chalets and campsites. Sossusvlei Karos Lodge is just outside the Sesriem-Sossusvlei entrance gate.

Other facilities: Walking is permitted in the northern part of the park as well as at Sesriem and Sossusvlei; a 120 km walking trail in the Naukluft sector must be booked in advance from Windhoek only. Fuel is available at Sesriem and Solitaire but otherwise this and food must be purchased at Walvis Bay, Swakopmund and Maltahöhe.

Climate: Much of the Namib receives its meagre rains during the summer months but to the south of Lüderitz winter rainfall is the norm. Temperatures in the coastal belt are mild to cool throughout the year. The further one goes inland the warmer it gets, and in summer it can be very hot in the interior. Probably the single biggest influence on the Namib's climate is the fog, which frequently rolls inland for more than 50 km from the coast.

Best times to visit: Any time of the year, although daytime temperatures can be high in the interior during summer.

Main attractions: True wilderness; deafening silence; unique animal and plant life; low visitor densities.

Hazards: Carry adequate water and food supplies in case of a breakdown; always carry a compass and a sketch map when walking (these can be obtained from the permit offices in Windhoek and Swakopmund) as it is very easy to lose one's bearings.

For further information: Ministry of Environment and Tourism. Sossusvlei Karos Lodge: tel. 061-248338 or Johannesburg 011-486 1641.

SKELETON COAST PARK

Travel and access: From Swakopmund follow the C34 northwards to Henties Bay; continue past Henties Bay on the C34 to the entrance gate at the Ugab River. From Henties Bay the road is salt and is usually in good repair. Alternatively, from Khorixas follow the C39 westwards via Springbokwasser to the C34 along the coast. This road is graded gravel but is often corrugated in sections. Permits or accommodation receipts are required.

Accommodation: Terrace Bay has rooms, each with a bathroom; the tariff includes three meals a day and freezer space. Book well in advance. Torra Bay has a camping and caravan site. Torra Bay is open from 1 December to 31 January only.

Other facilities: Accompanied 3-day hiking trail starting at the Ugab River crossing (book well in advance; 6 to 8 persons only); fishing from the beach; shops selling basic supplies and a restaurant at Terrace Bay; fuel at Terrace Bay and Torra Bay.

Climate: As for the Namib-Naukluft.

Best times to visit: All year, although summer days can be hot. Try to avoid the South African and Namibian school holidays as the camps are then overcrowded.

Main attractions: Unique animal and plant life; desert scenery.

Hazards: As for Namib-Naukluft.

For further information: Ministry of Environment and Tourism.

Below: The Namib coastal belt is an important habitat for resident and migratory birds. These white pelicans (Pelecanus onocrotalus) probably breed on the small off-shore islands where they are safe from predators.

Chapter 4

ETOSHA

THE MYTHICAL LAKE
OF TEARS

*It was the Africa I had read of in books of travel.
All the menageries in the world turned loose would
not compare to the sight I saw that day.*

Gerald McKiernan, 1876

The late morning summer heat is drawing herds of springbok and oryx (gemsbok) to slake their thirst at the Okaukuejo waterhole, some animals wading belly-deep into the cooling liquid. Without any warning the lioness, up to now lying unseen among the scrub and calcrete rubble some 20 m away, explodes from cover, scattering dust and small rocks in a charge that carries her into the water, launching herself onto the back of a luckless oryx yearling. Both predator and prey disappear below the surface; the lioness has misjudged the depth and is forced to relinquish her hold on the oryx. Here the antelope

sees its chance, lunging from water to bank, but the hungry cat is soon hot on its heels and the waterlogged, confused animal is pulled down after a short chase. Within a few minutes the lioness drags her feast to nearby shade and the waterhole again plays host to the thirsty animals that fled the charge. They will be safe until the lioness gets hungry again.

History

Although not the first European to set eyes on the Etosha area, Gerald McKiernan, an American trader hoping to deal in cattle and ivory with local tribes, travelled by ox-wagon across some of the harshest and least forgiving areas in southern Africa. Crossing the Namib Desert from the coast, he eventually arrived in the Etosha region, which is best described in his own words:

Travelled all day through a beautiful country, almost a level plain dotted with clumps of timber, in the middle of which pools of water left by rains were to be found, some of them of considerable extent. Wild ducks and geese were plentiful, the latter of beautiful plumage and with crested heads. It was by far the pret-

Above: *A family herd of elephant preparing to cross an open plain after visiting a waterhole.*

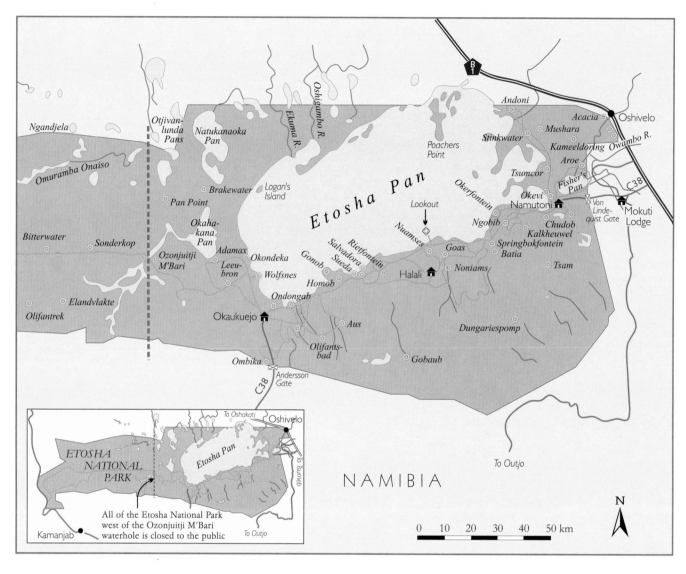

Below: *The Namutoni fort in the east of the Etosha National Park has been incorporated into the tourist camp.*
PHOTO: HERTA DÜRK

tiest scene I had met with, and I find it difficult to realize that I was in desert Africa. That afternoon we fell in with immense numbers of animals beyond anything I had yet seen. I would scarcely be believed, if I should state that there were thousands of them to be seen at a sight. Gnus in herds like buffalo on the plains, hundreds of zebras, beautiful in their striped coats, springboks by tens of thousands, ostriches, gemsboks and steenboks, hartebeeste and elands.

It was the Swedish naturalist and explorer, Karl Andersson, and his travelling companion the English scientist Francis Galton, who are believed to have been the first Europeans to visit and describe Etosha, in 1851. Arriving at Omutjamatunda, or Namutoni as we call it today, Andersson described it thus:

There is a most copious fountain, situated on some rising ground and commanding a splendid prospect of the surrounding country. It was a refreshing sight to stand on the borders of the fountain [this fountain is still there], *which was luxuriously overgrown with towering reeds and sweep with the eye the extensive plain encircling the base of the hill; frequented as it was, not only by vast herds of domesticated cattle, but with the lively springboks and troops of striped zebras.*

At the time when Andersson arrived in the Etosha area, the only human residents were the hunter-gatherer Heikum, a San people frequently referred to as Bushmen. Herero pastoralists herded their cattle into the area on a seasonal basis, benefiting from the rich pastures and the few permanent water points.

By the end of the 19th century, the Germans had a firm hold over what was then German South-West Africa – now Namibia – another large chunk of African real estate claimed by a European power during the infamous "scramble". The German administration established a border post at Namutoni in 1897 in an effort to control the spread of rinderpest, which was killing large numbers of cattle in the northern part of the territory. In 1903 this post was upgraded to a fort. The following year was marked by the beginning of a rebellion that eventually resulted in massive and brutal German reprisals against, in particular, the Herero nation.

Some 500 Ovambo warriors attacked the Namutoni fort early in 1904. Although the military garrison was defended by only a handful of men, they repulsed the attack and killed an estimated 80 warriors in the first assault. However, realising their luck could not last against such odds, the defenders made good their escape during the hours of darkness, and the next day the fort was torched. It was rebuilt in 1905.

Even before the end of the first decade of this century, game numbers had been severely depleted by hunting and by increased competition for grazing and water with domestic herds and flocks, and in 1907 Governor Von Lindequist proclaimed what was then the largest conservation area in the world: Etosha. This superpark extended over 93 000 km². The Atlantic Ocean was its western boundary; its northern boundary was the Cunene River.

Given the seasonally dry nature of this area, several of the larger game species followed traditional migration routes and the large size of the park allowed these traditional patterns to continue unhindered. This relatively natural

system was dealt a severe blow by the South African government's erstwhile policy of establishing separate homelands for each of the ethnic groups. Large parcels of land were excised from Etosha for this purpose. At the whim of a few politicians sitting in Pretoria, and at the stroke of a pen, 71 000 km² were no longer held in conservation trust but put up for overgrazing and degradation.

In 1970 the Etosha Game Reserve was upgraded to national park status in its diminished form, but worse was yet to come when the decision was taken to fence the park, cutting off the traditional migration routes. This resulted in overgrazing around water points and a general decline in certain game species, such as blue wildebeest. So here in a matter of a few decades a relatively natural ecosystem was turned into one that had to be managed by culling certain species, curbing population growth in lion by using contraceptives and manipulating waterholes.

The excised northern section of the original reserve, Ovamboland, is the most densely populated area of Namibia and has little conservation value, but the area of land stretching westwards to the coast, with its minimal agricultural value, is now largely set aside for conservation. Actual expansion of Etosha National Park beyond its present fenced boundaries is highly unlikely, however.

Geography

Extending over some 5 000 km², with a maximum length of 120 km and a breadth of approximately 50 km, the saline desert of the Etosha Pan is the

Above: Bat-eared foxes foraging for insects; the large, sensitive ears pick up the slightest subterranean movements. As elsewhere throughout their range these foxes are subject to considerable population fluctuations, principally as a result of disease, and at times they may be abundant and at others extremely scarce.
Below: A male Damara dik-dik, clearly showing the characteristic head crest.

Above: Plains zebra in Etosha have clearly defined shadow-stripes overlaying the white stripes.
Right: After a long dry season the first rains bring a sense of relief to Etosha; one can almost hear the earth and the vegetation breathing a great sigh.

dominant landscape feature in the park. During the Pliocene, some two to ten million years before present, a vast lake known as Ekuma, and including the Etosha extension, was fed by the life-giving waters of the Cunene River. However, this was a turbulent and restless time for Africa, and movements of the earth's crust and the continental plates caused the course of the Cunene to shift to the north and west, pouring its waters into the Atlantic Ocean. Without any major freshwater feeder the lake started to dry out, exposing fertile silts that were removed by wind erosion, and leaving in their place a very saline substrate and in places impermeable clays up to 240 m deep.

Although the above is the geomorphologically correct explanation, a more romantic version has been passed down in the oral tradition of the Heikum people. Long ago – too many years to count – a band of people travelling through the Etosha area were surrounded by local hunters who put the invaders to knife and arrow, sparing only the women. One of the captured women sat weeping under a tree and her tears were so copious that they formed a vast lake, but when it dried out it left in its stead a barren wasteland. The lady in question must have had salty tears indeed, as standing water in Etosha Pan may contain twice as much salt as is found in sea water!

Today Etosha Pan is fed by the seasonal Ekuma, Oshigambo and Omuramba Owambo rivers, but even in good rain years their flow is never enough to fill the pan; only partial flooding occurs. To the west and north-west of the main pan lie several smaller shallow saline basins that cover somewhat less than 1 000 km². Much of the surrounding terrain is overlaid with calcrete, a limestone product of the evaporation of subterranean waters.

Although precipitation is meagre in the park, with most rain falling during the summer months from January into April, there is a distinct incline from west to east. In an average year the hill-dotted west receives about 300 mm of rain, but as one moves eastwards this rises to some 450 mm. Some years are of course more generous than others. When the black, rain-filled clouds have rolled in over the brilliant white pan and the fork- and sheet-lightning offers further contrast, the first large life-giving drops disturb the fine dust. The rainfall increases in tempo and the dust turns rapidly to mud. The leaves of the trees and bushes are washed clean. Within but a few days the seedstock that has lain dormant throughout the dry season comes to life.

Flora

What is remarkable is that on and around the fringes of the dazzling white, saline Etosha Pan there is a grass species, *Sporobolus salsus*, that thrives on this inhospitable substrate. During the dry winter months when grazing is scarce elsewhere, the game herds concentrate on these protein-rich pastures. During the rains, when the pan holds water with massive "blooms" of blue-green algae – Namibia's own primordial soup – this is the feeding ground for up to a million flamingos.

The edges of the pan can support only a few species of halophytic plants, meaning those evolutionary selected few that can survive with their roots buried in a salty mix. Vast areas of the eastern part of the park are dominated by mopane *Colophospermum mopane* woodland and thicket, and it has been estimated that 80% of Etosha's trees are of this species. Around Namutoni there are mixed tamboti and *Terminalia* woodlands, with many *Acacia* species growing singly and in thickets throughout the park.

Fauna

During the dry season much of the game concentrates around the fringes of the main pan and within walking distance of those waterholes that are kept open. In order to reduce the impact of the game concentrations on the vegetation around waterholes, some 50 artificial boreholes are opened and closed on a rotational basis.

Above: *The Cape hares in northern Namibia have very pale coloured fur. Although they are mainly nocturnal these hares do emerge to feed on cool, overcast days.*

SPECIES TO WATCH FOR

MAMMALS

Elephant	*Loxodonta africana*		Kirk's (Damara) dik-dik	*Madoqua kirkii*
Hook-lipped (black) rhinoceros	*Diceros bicornis*		Lion	*Panthera leo*
Giraffe	*Giraffa camelopardalis*		Leopard	*Panthera pardus*
Plains zebra	*Equus burchellii*		Cheetah	*Acinonyx jubatus*
Southern oryx (gemsbok)	*Oryx gazella gazella*		Black-backed jackal	*Canis mesomelas*
Blue wildebeest	*Connochaetes taurinus*		Bat-eared fox	*Otocyon megalotis*
Red hartebeest	*Alcelaphus buselaphus caama*		Yellow mongoose	*Cynictis penicillata*
Greater kudu	*Tragelaphus strepsiceros*		Slender mongoose	*Galerella sanguinea*
Springbok	*Antidorcas marsupialis*		Ground squirrel	*Xerus inauris*
Black-faced impala	*Aepyceros melampus petersii*		Striped tree squirrel	*Funisciurus congicus*

BIRDS

Ostrich	*Struthio camelus*		Barred owl	*Glaucidium capense*
White-backed vulture	*Gyps africanus*		Palm swift	*Cypsiurus parvus*
White-headed vulture	*Trigonoceps occipitalis*		Olive bee-eater	*Merops superciliosus*
Tawny eagle	*Aquila rapax*		Purple roller	*Coracias naevia*
Martial eagle	*Polemaetus bellicosus*		Violet wood-hoopoe	*Phoeniculus purpureus*
Ovambo sparrowhawk	*Accipiter ovampensis*		Monteiro's hornbill	*Tockus monteiri*
Gabar goshawk	*Micronisus gabar*		Stark's lark	*Alauda starki*
Red-necked falcon	*Falco chicquera*		Mosque swallow	*Hirundo senegalensis*
Pygmy falcon	*Polihierax semitorquatus*		Carp's black tit	*Parus carpi*
Red-billed francolin	*Francolinus adspersus*		Black-faced babbler	*Turdoides melanops*
Hartlaub's francolin	*Francolinus hartlaubi*		Bare-cheeked babbler	*Turdoides gymnogenys*
Blue crane	*Anthropoides paradisea*		Rockrunner	*Achaetops pycnopygius*
Kori bustard	*Ardeotis kori*		Crimson-breasted shrike	*Laniarius atrococcineus*
Ludwig's bustard	*Neotis ludwigii*		White-tailed shrike	*Lanioturdus torquatus*
Spotted sandgrouse	*Pterocles burchelli*		Long-tailed starling	*Lamprotornis mevesii*
Rüppell's parrot	*Poicephalus rueppellii*		Great sparrow	*Passer molitensis*
Rosy-faced lovebird	*Agapornis roseicollis*		Chestnut weaver	*Ploceus rubiginosus*
White-faced owl	*Otus leucotis*			

In times of good rain, when the pan is partially filled in a brief shadow of its lake ancestor, the shallow alkaline waters have served as breeding grounds for huge hordes of lesser and greater flamingos. Little is known about their movements and what triggers breeding in these flamingos; we do know that the principal nesting ground is centred on Lake Natron in northern Tanzania. It is also known that where both species occur together the greater breeds before the lesser. In 1969 and 1971 this breeding pattern caused problems for the lesser flamingos. In 1971 it was estimated that some one million flamingos were on the partially flooded pan, with the greaters constructing their mud-nest mounds, laying eggs and rearing the young between February and May. Then it was the turn of the lessers but by August they had serious problems as the waters evaporated rapidly, leaving the breeding colonies stranded and the pulli (fledglings) increasingly vulnerable to land-based predators. But unlike the incident in 1969 when thousands of pulli had to be caught by hand and trucked to the water remaining in the Ekuma Delta – dubbed Operation Flamingo – in 1971 the lessers took matters "under their own wings". Large groups of adults and youngsters deserted the dried-out nesting grounds and walked day after day across the pan, and in one month they reached the last water that remained in the delta of the Ekuma River. Of the 30 000 pulli that started the odyssey an amazing 25 000 survived to fly to the alkaline lakes of the Great Rift Valley in East Africa.

After the erection of the park's boundary fence and the consequent cutting of traditional migration routes, the animals' movements, dictated by the abundance and quality of food and the availability of water, continued but to a much more limited extent.

Natural surface water and improved grazing and browsing allow the animals to disperse throughout the park. The blue wildebeest, plains zebra and elephant are particularly dispersive and move mainly westwards at the onset of the rains, but other species such as springbok and giraffe tend to undergo less extensive movements. Ungulates that are even less inclined to undertake seasonal migrations include greater kudu and black-faced impala. The warthog also falls in this category. It is primarily the mixed feeders and browsers with a greater diversity of food plants available to them that are the most sedentary.

The dry season has obvious advantages for the human visitor in that the game animals are concentrated in the vicinity of the pan edge and around waterholes, but for us the wet season holds the most appeal; in part because there are fewer visitors! This is also the time when most animals are dropping their young and the birds are nesting. Some of our finest memories of Etosha emanate from the rains: the fine-maned lion standing on the rim of the pan haloed in sunlight with a backdrop of velvet black storm clouds, a herd of springbok on the open plain, all with their white rump patches open to dry after a downpour, three bat-eared fox cubs playing among the green grass and yellow flowers. Of course this does

Above: With the onset of the rains in Etosha at least ten species of frog and toad emerge to breed and among the most vocal are the latter. Pictured here is a male olive toad (Bufo garmani) doing his best to attract females.
Right: Blue wildebeest (Connochaetes taurinus) have declined in numbers over the past two decades but are still frequently seen in small herds, often mingling with groups of plains zebra.

not mean we no longer visit Etosha in the dry season, which has also produced its share of special moments.

In the dry season Etosha is a real "waterhole park". Most animals have to drink, although some, such as the diminutive Damara dik-dik, common duiker and steenbok, obtain sufficient moisture from their plant food. Some waterholes lend themselves better than others to close viewing and photography and we have our favourite morning and afternoon locations. In the course of a five or six-hour session we sometimes see the same cars several times; they arrive in a cloud of dust, the drivers keep the car engines running and zoom off again after two or three minutes if nothing awaits their visitation! Little do they know what we have seen and what we will see at this one spot while they race around getting hot, dusty and irritable, particularly if at the end of the day they haven't seen lion, leopard or cheetah. In a typical viewing session we record nine species of large game animals, including elephant, greater kudu, gemsbok, springbok, red hartebeest and lion. The smaller beasties usually include a resident slender mongoose, yellow mongoose and African wild cat stalking doves.

The early morning and late afternoon hours are generally the busiest at waterholes but each species has its favoured time to slake its thirst. Gemsbok, giraffe and ostrich can be expected at any time but if you want to see large predators then you have to be in place very early.

With its all-encircling fence and because it is only a shadow of its original self, albeit a very large one, Etosha has been likened to a huge zoo, but unlike its South African cousin the Kruger National Park, it is not as yet a Disneyland.

Above: Giraffe are commonly seen in Etosha but they rarely wander onto the open plains, being mainly found in the vicinity of their food trees.

ETOSHA NATIONAL PARK

Travel and access: There are two entrance gates, one to Okaukuejo Camp in the south and the other to Namutoni Camp in the east. To reach Okaukuejo from Windhoek, follow the B1 for 242 km to Otjiwarongo; turn left onto the C33 and drive for a short distance before turning right onto the C38 to Outjo; from Outjo follow the C38 for 117 km to the entrance gate; the distance from the gate to Okaukuejo is 18 km.

To reach Namutoni from Windhoek, follow the B1 for 242 km to Otjiwarongo and proceed north-eastwards for 182 km to Tsumeb; from Tsumeb continue on the B1 for 73 km and turn left onto the C38 to the entrance gate (Von Lindequist gate). The camp is 8 km from the gate. Access to Halali Camp is by internal roads only. Etosha Fly-in Safaris operates a flying service at all three camps; there are also charter flights to Tsumeb.

Mobility: With the exception of the roads between the gates and Namutoni and Okaukuejo, which are tarred, all internal roads are gravel and well maintained. There is an extensive network of game-viewing roads. Halali Camp is closed between 1 November and 15 March.

Accommodation: OKAUKUEJO CAMP has 2-, 3- and 4-bed self-contained bungalows, each with a bathroom, cooking facilities, a refrigerator and bedding; 4-bed tents using communal ablution facilities and kitchen; 2-bed rooms, each with a bathroom and bedding.

NAMUTONI CAMP has 2-, 3- and 4-bed rooms with bedding, some with a bathroom, in the Namutoni Fort (the 4-bed rooms also have cooking facilities); 2-bed rooms, each with a bathroom and bedding; 4-bed mobile homes, each with a bathroom, kitchen facilities and bedding; a camping and caravan site with communal ablution and cooking facilities.

HALALI CAMP has self-contained, 4-bed bungalows, each with a bathroom, cooking facilities, a refrigerator and bedding; 4-bed tents using communal ablution and kitchen facilities; 2-bed rooms, each with a bathroom and bedding; 4-bed tents with bedding, using communal ablution and cooking facilities; 10-bed dormitory rooms. There is a camping and caravan site with ablution and cooking facilities. It is necessary to book well in advance during school holidays.

MOKUTI LODGE – 500 m from the Von Lindequist gate near Namutoni – has double-bedded chalets and 5-bed family units, all with en-suite bathrooms, a total of 96 rooms.

Other facilities: All three camps have a licensed restaurant; a shop with a wide selection of goods; petrol and diesel supplies; mail facilities; swimming pools; picnic sites. Okaukuejo Camp has an information centre and limited car repair facilities. Namutoni Camp has a museum. Mokuti Lodge has two restaurants, a bar, conference centre, swimming pool and a short walking trail in the private reserve.

Climate: This is a summer rainfall area, with the bulk falling between November and May. At this time temperatures are usually high and this is not the time to visit if you don't like the heat. Winter days are mild to warm but the nights are often cold.

Best times to visit: Most people visit the park between April and September when temperatures are at their most pleasant and the game concentrates around the waterholes. However, if your primary goal is to see the greatest diversity of birds, then the wet summer months are the best. March and April are especially productive.

Main attractions: Large diversity of wildlife; excellent waterhole observations during dry season; good infrastructure.

Hazards: Malaria; don't get out of your car except at camps and demarcated picnic sites.

For further information: Ministry of Environment and Tourism.

① *Chobe National Park*
② *Moremi Wildlife Reserve*

Chapter 5

OKAVANGO

THE WORLD'S LARGEST INLAND DELTA

Thy voice is on the rolling air;
I hear thee where the waters run;
Thou standest in the rising sun,
And in the setting thou art fair.

Alfred Tennyson, *In Memoriam*

There was a time in the recent past when tens of thousands of red lechwe walked, trotted and waded across the floodplains of the Linyanti Swamp, but then came the time for vultures! It was a period of political and human transition and the rule of law seemed to have been abandoned. Great palls of smoke from deliberate grass burns blotted out the sunsets and gunfire became as often heard as the call of fish eagles and coucals. The lechwe herds were massacred; poachers hacked off only the haunches and shoulders of the antelope, leaving the remainder for the vultures and jackals. The greatly reduced herds, perversely, moved closer to the game guard posts, seemingly expecting protection which they

never received. Then the guns were turned on the elephants. We can still hear the screams of terror and the trumpeting of rage, with great dust clouds raised by the mighty cushioned feet, and in particular the silence that followed. It was probably the silence, the lack of bird song or call, that left the greatest impression upon us. Today the gunfire has gone and two conservation areas have been proclaimed, but the lechwe herds will never recover their former glory.

Rising in the Angolan highlands, various tributaries feed their waters into the Okavango River. The river flows into the largest inland river delta in the world, a vast complex of channels, lagoons and floodplains extending over 15 000 km² that overlies the deep Kalahari sands of northern Botswana. The Okavango Delta has been described as "one of the last best places on earth" – and with some justification, although it has not been immune from man-made problems.

Prehistory

Little has been recorded about the prehistory of the Okavango region. It is believed that the ancestors of the San arrived in Botswana at least 25 000 years ago – probably earlier – but when they reached the area of the delta is unknown. No major archaeological site is known here but the Tsodilo Hills, lying to the

Above: *The sitatunga is the most aquatic of all the antelope occurring in the delta, swimming freely between feeding grounds, or to escape danger.*
PHOTO: IAN MANNING

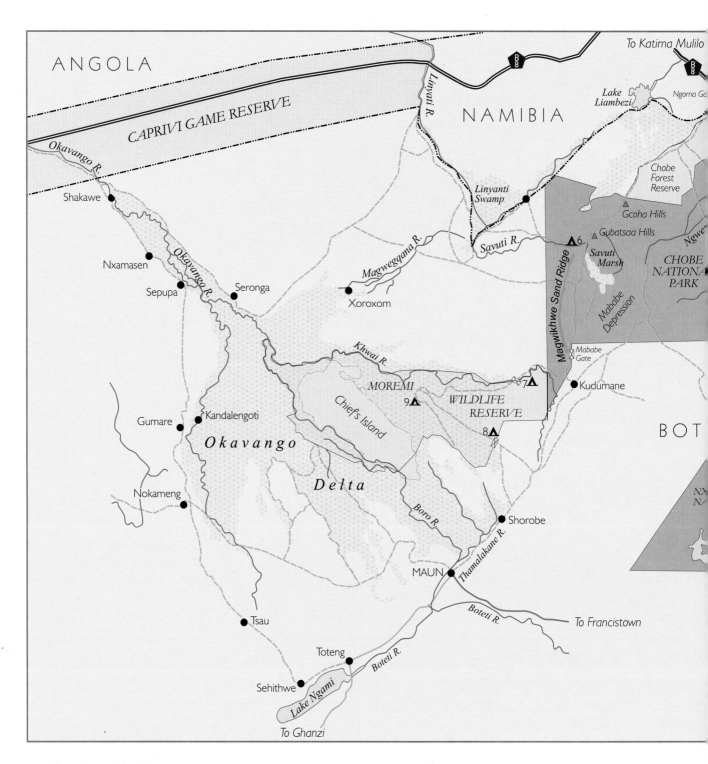

west of the central Okavango Panhandle, are a veritable gallery of San art, and that of their ancestors, with numerous well preserved rock paintings on the walls of overhangs.

History

Several different clan groupings of San people live in Botswana, with for example the Dzu in the region of the Tsodilo Hills. Although traditionally hunter-gatherers, the San in Botswana have largely given up this way of life but in the delta they still fish and hunt, as do other indigenous tribes.

By the 13th century the first pastoral ancestors of the modern-day Tswana peoples filtered into the area from the north. In the 18th century a further influx of members of this

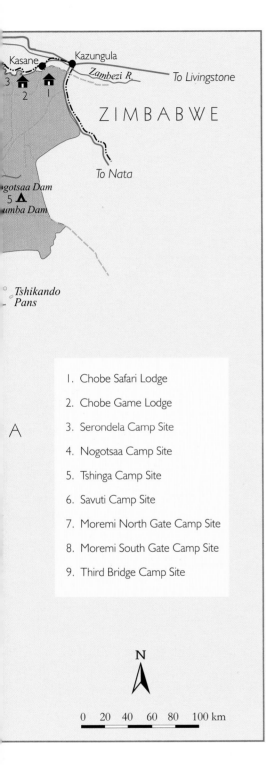

Map legend:

1. Chobe Safari Lodge

2. Chobe Game Lodge

3. Serondela Camp Site

4. Nogotsaa Camp Site

5. Tshinga Camp Site

6. Savuti Camp Site

7. Moremi North Gate Camp Site

8. Moremi South Gate Camp Site

9. Third Bridge Camp Site

A

N

0   20   40   60   80   100 km

Europeans first entered the area of the Okavango and Lake Ngami in the early part of the 19th century, although it is certain that elephant hunters and traders – Portuguese, half-caste *pombeiros* and Boers – penetrated the area in the previous century in search of the white gold, ivory. Explorers such as Andersson and Livingstone passed through such locations as Lake Ngami, and numerous missionaries attempted to impose their alien religion on the "innocent savages". It is of interest to note here that when David Livingstone first observed Lake Ngami in 1849, he estimated that it was 120 km in circumference and more than 2 m deep in some spots.

Towards the end of the last century Cecil John Rhodes tried by devious means to take over the control of the then Bechuanaland territory, annexed in March 1885, from the British colonial office in order to bring it under the control of his British South Africa Company. However, three Batswana chiefs, Bathoen, Sebele and Khama, who were opposed to this move, travelled to London to petition the crown with "We fear they will fill our country with liquor." With the assistance of the London Missionary Society they took the case to the English press and public and Rhodes failed in his landgrab attempt. The colonial authority retained power until 30 September 1966 when Bechuanaland, now Botswana, became an independent state.

Geography

Northern Botswana once held a large lake that was made up of two parts. A long and narrow section encompassed the present Lake Ngami and extended in a north-easterly direction as far as western Zambia. This was joined by a channel perhaps 10 km wide that linked it to the south-eastern part of the lake, which inundated the entire Makgadikgadi Pan system from the eastern boundary of the central Kalahari to the present Zimbabwe border.

Before the advent of an episode of faulting in the earth's crust, the Okavango River formed part of the watershed of the mighty Zambezi River. There is geological evidence that the Okavango once flowed into the Indian Ocean via the Shashe and Limpopo rivers. The fact that these two eastward-flowing rivers run mainly through deeply incised valleys is an

Above: *A giant among wading birds, the goliath heron (Ardea goliath) is a rather uncommon resident in the Okavango.*
Below: *The flap-neck chameleon (Chamaeleo dilepis) is the only member of the family known to occur throughout northern Botswana.*
Far left: *The bubbling kassina (Kassina senegalensis) is one of many amphibian species associated with the Okavango. Unlike many frogs that hop, the kassina either walks or runs, giving it its alternative name of running frog.*

tribe penetrated what is now Botswana from the south to escape the depredations of the Zulu army.

Delta-dwelling tribes now include the Bayei, Seyei and Mbukushu, with people from all over Botswana and neighbouring countries living on the periphery of the delta with its abundant fish and the draw of jobs in the burgeoning tourist industry.

indication that in past geological periods they carried much greater quantities of water than they do today. It was during a period of warping and faulting of the earth's crust, particularly in north-central Botswana, that the flow of the Okavango was cut off from the Shashe and Limpopo system and the Okavango poured its waters into the Makgadikgadi, the

number of major tributaries, the Luasingua, Langa, Curiri, Cuito, Cuebe and Cuanavale, contribute their waters to the flow of the Cubango, the name that this river takes in Angola. Where it forms the international boundary between that country and Namibia, the southerners refer to it as the Okavango and so it remains for the rest of its journey. The river crosses Namibia in that narrow belt of land separating Kavango from western Caprivi and then meanders along what is known as the Panhandle floodplain for some 96 km, sandwiched between two parallel crustal faults.

The Gomare Fault, cutting across the lowest point of the Panhandle and creating a slight drop in elevation to its south, causes the Okavango River to split into several main channels and an intricate network of shallower watercourses. This complex of channels, lagoons, floodplains and islands is at its driest during the summer months when inflow is at

Top: Beds of Phragmites *reeds and woodland on the northern fringe of the Linyanti Swamp.*
Above: *One of the common trees in the region is* Baikiaea plurijuga, *heavily harvested in many areas for its fine timber.*
Right: *Bushbuck (*Tragelaphus scriptus) *occur throughout the area but rarely venture out into open locations. Only the rams carry horns.*

world's largest saltpan. Today, the flow is lost in the delta, although in years of bountiful rain the floodwaters may reach Lake Ngami in the south-west, or flow down the Boteti River to the pans in the south-east.

The delta receives some two thirds of its waters from deep in the central Angolan Highlands: Huambo and Bié provinces. A

its lowest and most water is found only in the deeper channels and some areas of standing water. It is during these summer months that the rains are falling far to the north in Angola but it takes until March or April before the inflow causes a rise in the delta water levels. These increased flows reach the base of the delta only in June or July, an indication of the vast area over which the waters must be distributed. Rain falls locally over the area of the Okavango Delta from October to May, an average of 500 mm per year but often patchy. Local rains contribute only about a third of the delta's water.

Water flow varies according to how much rain has fallen in the Angolan catchment but an average flood carries in 10 billion cubic metres of that essential liquid and deposits as much as 727 000 tons of fertile sediment over the Kalahari sands, to form a vast alluvial fan – the world's largest inland delta. A river to nowhere! The waters spill over the banks and spread across the plains, in the process isolating higher patches of ground. Many of these are well wooded.

Amazingly, much of this prodigious quantity of water evaporates or is lost through transpiration (water loss through plant stomata) but in good years the flow disperses along the Boteti River and into Lake Ngami. In exceptional years there is water flow from the delta north-eastwards into Chobe's Savuti Marsh via the Selinda Spillway. The continuous depositing of sediment and blocking of waterways by vegetation, thus changing the courses of the waterways and creating new courses, ensure that the Okavango is a dynamic and ever-changing system.

To the north-east of the Okavango is the Linyanti Swamp, much smaller but in many ways similar. The Linyanti straddles the Namibia-Botswana border and is fed by the Kwando River, which rises in the southern highlands of Moxico Province, Angola. The Kwando runs into the Linyanti, then the Chobe and finally mixes its waters with the Zambezi in far north-eastern Botswana. We mention the Linyanti Swamp because during the best rainy seasons water spills over from the Okavango via the Selinda Spillway to connect the delta with its system of rivers and wetlands. The Linyanti, despite the relatively small area it covers, was until the late 1980s one of our favourite southern African wild areas but heavy poaching pressure and incursions by cattle have diminished its appeal for us. However, the proclamation of two small game reserves, Mamili (355 km²) and Mudumu (850 km²), will hopefully go some way towards its salvation.

Nowhere in the Okavango Delta is the water deep, averaging perhaps 7 m in the main channels of the upper reaches, to as little as 20 cm in some lagoons. As the floodwaters overspill the channels and spread over the floodplains, many islands stand in splendid isolation, their existence having begun as large termite mounds, around which silt and sediments built up. Here plant seeds could germinate and take root. The largest island at almost 1 000 km², Chief's Island, is however a long, flat ridge with calcrete-type material forming its backbone. At its northern point the water flow is deflected north and south. Approximately 60% of the flow passes to its northern flank where it runs in large part into the lagoon network in, and close to, the Moremi Wildlife Reserve, the only formal conservation area in the delta. The remainder flows to the south of the island to the Thamalakane Fault. Large areas of the western delta are characterised by shallow lagoons that are mostly dry outside the months of flooding but form rich grazing at this time.

Flora

One of the most attractive features of the delta is its crystal clear waters, thanks mostly to the filtering action of the great expanses of aquatic vegetation, which act both as filters of sediment and sponges, absorbing and releasing water gradually.

Beds of tall papyrus dominate the waterways and other areas of permanent water in both the Okavango River and its delta, and in places grow so densely that the water flow is diverted to create new channels. As one moves to the south of the delta where permanent water is less abundant the papyrus is largely replaced by feather-plume, or *Phragmites*, reeds. These are harvested extensively by people living around the delta for use as roof-thatching and for other domestic needs.

Throughout the delta there are small islands, on which grow such tree species as the wild date palm, the abundant real fan palm, as well as the pale-barked appleleaf, sycamore and water figs, sickle-leafed *Albizia*, several *Acacia* species and the red seringa. On the drier eastern and southern fringes of the delta the mopane tree is dominant – a favoured food plant of the numerous elephants in the delta, and many have been levelled by these pachyderms.

In the middle and lower reaches of the delta lie extensive seasonally flooded grasslands which attract thousands of head of game as

Above: *Two types of reed dominate in the Okavango and Linyanti swamps, the* Papyrus *and, pictured here,* Phragmites. *These reedbeds are important habitats for a wide range of animals, ranging from numerous aquatic insects to the shaggy-coated swamp antelope, the sitatunga* (Tragelaphus spekei).

the waters recede, exposing fresh growth. It has been estimated that as much as 70% of the delta's grasslands burn each year, some of the fires caused by lightning but most by hunters and cattle herders.

Fauna

Probably the mammal with the most important ecological influence in the delta is that barrel-chested, heavy-muzzled beast, the hippopotamus. Hippo numbers are not particularly high; probably the fairest estimate is around 1 500 individuals, with perhaps an additional 500 in the Linyanti and Chobe

Right: Despite its distinctive coloration the pygmy goose (Nettapus auritus) is difficult to spot among the aquatic vegetation it favours. At certain times flocks of several hundred geese may gather but pairs and small groups are more usual.

SPECIES TO WATCH FOR

MAMMALS

Elephant	*Loxodonta africana*	Common waterbuck	*Kobus ellipsiprymnus ellipsiprymnus*
Plains zebra	*Equus burchellii*	Lion	*Panthera leo*
Hippopotamus	*Hippopotamus amphibius*	Leopard	*Panthera pardus*
Buffalo	*Syncerus caffer*	Serval	*Felis serval*
Sable antelope	*Hippotragus niger*	Spotted hyaena	*Crocuta crocuta*
Roan antelope	*Hippotragus equinus*	Side-striped jackal	*Canis adustus*
Tsessebe	*Damaliscus lunatus lunatus*	Wild dog	*Lycaon pictus*
Sitatunga	*Tragelaphus spekei*	Cape clawless otter	*Aonyx capensis*
Bushbuck ("Chobe")	*Tragelaphus scriptus*	Spotted-necked otter	*Lutra maculicollis*
Red lechwe	*Kobus leche leche*	Banded mongoose	*Mungos mungo*
Puku	*Kobus vardoni*	Peters's epauletted fruit-bat	*Epomophorus crypturus*

BIRDS

White pelican	*Pelecanus onocrotalus*	Water dikkop	*Burhinus vermiculatus*
Pink-backed pelican	*Pelecanus rufescens*	Red-winged pratincole	*Glareola pratincola*
Darter	*Anhinga melanogaster*	Meyer's parrot	*Poicephalus meyeri*
Goliath heron	*Ardea goliath*	Ross's turaco	*Musophaga rossae*
Black egret	*Egretta ardesiaca*	Coppery-tailed coucal	*Centropus cupreicaudus*
Slaty egret	*Egretta vinaceigula*	Senegal coucal	*Centropus senegalensis*
Rufous-bellied heron	*Butorides rufiventris*	Pel's fishing owl	*Scotopelia peli*
White-backed night heron	*Gorsachius leuconotus*	Giant kingfisher	*Ceryle maxima*
Saddle-billed stork	*Ephippiorhynchus senegalensis*	Blue-cheeked bee-eater	*Merops persicus*
White-backed duck	*Thalassornis leuconotus*	Southern carmine bee-eater	*Merops nubicoides*
Red-billed teal	*Anas erythrorhyncha*	Broad-billed roller	*Eurystomus glaucurus*
Pygmy goose	*Nettapus auritus*	Bradfield's hornbill	*Tockus bradfieldi*
Hooded vulture	*Necrosyrtes monachus*	Mosque swallow	*Hirundo senegalensis*
Western banded snake eagle	*Circaetus cinerascens*	Black-faced babbler	*Turdoides melanops*
Palmnut vulture	*Gypohierax angolensis*	White-rumped babbler	*Turdoides leucopygius*
African fish eagle	*Haliaeetus vocifer*	Arnot's chat	*Thamnolaea arnoti*
African marsh harrier	*Circus ranivorus*	Greater swamp warbler	*Acrocephalus rufescens*
African hobby falcon	*Falco cuvierii*	Stierling's barred warbler	*Camaroptera stierlingi*
Dickinson's kestrel	*Falco dickinsoni*	Black-backed cisticola	*Cisticola galactotes*
Red-billed francolin	*Francolinus adspersus*	Chirping cisticola	*Cisticola pipiens*
Wattled crane	*Grus carunculata*	Pink-throated longclaw	*Macronyx ameliae*
Crowned crane	*Balearica regulorum*	Sousa's shrike	*Lanius souzae*
Striped crake	*Aenigmatolimnas marginalis*	Swamp boubou	*Laniarius bicolor*
Lesser gallinule	*Porphyrula alleni*	Yellow-billed oxpecker	*Buphagus africanus*
Lesser moorhen	*Gallinula angulata*	Golden weaver	*Ploceus xanthops*
African finfoot	*Podica senegalensis*	Brown-throated weaver	*Ploceus xanthopterus*
African jacana	*Actophilornis africanus*	Brown firefinch	*Lagonosticta nitidula*
Long-toed plover	*Vanellus crassirostris*		

rivers. Nevertheless they play an essential role in keeping the waterways open and fertilising the channels and lagoons. In certain African wetlands where hippos have been eradicated or greatly reduced in numbers, waterways and pans have become choked with aquatic vegetation. The hippo has been referred to as the "dredger of channels, keeper of swamps, fertiliser of plants and feeder of fish". Quite a reputation! In addition these animals serve to crop long, coarse grasses and reeds, making short, new growth available to more selective grazing species. Hippos tend to be closely attached to permanent waters but during the flood season they disperse to the larger temporary water bodies. This gives them access to new grazing grounds. For us there are three sounds that epitomise Africa – the snort-grunts of the hippo, the call of the fish eagle and the roaring of a lion – and all three can be regularly heard in the delta.

But if the hippo has a massive influence on the waterways, it has to be the elephant that has played the biggest role in modifying the ecosystem that encompasses the delta, the Linyanti Swamp and their associated river systems. Northern Botswana plays host to Africa's last great unharassed elephant herd, although more accurately we should say that many of these animals are internationalists. During the wet season large numbers of elephants disperse away from the delta and occupy the eastern woodlands of Botswana where clay-bottomed seasonal pans hold water and new plant growth provides adequate nourishment. During the dry season when the sea-

sonal pans no longer hold water the pachyderm herds move back into the delta, northwards to the Kwando, Linyanti and Chobe rivers, and not needing passports they freely cross into Zimbabwe, Namibia, Zambia and Angola. Little accurate information has been collated on these movements but the Botswana authorities have been very vociferous about "their" elephants that are being culled in Zimbabwe's Hwange National Park and adjacent state woodlands. Hwange has artificial waterholes that allow elephants to withstand the protracted dry season but the large numbers that utilise the park also, according to the Zimbabweans, threaten its vegetation structures and in turn certain of its animal biota.

Although elephant numbers in northern Botswana vary according to the season, a whopping 65 000 animals are believed to be present at its peak. The impact of these great herbivores on the vegetation was clearly seen during the seven-year drought that occurred in the 1980s, and is still being felt today. The elephants were forced to remain close to permanent water: the main channels of the upper delta and in particular the border rivers of the north-east. Forced to stay close to places where they could drink, they turned riparian woodland into bare, eroded landscapes. Some argue that as these elephants can range over tens of thousands of kilometres, and vast tracts of woodland remain undamaged, most of which is of little agricultural use to humans, nature should be allowed to take its course. Others advocate culling to reduce elephant numbers but perhaps this role is already being filled by the Zimbabwean authorities. Despite the large size of this elephant population it remains remarkably poorly understood, compared with say those of Kruger, Amboseli or Lake Manyara. What will be important for this vast national herd to sustain its numbers is the continuance of free movement unhindered by artificial barriers, and protection of the eastern dry forests that sustain them during the rains.

Throughout northern Botswana it has been estimated that there are at least 45 000 buffaloes, that dark, unpredictable, cow-like beast that lacks the ability to arouse people's emotions when it is hunted or poached, tinned or turned into biltong. The veterinary cordon fences erected all over Botswana to protect the cattle industry have had a cata-

Top: *The placid waters of the Okavango River just above the Popa Falls, actually a series of shallow rapids.*
Above: *Despite heavy hunting pressure in the past for their valuable belly hides, there are still substantial numbers of Nile crocodiles (Crocodylus niloticus) in the Okavango Delta.*
Left: *Red lechwe on the alert in the Panhandle.*

strophic impact on a number of game species but possibly least on the buffalo.

Although the northernmost arm of the Makalamabedi fence crosses the Thamalakane River and extends marginally into the southern delta, affecting movements of such species as plains zebra, it is the western buffalo fence that has had the biggest impact on the delta, and as a rare exception it has proved beneficial. The only check to the full-scale invasion by cattle and goats deep into the delta has been this fence, which was erected in 1982. Unfortunately it was not put in place to protect the wildlife from this competition, but to prevent the transfer of foot and mouth disease from buffaloes, suspected of carrying it, to cattle. To the west of the buffalo fence the

thousands here, its only stronghold in southern Africa. The Namibian Linyanti was home to more than 50 000 of these handsome slope-backed animals in the early 1980s but uncontrolled poaching has seen their numbers dwindle to perhaps less than 1 000, a tragedy from which they are unlikely to recover.

Other game species in the delta and its fringes to the north and east include giraffe, impala, greater kudu, common waterbuck, blue wildebeest, bushbuck, tsessebe, southern reedbuck, sable, roan, warthog and plains zebra. All of the attendant predators occur in the delta and in areas to the north and east.

Although crocodiles are frequently sighted in the waterways of the Okavango, most visitors are not aware that as a result of hide-hunt-

Above: Two local youngsters catching small fish in traditional fishing baskets in a side pool of the Okavango River. Fish form the principal source of protein for many people living in association with the river and its delta.
Above right: During the breeding season the white-faced duck (Dendrocygna viduata) is generally seen in pairs and small parties but at other times may congregate in flocks numbering in the thousands.

vegetation has been overgrazed; the soil is trampled and the area dust-blown, but to the east the vegetation is intact and carries a diversity of game animals that do not have the anti-environmental manners of their domesticated cousins.

Other game species have not been as lucky as the elephant or buffalo. Deep in the papyrus swamps lives a substantial population, in fact the only viable one in southern Africa, of that true swamp antelope the sitatunga. With its long, splayed hoofs it is able to walk over floating vegetation mats, and will take readily to water if moving between feeding grounds or to escape enemies.

Another water-loving antelope, the red lechwe, occupies the vicinity of the shallows and the floodplains, and occurs in the low

ing over the past 40 or so years their numbers have been reduced by as much as 80%. The crocodile plays an essential role in Africa's water bodies, as scavenger and fish-control specialist. Today this giant reptile is protected in Botswana, although 50 licences are issued each year to non-resident, high-paying trophy hunters, and registered crocodile farms are allowed to harvest breeding stock and eggs.

It is probably the delta's rich and diverse bird populations that act as the drawcard for many of the human visitors who roll into Maun in safari vehicles, or buzz around in light aircraft like so many agitated dragonflies seeking out a resting place at one of the numerous safari camps scattered throughout the delta. An aside: Maun is one of southern Africa's busiest airports, and the near constant whine of aircraft flitting to and fro during daylight hours seriously intrudes into the feeling of untouched wilderness.

Aquatic life

Apart from the anglers out to land the world-record tiger fish, very few visitors give any thought to the aquatic diversity passing below their *mokoro* or – perish the thought – their powerboat. Here in open water, among the matted vegetation or on the bottom live such piscine glories as the slender stonebasher, Zambezi parrotfish, bulldog, Churchill (minus trademark cigar), striped robber, Zambezi grunter, Okavango suckermouth, Zambezi happy, banded jewelfish and spotted squeaker. Never let it be said that the net-wielding ichthyologist does not have a sense of humour in naming fishes!

Apart from the great aquatic diversity, the biomass of fish in the delta and its feeders is also considerable. There are numerous fish predators including otters, kingfishers, fish eagles and cormorants, but humans are the primary piscivores. Although traditional fishing methods such as thrust baskets and traps are still widely used, nets are increasingly employed and hold long-term threats to the well-being of the delta's fish fauna. Traditional fish drives take place when the water level is receding or low and the fish are concentrated in pools and pans, but nets can be used at any time. An indication of the importance of these fisheries to local people: in the stretch of the Okavango River that passes through the Kavango region of Namibia it is estimated that more than 800 tons of fish are harvested each year. For the system as a whole the figure runs into several thousand tons. In many cases fish is the only source of protein regularly available.

Conservation issues

The Okavango Delta as a whole can no longer be regarded as one of Africa's greatest wild areas, at least not in our eyes. Nevertheless, it is still a magnificent wildlife refuge that is deserving of every effort to preserve its integrity. Massive spraying campaigns have all but eliminated the "principal game ranger", the tsetse fly, although small pockets of these valuable small insects still hang onto survival by the tips of their proboscises. Only the tsetse fly and the western buffalo fence are prevent-

ing a wholesale invasion of the delta by thousands of cattle. Fortunately the Botswana authorities are aware of the commercial value of the wildlife as the drawcard that attracts high-paying foreign tourists and trophy hunters. However, there is a feeling among many conservationists that the delicate ecosystem of the delta is already overloaded by the ecotourist hordes. There is also the threat of water extraction from the delta to feed other parts of this largely arid nation, notably the diamond mines to the south.

Chobe National Park – a neighbour on the eastern flank

Chobe National Park in extreme north-eastern Botswana, with the river of the same name forming its northern boundary, is one of southern Africa's finest conservation areas. Covering approximately 12 000 km^2 it was first proclaimed as a game reserve in 1961 and elevated to national park status in 1968. This vast park is mostly flat and featureless, with the exception of the low hill ridges of Gubatsaa, Gcoha and Magwikhwe, and the Mababe Depression, all situated in the south-west. Throughout north-eastern Botswana there are numerous clay-bottomed pans that hold water only during and shortly after the rains. This availability of water away from the delta and the northern border rivers allows thousands of head of game to disperse to graze and browse on the grasslands and mopane and mixed woodlands that dominate the park's vegetation.

Top: *The blackback barb (*Barbus barnardi*) is a small species, seldom exceeding 70 mm in length and living in small shoals among aquatic vegetation.*
Above: *Johnston's topminnow (*Aplocheilichthys johnstoni*) occurs throughout the Okavango system, even in very shallow water.*
Below: *A group of young wild dogs (*Lycaon pictus*) in the Moremi Wildlife Reserve in the east of the delta.*

Right: Sunset over the
Chobe River, drawing its waters
from the Linyanti Swamp which
in good rain years receives flow
from the Okavango via the
Selinda Spillway.

There are several elements that make Chobe a great park: the concentration of elephants along the river during the dry season, the rainy-season migration of tens of thousands of plains zebra, the great herds of buffalo – some a thousand strong. The short-grass plains fringing the Chobe River is the only locality in southern Africa where you will see puku. In the recent past they were also present in the eastern Caprivi of Namibia but heavy poaching has resulted in their extinction there. This is also one of the best locations to see the most brightly coloured and patterned of the southern African bushbuck races.

Some readers may ask why we did not afford Chobe more comprehensive coverage. Although we do consider it to be a great park we are disturbed by the increasing trend towards the East African-type tourist brigade of safari vehicles, each's occupants swallowing the others' dust, encircling lions and other predators and harassing elephants. However – a blessing for the wildlife – great tracts of the park remain inaccessible to humans.

CHOBE NATIONAL PARK

Travel and access: From Francistown follow the main road north-westwards for about 495 km towards Kazungula; just before Kazungula take the signposted turn-off to Kasane village and follow this road to the reserve. If approaching from Victoria Falls in Zimbabwe, follow the main road westwards to the border control at Kazungula and continue westwards to Kasane village.

Coming from north-eastern Namibia travel through the Caprivi Strip to Katima Mulilo and turn right to Ngoma passport control; visitors taking this route must continue eastwards through the park to report to border authorities at Kasane or Kazungula. An alternative route for 4x4 vehicles is from Maun: drive north-eastwards for 138 km to Mababe gate.

There are landing strips for light aircraft at Kasane, Savuti and Linyanti, but conditions need to be checked.

Mobility: The road from Maun to Mababe gate is closed during the rainy season. The all-weather road between Sedudu and Ngoma gate is suitable for most vehicles, but in all other sections of the park the roads are generally very sandy and can only be negotiated by 4x4 vehicles. Movement can be very difficult during the rains.

Accommodation: Several privately owned safari camps operate from Savuti and Linyanti, and offer luxury tented accommodation. The Chobe Safari Lodge at Kasane has chalets and a camping and caravan site. The luxury Chobe Game Lodge is situated a short distance from Kasane, just inside the park.

There are four public campsites: Savuti, Serondela, Nogatsaa and Tshinga. Savuti and Serondela have basic ablution facilities, but there are no facilities at Nogatsaa and Tshinga. Camping is not allowed elsewhere in the park. The number of camps and lodges in and around Chobe is growing constantly; it is advisable to approach one of the larger specialist travel agents.

Other facilities: Fishing is permitted at Bushbuck Drive, Puku Flats and Serondela campsite; permits are required. There is a store selling liquor and a bar at Chobe Safari Lodge. Petrol and diesel and most supplies are available at Kasane. Clive Walker Trails conduct the Chobe section of their guided Fish Eagle Trail (Okavango-Chobe) from a mobile camp at Savuti.

Climate: As for Moremi.

Best times to visit: As for Moremi.

Main attractions: Diverse and abundant game, including very large numbers of elephants and buffaloes; rare and localised species such as puku and red lechwe; excellent bird-watching with more than 450 species; plains zebra migration between Linyanti and Savuti – November-December and then between February and April.

Hazards: Malaria; crocodiles and other potentially dangerous animals; do not drive at night.

For further information: The Warden, Department of Wildlife and National Parks, Kasane. Chobe Safari Lodge, P.O. Box 10, Kasane. Chobe Game Lodge, P.O. Box 32, Kasane. Clive Walker Trails, P.O. Box 645, Bedfordview 2008, South Africa; tel. (011) 453 7645/6/7; fax (011) 453 7649.

MOREMI WILDLIFE RESERVE

Travel and access: From Maun follow the track north-eastwards in the direction of Chobe National Park; after 64 km turn left and continue for another 34 km to the Moremi South gate. Alternatively, from Savuti in the north, drive southwards, turn right at the signpost to the reserve and follow this track to Moremi North gate. Both these routes require a 4x4 vehicle; the latter route has long stretches of deep sand, remember your fuel consumption will increase.

Mobility: There are game-viewing drives on sandy tracks. Movement is severely limited in the rainy season and in very wet years is impossible. Boat trips can be made from Xakanaxa Camp near Third Bridge by arrangement with the safari operators.

Accommodation: A number of safari companies operate lodges and camps on the edge of the reserve, most of which are expensive. Booking for these is essential. There are three public campsites, at South gate, North gate and Third Bridge. South gate and North gate camps have basic, and usually overworked, ablution facilities and tapped water. Third Bridge has a few pit toilets and the only water source is the river.

Other facilities: The nearest fuel and food supplies are at Maun.

Climate: This is a summer rainfall region with most rain falling from December to February. The driest period is from May to October. Summer temperatures are generally warm to very hot. Winter days are usually mild but nights can be cold.

Best times to visit: The drier months are the best for game-viewing, as mobility during the rains can be severely restricted with many roads becoming impassable.

Main attractions: Abundant game and bird life; crystal clear water.

Hazards: Malaria; bilharzia; crocodiles and other potentially dangerous animals.

For further information: Department of Wildlife and National Parks, Maun.

OKAVANGO DELTA

Travel and access: Maun is the main access point to the delta and it is here that most safari companies collect their clients, some flying them from the airstrip at Maun to their bush camps deep in the delta. Dug-out canoes (mekoro) and other watercraft can be hired.

Mobility: It is strongly recommended that you make use of the services offered by one of the many companies operating from Maun and do not attempt to enter the delta unaccompanied. Walking is permitted, but limited; the best way to move around is in a boat.

Accommodation: There is a hotel in Maun. Privately run camps a short distance outside Maun on the road to Moremi offer chalet-type accommodation, campsites, bars and eating facilities. Safari companies offer all-inclusive camps, but most are expensive and prebooking is essential.

Other facilities: Fishing; boats for hire. The nearest food and fuel supplies are available in Maun.

Climate: As for Moremi.

Best times to visit: As for Moremi.

Main attractions: Crystal clear waters; diversity of game and bird species; there are still places where one can escape the tourist trade.

Hazards: Malaria; bilharzia along the southern and western fringes of the delta; sleeping sickness (tsetse fly); crocodiles, hippos and other dangerous animals.

Above: *Troops of savanna baboons* (Papio cynocephalus) *are frequently sighted in the area, feeding in woodland or on the open floodplains. Before nightfall they always retreat to tall trees to escape the attention of predators. When tiny the youngsters cling to the chest of the mother but as they become stronger they ride jockey-style on her back.*

For further information: There are many tour operators with tourist camps in the delta and we would advise that you contact your travel agent and shop around for the deal that best suits you.
Department of Wildlife and National Parks, P.O. Box 131, Gaborone; tel. (267) 371405.

Chapter 6

HWANGE

PLACE OF THE ELEPHANTS

Nature's great masterpiece, an elephant
The only harmless great thing.

John Donne, *The Progress of the Soul*

The male Swainson's francolins are harshly proclaiming their small piece of Africa, from the top of termite mounds and dead trees. Doves are winging in for the first drink of the day and a sway-bellied hyaena, bloated from some unseen midnight feast, makes its way denwards before the blood-red sun should rise too high in the sky. A pall of dust extending over a distance of at least 2 km hangs in the cool, still air, raised by the hoofs of more than 1 000 buffalo snaking towards the waterhole. With much bellowing and lowing the leaders

emerge from the bush, intent on slaking their thirst. Within minutes the first to drink are pushed into chest-deep water. It takes 30 minutes before all have had their fill. Two matriarchal elephant herds emerge silently from the woodland and the buffalo move slowly and seemingly reluctantly from the water. In the distance a lion roars, either satisfied with the night's hunting or warning others to avoid his beat. All of this in less than an hour on one of our dry-season visits to Zimbabwe's Hwange National Park!

Prehistory

Hwange lies in north-western Matabeleland Province and it is the largest conservation area in the country, covering some 14 651 km². Archaeologists tell us that humans first entered the Hwange area between 20 000 and 10 000 years before present and represented the Stone Age Wilton Culture. It is believed that the rock engravings of animal tracks, located at Bambusi and Deteema, were executed by these early settlers.

Above: During the dry season thousands of elephant move into Hwange from surrounding areas in order to gain easy access to its artificial water-points.

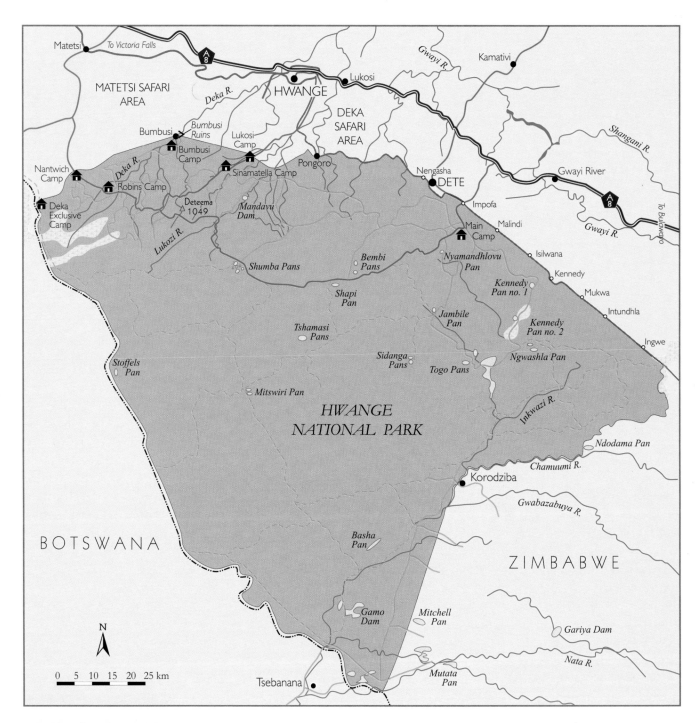

Signs of old fields and the ruins at Matoa indicate that people of later cultures also called Hwange (the incorrect version Wankie was used for many years) home. Hwange Rosumbani, a sub-chief of the Rozvi tribe, and his people lived peacefully in the area until the great warrior chief Mzilikazi, founder of the Ndebele nation, arrived with his army. Fleeing the wrath of Chaka, the Zulu king who held sway over large areas in what is now KwaZulu-Natal, Mzilikazi was intent on carving for himself an empire. Hwange and his followers were massacred but his name lives on in one of Africa's greatest game sanctuaries. The area to the south of the present park was proclaimed as Mzilikazi's royal hunting preserve and remained so until the entry of Cecil John Rhodes and British Empire, and a goodly bit of greed, destroyed his power.

But long before the arrival of Mzilikazi or Rhodes, those hardy desert-dwellers the San (often referred to as Bushmen) roamed the central and western areas of Hwange. They hunted only for their immediate needs, living a hard life but one that was in harmony with nature. It was only after the proclamation of the Wankie Game Reserve in 1928 that the last San hunter-gatherer bands returned forever to Bechuanaland, or Botswana as we know it today.

History

Hwange had its beginnings as a result of a questionnaire survey, rather an inglorious start to this fine park! The government requested that native commissioners and people with knowledge of game populations select the most suitable area for the country's first game sanctuary, and fortunately Hwange (Wankie) was selected. In 1928 Ted Davison, then only 22, was appointed the park's first warden, a post he held for 33 years. When he arrived there were no roads – he patrolled with horses and pack donkeys; water was scarce in the dry season and he had to build his own home. At the time of his arrival in the area, two commercial activities were taking place under permit within the reserve's boundaries: timber extraction and the capture of wild animals for the international zoo trade. Lundin and Herbst had their base camp at Kennedy where the animals were held in bomas to condition them to captivity before the journey to the railhead and the long, slow trip to one of the South African or Mozambican ports. The permits were not renewed after the game reserve was proclaimed but apparently timber extraction, mainly of Zimbabwe teak, continued in the eastern section of the park and in the Linkwasha valley until 1937.

In the 1930s the threat of sleeping sickness, carried by the "needle-biting" tsetse fly, resulted in the slaughter of many head of game in a buffer zone between the railway line that forms part of the park boundary and the Gwaai River. The government allowed free hunting and employed African hunters. This resulted in a drain of game stocks in the park, as animals were forced to leave its sanctuary and cross the buffer zone for water, which was very limited during the dry season within the park. It was soon realised that water would be the key to the future of Hwange and in 1936 a start was made to erect windmills to provide a year-round supply of this necessity. These were later replaced with diesel pumps to

ensure a more reliable supply and to increase the quantity of water reaching the surface. The presence of permanent water inside the park ensured that most of the game remained out of reach of the hunters' guns. It is of interest, albeit of a depressing nature, that the slaughter of tens of thousands of head of game here and at other African locations, in the belief that it would control sleeping sickness, was in vain, as it was later found that the primary carriers were warthog and bush pig – neither of which was targeted!

Although tourists came to the park in the early years there were no facilities and they viewed the game on foot. The first huts were built with large green "Kimberley" bricks, made from soil taken from termite mounds. These structures remained in use until 1966. Huts built later were constructed with poles and cement, and without windows. In an attempt to improve the standard of accommodation for visitors, a number of second-hand wooden prefabs were erected, but these good intentions were foiled by a minuscule but disturbing creature already in residence: the bedbug. The huts were never used.

It was only in 1950, when Hwange was proclaimed a national park, that the development of tourist facilities really got off the ground. Today there are three camps: Main, Robins/Nantwich and Sinamatella. Robins takes its name from the eccentric Herbert Robins, who bequeathed his two farms *Big Toms* and *Little Toms* to extend Hwange in the north.

Geography

The greater part of Hwange, in the central and western regions, is covered by the sands of the Kalahari. This largely unbroken mantle of sand has no major rivers but there are many natural, shallow pans that hold water during the rainy season and a number of these have water artificially pumped into them during the dry season. The northern section of the park is covered with basaltic rock and it is drained by the Deka River system. This watershed is the most significant topographical feature in Hwange, stretching as it does across the park from Ngamo and Kennedy towards Main Camp and then north-westwards to Shumba. North of the watershed

Above: *Impala* (Aepyceros melampus) *rams waiting out a rain shower.*
Far left: *A mantis female in the act of devouring her mate.*
Below: *European rollers* (Coracias garrulus) *are common summer visitors to the park.*

the landscape is dominated by granite outcrops, which are in sharp contrast to the surrounding areas and are located in shallow, sandy soils.

In November the great, water-filled clouds bring relief to the parched earth and the plant and animal worlds begin to stir. After a long dry season the first raindrops dampening the ground produce a fragrance that equals any fine French perfume. In some years the clouds are bountiful and generous, in other years they can be lean and mean, with some seasons delivering more than 800 mm, others as little as 320 mm. With a peculiar sense that man does not yet fully understand, the plants and many of the animals gear their reproduction to suit the level of the coming rainfall. If only our weather forecasting could be as accurate!

teak *Baikiaea plurijuga* (or kiaat as it is known in the timber trade), bloodwood or mukwa *Pterocarpus angolensis*, mangwe or silver terminalia *Terminalia sericea*, mufuti *Brachystegia boehmii*, large stands of mopane *Colophospermum mopane* with its characteristic "butterfly" leaves, and 17 species of the genus *Acacia*. At least 255 species of trees and tall shrubs grow in Hwange. A grand total of 1 070 plant species have been collected to date.

Fauna

That hunter's hunter, Frederick Courteney Selous, hunted in the Hwange area in the 1870s, travelling as far north as Linkwasha and Dopi vleis by oxwagon, but from here he proceeded on foot for fear that he would lose his

Right: Mukwa, or bloodwood (Pterocarpus angolensis), is a conspicuous tree in Hwange, particularly when it is carrying its large, distinctive fruits. Although not cut in the park, elsewhere it is much sought after as a fine furniture timber and for the manufacture of dugout canoes.
Far right: The flame lily (Gloriosa superba) has been given its common name for obvious reasons.
Below: Large herds of buffalo raise clouds of dust as they make their way to waterholes during the dry season.

Above right: The mongoose species most frequently observed in Hwange is the banded (Mungos mungo), as it is diurnal and highly social, living in groups of five to thirty individuals.

Flora

The vegetation in Hwange is rich and varied, with the different plant communities showing the influence of the rainfall, which is lowest in the Kalahari sands of the west. Nine major vegetation structures are recognised in Hwange. Apart from limited areas of open grassland and mixed scrub the park consists mainly of a variety of woodland types. There are extensive areas dominated by Zimbabwe

oxen to the potentially deadly parasite carried by the then numerous tsetse fly. The lack of surface water in the extensive area covered by the Kalahari sands forced the game to move towards the Gwaai River and it was here that the famous hunter and naturalist was most active. Before 1896 he recorded black rhinos as occurring in fair numbers in the well bushed north of what is now the park but by 1912 it is believed that they had all been hunted out. Only in 1942 was this weak-sighted, bad-tem-

SPECIES TO WATCH FOR

MAMMALS

Elephant	*Loxodonta africana*		Lion	*Panthera leo*
Buffalo	*Syncerus caffer*		Leopard	*Panthera pardus*
Plains zebra	*Equus burchellii*		Spotted hyaena	*Crocuta crocuta*
Giraffe	*Giraffa camelopardalis giraffa*		Black-backed jackal	*Canis mesomelas*
Sable antelope	*Hippotragus niger*		Side-striped jackal	*Canis adustus*
Roan antelope	*Hippotragus equinus*		Bat-eared fox	*Otocyon megalotis*
Southern reedbuck	*Redunca arundinunus*		Banded mongoose	*Mungos mungo*
Common waterbuck	*Kobus ellipsiprymnus ellipsiprymnus*		Slender mongoose	*Galerella sanguinea*
Greater kudu	*Tragelaphus strepsiceros*		Dwarf mongoose	*Helogale parvula*

BIRDS

Ostrich	*Struthio camelus*		Barred owl	*Glaucidium capense*
White stork	*Ciconia ciconia*		Southern carmine bee-eater	*Merops nubicoides*
Abdim's stork	*Ciconia abdimii*		White-fronted bee-eater	*Merops bullockoides*
Marabou	*Leptoptilos crumeniferus*		Racket-tailed roller	*Coracias spatulata*
Hooded vulture	*Necrosyrtes monachus*		Broad-billed roller	*Eurystomus glaucurus*
Lappet-faced vulture	*Torgos tracheliotus*		Bradfield's hornbill	*Tockus bradfieldi*
Tawny eagle	*Aquila rapax*		Wire-tailed swallow	*Hirundo smithii*
Martial eagle	*Polemaetus bellicosus*		Pied babbler	*Turdoides bicolor*
Lizard buzzard	*Kaupifalco monogrammicus*		Arnot's chat	*Thamnolaea arnoti*
Dickinson's kestrel	*Falco dickinsoni*		Red-faced crombec	*Sylvietta whytii*
Coqui francolin	*Francolinus coqui*		Tinkling cisticola	*Cisticola rufilata*
Crowned crane	*Balearica regulorum*		Crimson-breasted shrike	*Laniarius atrococcineus*
Kori bustard	*Ardeotis kori*		Long-tailed starling	*Lamprotornis mevesii*
Black-bellied korhaan	*Eupodotis melanogaster*		Golden-backed pytilia	*Pytilia afra*
Three-banded courser	*Rhinoptilus cinctus*		Black-cheeked waxbill	*Estrilda erythronotos*
Meyer's parrot	*Poicephalus meyeri*		Black-eared canary	*Serinus mennelli*
Scops owl	*Otus senegalensis*			

pered animal recorded again in the area, but population growth was so slow that during Operation Noah some 50 rhinos were transferred to Hwange from the Zambezi Valley, where waters were rising behind the great, newly built Kariba dam wall.

In the 1970s and 1980s the growing demand for rhino horn, for the production of traditional Asian medicines and Yemeni dagger handles, put massive pressure on the Zimbabwean rhino population, then the largest national herd in Africa. Most of the poaching, usually involving large, heavily armed gangs entering the country from Zambia and decimating the rhinos, was taking place in the Zambezi Valley. In a desperate last-ditch effort to save them, many rhinos were caught and transported to Hwange and private conservancies in the midlands. The latter rhinos have continued to fare well but the poachers moved into Hwange and killed most of the black rhinos there. The few surviving black rhinos hide out mainly in the dense bush in the vicinity of Sinamatella. It

would seem that poaching is continuing.

The white rhino, which unlike its black cousin is a grazer, was said to have been fairly common on the grassed pans and in open country but it is believed that the animals observed by Selous in 1873 in the vicinity of Dett Vlei, some 8 km north-east of Hwange's eastern boundary, were the last survivors. In the 1960s the decision was made to reintroduce white rhinos from Natal, South Africa, where they occurred in high enough numbers for animals to be returned to "safe areas" in their former range. Between November 1966 and March 1967 35 white rhinos were released but now all have fallen to the poachers' bullets!

Fortunately, the tale of the elephants is much happier, as ivory poaching has never developed into a major problem in modern-day Zimbabwe, nor in other parts of southern Africa for that matter, unlike the disastrous situation that developed elsewhere in Africa. During the dry season there are more than 20 000 elephants in the park, one of the

Above: *The grey crowned crane is frequently sighted in Hwange, where it also breeds.*

largest protected herds in Africa, but with the onset of the rainy season many thousands of these gentle giants disperse, a great number into northern Botswana. The main attraction of the dry season is the availability of artificially pumped water at many locations and an abundance of food.

Ironically, this elephant population has done so well that it has gone beyond its sustainable limit and a percentage are culled each year to prevent extensive vegetation destruction and modification. Because many thousands of these elephants cross the international boundary between Botswana and Zimbabwe with impunity, the former country claims that Zimbabwe is not legally entitled to shoot what they claim to be "their" elephants. The culling policy in Hwange is to remove every member of selected matriarchal herds, from the oldest *"grand dame"* to the youngest calf, on the presumption that these tightly knit groups would be thrown into chaos and trauma if only some individuals were harvested. Whatever is correct this controversial issue is certain to foment argument and discussion for as long as culling is considered necessary.

Another denizen of Hwange that occurs in many thousands today is the buffalo, but in 1929 only a small number were confined to the dense bush along the southern fringe of the Deka basin, west of the Deteema River. The first big herd, some 500 strong, was observed at Shumba in 1937. Today herds of this size are commonly sighted and herds numbering up to 3 000 of these massive wild cattle tread the dust and mud of Hwange.

When Hwange was established as a conservation area a number of giraffe, eland, sable, roan, greater kudu, impala and lion were present but blue wildebeest was very rare. As an indication of how little game the reserve held at the time of its proclamation, on one of his early patrols in a period of two days Ted Davison saw only three giraffes and about 20 impalas, and he heard elephants and spotted hyaenas. Lions occurred throughout the area and were considered to be common. In the early years these fine predators were shot as a matter of policy in the belief that this would allow game populations to increase. Today lions occur throughout the park and are commonly heard and seen, particularly in the vicinity of Main Camp and the major waterholes.

Other major predators present include wild dog, spotted and brown hyaenas and the elusive leopard. It is known that 104 species of mammal occur in Hwange. The number used to be 105 but the poachers killed one species, the white rhino.

Over the years we have learned that in a park such as Hwange, particularly in the dry season, the most fruitful way of observing the wildlife is to select a waterhole with a clear all-round view, have food and drink to hand and settle down for the day. In Hwange there are several viewing platforms raised on stilts.

Below right: Lions are not as frequently observed in Hwange as in some other major national parks.
Below: The diminutive scops owl is one of eight owl species known to occur in Hwange.

HWANGE NATIONAL PARK

Travel and access: From Bulawayo take the main road towards Victoria Falls. To reach Hwange's Main Camp, about 17 km after Gwayi River (at the 264,5 km peg) turn left at the signpost to the park and proceed for 24 km to the camp. Alternatively, continue along the main road for another 16 km, turn left to Dete village and follow the signposts to Main Camp. To reach Sinamatella Camp: about 340 km from Bulawayo turn left and drive 45 km to the camp; this road should be suitable for most vehicles. Lukosi Exclusive Camp can be reached from Sinamatella. Bumbusi Exclusive Camp lies 24 km north-west of Sinamatella and can be reached by ordinary vehicles during the dry season, but a 4x4 vehicle is required during the rains. To reach Robins Camp: approximately 390 km from Bulawayo turn left; follow this road for about 70 km to the camp, along a clearly signposted route. Nantwich Camp is close to Robins Camp. Deka Exclusive Camp lies 25 km west of Robins Camp and can only be reached by 4x4 vehicles. During the rainy season a number of roads are closed; check with the park authority in advance.

There is an airstrip at Main Camp and Hwange National Park Aerodrome is nearby. The park can also be reached by train; Dete station is 19 km away. Transport and tours can be arranged through United Touring Company.

Mobility: The 480 km network of game-viewing drives consists mostly of dirt roads; some sections are closed during the rainy season. Heavy rains can isolate Sinamatella and Robins camps.

Accommodation: MAIN CAMP: cottages with 1 or 2 bedrooms, lodges and chalets. Cottages and chalets share cooking and dining facilities. There is a campsite with a limited number of stands and ablution facilities.

SINAMATELLA CAMP has similar accommodation to Main Camp. Bumbusi and Lukosi exclusive camps each have four 2-bed units and a 4-bed cottage; both have a fully equipped communal kitchen and communal ablution facilities.

ROBINS CAMP has chalets with 1 or 2 bedrooms.

Main, Sinamatella and Robins camps are open all year.

NANTWICH CAMP has 2-bedroomed lodges.

DEKA EXCLUSIVE CAMP has two 3-bedroomed family units, each en suite and serviced. There is a communal dining room, sitting room and fully equipped kitchen.

IVORY LODGE, just outside the park in its own wilderness estate, has 10 luxury thatched treehouses, each with a bathroom and a veranda overlooking a waterhole; shop, dining room and game-viewing platform.

HWANGE SAFARI LODGE lies outside the park not far from Main Camp and offers luxury accommodation and tours. With the permission of the warden, single groups of up to 8 persons may camp for a single night at 6 of the picnic sites in the park: Shimba, Mandavu Pan, Ngweshla, Jambile, Kennedy 1 and Deteema. These sites are enclosed and have ablution facilities and water.

There has been a proliferation of lodges and luxury camps in the vicinity of Hwange. These include Sikumi Tree Lodge, Kanondo Tree Camp, Makalolo Camp and Sable Valley Lodge, all run by Touch the Wild (tel. Bulawayo 74589; fax 44696); Jabulisa Lodge (tel. Dete 2306, fax 375); Nemba Safari Camp (fax Dete 375); Chokamella Camp (tel. Harare 702634; fax 737956).

Other facilities: Picnic sites, large hides at several waterholes. Main Camp offers game-viewing by moonlight, escorted walks, a shop

Above: *A pair of spotted dikkops, or stone curlews* (Burhinus capensis), *with an extra large prey item – a giant millipede – that they puzzled over for some time!*

selling basic supplies, a restaurant and a bar, petrol and diesel. Sinamatella Camp offers escorted walks, wilderness trails between April and October, a restaurant, a shop selling basic goods, petrol and diesel. Robins Camp offers escorted walks, wilderness trails between April and October, a shop selling basic goods, petrol and diesel. Ivory Safaris conducts game-viewing drives from Ivory Lodge. The nearest point for vehicle repairs is at Hwange town, 101 km from Main Camp and 46 km from Sinamatella.

Climate: The rains fall in the summer – November to March – and at this time temperatures are quite high but not unbearably so. During the dry season temperatures are cooler and nights can be quite cold.

Best times to visit: If game-viewing is the main aim of a visit then the dry winter months are most productive when animals are forced to concentrate close to the limited number of waterholes. This is also the time when elephants are present in large numbers. During the rains some roads may be closed but this is a good time for birds and many game species are dropping their young.

Main attractions: Great diversity of species; large elephant concentrations in the dry season; ease of access.

Hazards: Malaria; potentially dangerous animals may enter the tourist camps.

For further information: The Warden, Main Camp, Private Bag DT 5776, Dete; tel. Dete 331/2.

The Warden, Sinamatella Camp, Private Bag WK 5941, Hwange; tel. Hwange 44255.

The Warden, Robins Camp, Private Bag WK 5936, Hwange; tel. Hwange 70220.

Ivory Lodge, P.O. Box 55, Dete; tel. Dete 3402.

United Touring Company, Hwange Safari Lodge, Private Bag 5792, Hwange.

Ivory Safaris, P.O. Box 9127, Hillside, Bulawayo; tel. 61709. National Parks Central Booking Office (Wilderness Trails).

Chapter 7

LUANGWA

WONDERLAND CREATED BY A RIVER

I do not know much about gods;
but I think that the river
Is a strong brown god.

T.S. Eliot, *Four Quartets*

Nine hippo herds are spaced out on the sand-banks and in the river along this stretch of the Luangwa. Sitting on the steep eastern bank we have a grandstand view of the hippos' daytime world. A small group of puku are grazing on the short grass of the west bank and in the far distance a lion contributes his roaring to the clucking of nearby helmeted guineafowl and the ever-present hippo chorus. Two bull hippos, separated by some 100 m of sandbank, start a slow, ponderous approach. Are we to witness a territorial battle? Advance, stand,

advance, stand… Only a few metres now separate the potential adversaries but after a few "yawn threats" one of the bulls veers into the water and disappears in a trail of bubbles. Obviously discretion has been deemed to be the better part of valour! Further downstream a sun-basking group of more than 20 hippos take fright and with a cloud of oxpeckers in hot pursuit, they plunge into the river. As the hippos calm down and realise that nothing is amiss, the birds settle on the non-submerged parts of their anatomy – a halo of oxpeckers!

Prehistory

Humans, or rather their ancient ancestors, roamed areas adjacent to the Luangwa Valley of Zambia, possibly as long ago as 2,5 million years. It was at Malema, near the north-western shore of Lake Malawi, that the remains of *Australopithecus boisei* were discovered; this is the same "upright walker" that roamed the Olduvai Gorge of northern Tanzania and the vicinity of Lake Turkana in Kenya. It is almost certain that these humanoid creatures also

Above: The Luangwa River has one of Africa's greatest concentrations of hippos. Each herd bull controls sections of the river and the adjacent sandbanks.

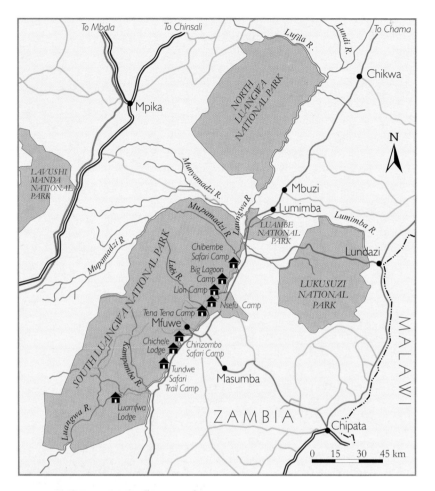

Above: *The characteristic paired leaves of the mopane tree (Colophospermum mopane).*

Right: *The common, or shovel-snouted, squeaker (Arthroleptis stenodactylus) lays small clutches of large eggs in shallow burrows among leaf litter.*

roamed through the Luangwa Valley but fossil evidence is lacking, probably because dense vegetation cover makes discovery difficult. Most of Africa's major human fossil discoveries have been made in areas of low rainfall and sparse vegetation. So far the oldest verified records for humans in the Luangwa Valley date back about 35 000 years, to a period known as the Middle Stone Age. They are based on several sites where artefacts have been discovered.

From the little evidence available it would seem that large areas of the central Luangwa Valley were not permanently occupied by the Bantu-peoples who migrated into central Africa from the north. This is almost certainly because of the extensive expansion of the river onto the floodplain during the rainy season. There can however be little doubt that this region was used as a hunting and foraging ground in the dry season. Between AD 1500 and AD 1700 several

kingdoms flanked the valley, such as the Bemba (Bena Nga'ndu), Bisa (Bena Ng'ona) and Lala in the west, and the Undi and Chewa in the east.

Between this period and the end of the 19th century, when the British colonisers arrived, a number of Bantu empires came and went, and by the beginning of this century the Bemba had greatly expanded their influence in the north, with the Chikunda occupying the area around the confluence of the Luangwa and Zambezi rivers. It is of interest that between AD 1700 and 1800 a number of kingdoms expanded their domains to incorporate substantial areas of the valley, but later retreated away from it or were absorbed by other tribes. It is possible that the expansion was a reaction to a drier period that made the valley more hospitable. Otherwise external pressures may have forced smaller, weaker tribes to occupy a more hostile and difficult environment.

History

Although little evidence exists it has been suggested that the Portuguese and half-caste *pombeiros* were already exploiting ivory around the middle Zambezi River, near its confluence with the Luangwa, by the end of the 15th century. A trade route linking coastal Portuguese East Africa (Mozambique) and Lake Mweru in north-eastern Zambia, passing through the Luangwa Valley, was opened by Lacerda in 1798. Other Portuguese, such as Baptista (1810) and Da Silva (1854) crossed the valley with the primary aim of establishing new trade routes.

The British explorer-missionary David Livingstone crossed the Luangwa in 1866, but with other issues on his mind! There was a trading post at Malambo, some 100 km north of Mfuwe, which was established in about 1810 but was already defunct by 1820. Of particular interest is that in 1876 some 18 tons of ivory, from perhaps 850 elephants, were shipped from the middle Zambezi River area, which includes the confluence with the Luangwa.

The first, ineffective, attempt at game conservation took place on 31 December 1904 with the proclamation of the Luangwa Game Reserve, which was located on the river's east bank, but the project received no further attention and was a failure. The Luangwa Valley Game Reserve was proclaimed on 27

May 1938 in roughly the form of the present-day South Luangwa National Park. The latter, incorporating a few additions, was finally established in 1972.

The first camp opened for tourists in 1949, with additional development taking place between 1955 and 1960. It is significant that the 1949 development took place on the then Nsefu Game Reserve, which had originally been set aside by Chief Nsefu. Four additional national park areas in the valley were afforded protection in later years: North Luangwa, Luambe, Lukusuzi and Lower Zambezi, but none is easily accessible and none has been developed to any degree for the tourist market. All are linked by a broad belt of so-called game management areas, whose original intention was to act as controlled-use buffers between the parks and areas of dense human population. From north to south these are Musalangu, Munyamadzi, Lumimba, Lupande, Sandwe, Chisomo, West Petauke, Luano and Rufunsa. However, the value of the game management buffers as controlled resource areas has to a large extent been diminished because of lack of interest and inadequate management.

Unlike many conservation areas that are on the tourist route, access for the visitor is limited to the dry season, as during the rains most roads become impossible to negotiate. This allows for a total wilderness state for several months every year.

Geography

The total national park area associated with the Luangwa Valley measures more than 16 600 km². We have excluded from this the large Lower Zambezi National Park because it only borders on the confluence of the Luangwa and Zambezi rivers.

The Luangwa Valley is a branch of the Great Rift Valley system, which intersects the main western and eastern branches just north of Lake Malawi, carving its path through the central plateau to the mighty Zambezi River. The Luangwa River runs some 700 km from its source in the Mafinga Mountains. At this point it is called the Chire and further along the Luwumbu. It flows along the border with Mozambique from just below the Luangwa Bridge and then pours its waters into the Zambezi at Feira. This is the lowest point in Zambia, at 330 m above sea-level.

There are a number of important feeder rivers that serve the Luangwa drainage, including the Lunsemfwa and the Mulungushi, which carve through the Muchinga Escarpment, flowing eastwards through the Luano Valley to join the Lukusashi River before it flows into the Luangwa. The Luangwa River flows through a broad valley that is bounded steeply in the west by the Muchinga Escarpment.

The Luangwa River, with its broad floodplain, is an ever-changing and variable watercourse: each flood creates new channels, meanders and oxbow lakes. This variability and the broad floodplain have allowed the development of one of Africa's most diverse wildlife locations, with very high carrying capacities.

Flora

Large tracts of the Luangwa Valley's floodplain are covered with short grass, fringed by mixed woodland which in large areas is dominated by that hardy tree, the mopane. Miombo woodlands, which cover almost 80% of Zambia's land surface, dominate the escarpment down much of the length of the Luangwa, with *Brachystegia* being particularly abundant. Open grassland is not restricted to the floodplain. There are two areas of grassed savanna totalling some 400 km², the largest being the Chifungwe Plain just south of the Munyamadzi River.

Top: Woodland in South Luangwa National Park, with a yellow-flowered sjambok tree (Cassia abbreviata) in the foreground. The tree takes its name from the long pods, almost one metre in some cases, which resemble the short hippopotamus-hide whips that were once common in Africa.
Above: A young diederik cuckoo (Chrysococcyx caprius); although a relatively common bird it is seldom seen, but its distinctive plaintive call is often heard.

S P E C I E S   T O   W A T C H   F O R

M A M M A L S

Elephant	*Loxodonta africana*	Lion	*Panthera leo*
Hippopotamus	*Hippopotamus amphibius*	Leopard	*Panthera pardus*
Buffalo	*Syncerus caffer*	Spotted hyaena	*Crocuta crocuta*
Thornicroft's giraffe	*Giraffa camelopardalis thornicrofti*	Wild dog	*Lycaon pictus*
Sable antelope	*Hippotragus niger*	Side-striped jackal	*Canis adustus*
Roan antelope	*Hippotragus equinus*	Honey badger	*Mellivora capensis*
Cookson's wildebeest	*Connochaetes taurinus cooksoni*	African civet	*Civettictis civetta*
Lichtenstein's hartebeest	*Alcelaphus lichtensteini*	Slender mongoose	*Galerella sanguineus*
Bushbuck	*Tragelaphus scriptus*	Banded mongoose	*Mungos mungo*
Puku	*Kobus vardoni*	Tree squirrel	*Paraxerus cepapi*
Common waterbuck	*Kobus ellipsiprymnus ellipsiprymnus*	Red-legged sun squirrel	*Heliosciurus rufobrachium*
Sharpe's grysbok	*Raphicerus sharpei*		

B I R D S

Goliath heron	*Ardea goliath*	Collared pratincole	*Glareola pratincola*
Black egret	*Egretta ardesiaca*	Blue-spotted wood dove	*Turtur afer*
Rufous-bellied heron	*Butorides rufiventris*	Lilian's lovebird	*Agapornis lilianae*
Woolly-necked stork	*Ciconia episcopus*	Pel's fishing owl	*Scotopelia peli*
Open-billed stork	*Anastomus lamelligerus*	Pennant-winged nightjar	*Macrodipteryx vexillaria*
Saddle-billed stork	*Ephippiorhynchus senegalensis*	Pygmy kingfisher	*Ispidina picta*
Marabou	*Leptoptilos crumeniferus*	Olive bee-eater	*Merops superciliosus*
White-faced duck	*Dendrocygna viduata*	Southern carmine bee-eater	*Merops nubicoides*
Pygmy goose	*Nettapus auritus*	Böhm's bee-eater	*Merops boehmi*
Knob-billed duck	*Sarkidiornis melanotos*	Raquet-tailed roller	*Coracias spatulata*
Hooded vulture	*Necrosyrtes monachus*	Southern ground hornbill	*Bucorvus leadbeateri*
Bat hawk	*Macheiramphus alcinus*	Miombo grey tit	*Parus griseiventris*
Martial eagle	*Polemaetus bellicosus*	Yellow-spotted nicator	*Nicator gularis*
Bateleur	*Terathopius ecaudatus*	Miombo rock thrush	*Monticola angolensis*
African fish eagle	*Haliaeetus vocifer*	Collared palm-thrush	*Cichladusa arquata*
Augur buzzard	*Buteo augur*	Black-throated wattle-eye	*Platysteira peltata*
Dark chanting goshawk	*Melierax metabates*	Livingstone's flycatcher	*Erythrocercus livingstonei*
African hobby falcon	*Falco cuvierii*	Sousa's shrike	*Lanius souzae*
Dickinson's kestrel	*Falco dickinsoni*	Long-tailed starling	*Lamprotornis mevesii*
Red-necked francolin	*Francolinus afer*	Lesser blue-eared starling	*Lamprotornis chloropterus*
Crowned crane	*Balearica regulorum*	Purple-banded sunbird	*Nectarinia bifasciata*
Red-crested bustard	*Eupodotis ruficrista*	Miombo double-collared sunbird	*Nectarinia manoensis*
African jacana	*Actophilornis africanus*		
White-crowned plover	*Vanellus albiceps*	Blue-throated sunbird	*Anthreptes reichenowi*
Long-toed lapwing	*Vanellus crassirostris*	Red-throated twinspot	*Hypargos niveoguttatus*
Water thick-knee	*Burhinus vermiculatus*	East African swee	*Estrilda quartinia*
Three-banded courser	*Rhinoptilus cinctus*	Locust finch	*Ortygospiza locustella*

Fauna

Like Hwange and Tsavo, Luangwa is one of Africa's greatest elephant reserves. In the early 1970s some 100 000 of the grey giants were estimated to roam the length and breadth of the valley. It is generally recognised that this huge population was seriously detrimental to the woodlands, modifying the vegetation in such a way that other browsing species, including black rhinos, were suffering. Not only was the valley population exploding, but increasing numbers of elephants from surrounding areas came seeking respite from the harassment and loss of habitat as a result of burgeoning human populations around the rim of Luangwa.

However, as we all know, this was to be the beginning of one of the continent's greatest recorded wildlife slaughters. Soon the pachyderms had their backs to the proverbial wall. By 1982 an estimated 20 elephants were being shot each day in the valley. In 1991, when the last major census was undertaken, only some 10 000 animals remained in South Luangwa National Park and the adjoining Lupande Game Management Area. From having one of Africa's largest national herds, Zambia now has an estimated 35 000 elephants, of which well over half make their home in the valley.

As was occurring throughout its former range, the black rhino suffered far more than the elephant, because its horns were, and still are, in unreasonable demand for their alleged medicinal properties and to be carved into dagger handles for Yemeni and Omani men.

Writing in 1978, W.F.H. Ansell summed up the position of the rhino in the Luangwa Valley as follows:

> In the Luangwa Valley it is particularly abundant and recent carefully conducted surveys indicate that the subjective estimates recorded previously were altogether too low, the minimum number now being assessed at 4 000.

With the exception of the high mountains where the Luangwa River rises, black rhinos occurred virtually throughout the valley, but the latest estimate indicates that probably no more than 30 individuals survived the slaughter. They all live in South Luangwa National Park. What a horrifying figure: in the space of some 20 years less than 1% of the original rhino population has survived the onslaught!

Today, much of the valley is no longer a wildlife slaughterhouse, but with ever-growing human populations, hungry for land and food, game animals will be increasingly restricted to the national parks. But, fortunately, all is not doom and gloom, as there are tens of thousands of buffaloes, one of Africa's most numerous hippo populations and an amazing diversity of antelope species.

It has been said that Zambia probably has more hippos than any other country. At least half of them, or some 25 000, live in the waters of the Luangwa Valley. With its relatively high earth banks the Luangwa River allows for easy observation of hippos. There are few areas on the continent where one can have so many of these great barrel-chested beasts in view at one time. Wherever there are pools and stretches of river with enough water to allow hippos to fully submerge themselves, they are there.

When camped in the Luangwa Valley in 1831-32, Captain Gamitto encountered a party of 50 hippo hunters operating during the dry season when the hippo schools were more concentrated. Apparently most animals were trapped, although the method used is not clear, and the meat harvested and then traded

Opposite: A puku ram on the edge of an oxbow lake in South Luangwa. This antelope reaches high densities here, where it is restricted to the short grasslands on the floodplains.
Below left: *Yellow-billed storks (Mycteria ibis) and sacred ibis (Threskiornis aethiopicus) feeding in a shallow oxbow lake.*
Below: *Buffalo, those black wild cattle, are common along the valley and herds numbering in the hundreds can be seen.*

Left: *Nile, or water, monitors (Varanus niloticus) are common along the valley, in close association with water. This individual was searching holes in the river bank for young birds, lizards and insects.*
Far left: *A small herd of puku ewes close to the Luangwa River.*

Below: The hippopotamus spends most of the daylight hours immersed in water, or basking in close proximity to it. Feeding is a mainly nocturnal activity and they may wander considerable distances to suitable grazing grounds.

for food, cloth, slaves and elephant ivory. Hippopotamus hunting undoubtedly took place on a considerable scale as by 1918 it was unusual to see a large hippo school; in fact hippo sightings had become unusual. However, once the area and of course the hippos were afforded protection, the population increased rapidly. It has now reached the point where there may be too many hippos for the available grazing.

ritories for short periods. Although fawns may be dropped at any time of the year, most birthings take place during the dry season when the maximum areas of floodplain grasses are exposed.

The range of antelope species occurring in the Luangwa is immense and includes both sable and roan antelope, Lichtenstein's hartebeest, southern reedbuck, impala, oribi, bushbuck, greater kudu, eland, common waterbuck, with plains zebra and large numbers of warthog. Of course, with such a host of potential prey, there is the complete spectrum of predators to eat them. At least one pride of lions has learned to specialise in hunting and eating the abundant hippos; even adults weighing well over a ton are not immune to their unwelcome attentions.

Above right: Foam nest frogs (Chiromantis xerampelina) are unique in that they "construct" a nest of a foam-like substance secreted by the female and then kicked into a froth, in much the same way as one whips cream. In this nest, usually attached to branches or other vegetation overhanging water, the female lays the eggs and the tadpoles on hatching spend several days in the nest before falling to the water. This frog is common in the vicinity of the Luangwa River.

Below right: *Red-necked francolin are common along the Luangwa valley.*

There are two distinctive and isolated races of large mammal in Luangwa: Thornicroft's giraffe and Cookson's wildebeest. This giraffe race differs in having large areas of light-coloured hair on the neck and an almost complete absence of spotting on the lower part of the legs. Cookson's wildebeest generally has more brown on the body than other races. Neither mammal comes in contact with others of its kind, being separated by several hundred kilometres. It is presumed likely that they were isolated in the valley when climatic changes influenced vegetation in the intervening areas, making them unsuitable for their survival.

Zambia is the only country outside Tanzania that has substantial numbers of puku, an antelope restricted to the short-grass floodplains of rivers and other water bodies. The main concentrations are in the Kafue region and the Luangwa Valley. Occurring in large numbers along the Luangwa, they are generally observed in herds numbering from 5 to 30 animals, with adult rams defending small ter-

SOUTH LUANGWA NATIONAL PARK

Travel and access: From Lusaka take the main road eastwards to Chipata, and from there a secondary road north-westwards to the park's main entrance at Mfuwe. Access roads are suitable for all vehicles, although the road between Chipata and Mfuwe is often in poor condition.

Safari operators meet clients at Lusaka, and Zambian Airways run regular flights to Mfuwe Airport, 25 km from Mfuwe Lodge.

Mobility: Within the park there is an all-weather game-viewing circuit in the Mfuwe area, but elsewhere 4x4 vehicles are recommended. The park is open throughout the year, but movement is restricted during the rainy season.

Accommodation: 14 lodges and camps operate in South Luangwa, several of which are privately run.

KAPANI SAFARI CAMP: 4 double chalets, each with a bathroom and electricity, US$100 per person per night, all inclusive.

LUWI BUSH CAMP: available to visitors staying for 5 or more nights at Kapani, for an extra charge of US$50.

CHINZOMBO SAFARI LODGE: fully-catered accommodation in 9 thatched chalets, each with a bathroom. Open from late April to mid-January.

CHIBEMBE LODGE: wooden chalets for a maximum of 40 people, some with their own bathrooms, others using separate ablution facilities. Full catering is provided. Open between June and November.

NSEFU CAMP: 6 thatched rondavels, each with a bathroom. Full catering is provided. Open between June and November.

TENA TENA CAMP: tented camp for a maximum of 12 people, with ablution facilities and full catering. Open between June and October.

For all the above camps book well in advance. Casual visitors are not admitted to the private camps.

Official lodges offer both full-catering and self-catering accommodation. Contact the Zambia National Tourist Board for details.

The Wildlife Camp offers self-catering chalets and camping on the river bank, just outside the park near the main entrance – a good, cheap option, with restaurant and bar (run by Wildlife Conservation Society of Zambia, tel./fax (062) 21596 or (062) 21781).

Other facilities: KAPANI SAFARI CAMP: swimming pool, guided game-viewing drives, including night drives, and walking safaris.

CHINZOMBO SAFARI LODGE: game-viewing drives, night drives and accompanied walks.

CHIBEMBE LODGE: accompanied walks, bush camps, game-viewing drives, night drives, swimming pool.

NSEFU CAMP: game-viewing drives, night drives and a photographic hide.

TENA TENA CAMP: accompanied game-viewing walks and drives, including night drives.

There is a petrol pump at Mfuwe.

Climate: This is a summer-rainfall area. At this time large areas of the park are flooded, with temperatures and humidity high. The dry winter months are mild, although nights can be cool to cold.

Best times to visit: The dry season is favoured because game-viewing is at its best. During the rains mobility is severely restricted but bird diversity is at its greatest. However, many of the tourist camps are closed during summer.

Main attractions: Great diversity and numbers of game species, including one of Africa's densest hippo populations; it is also one of the best parks to observe puku. Bird diversity is great.

Hazards: Malaria, bilharzia, tsetse fly; potentially dangerous animals such as lion, elephant and buffalo as tourist camps are not fenced.

For further information: The Zambia National Tourist Board.

Kapani: Norman Carr Safaris, P.O. Box 100, Mfuwe; telex ZA 45940; tel. 1-21636.

Chinzombo: Save the Rhino Trust, P.O. Box 320-169, Woodlands, Lusaka; telex ZA 42570; tel. 1-211644; fax 1- 226736.

Chinzombo campsite: The Secretary, the Wildlife Conservation Society of Zambia, Chipata Branch, P.O. Box 510358, Chipata.

Chibembe, Nsefu: Wilderness Trails Ltd, P.O. Box 30970, Lusaka; telex ZA 40042.

Tena Tena: Robin Pope Safaris Ltd, P.O. Box 320-154, Lusaka; or Andrew's Travel and Safaris Ltd, P.O. Box 31993, Lusaka; telex ZA 40104; tel. 1-213147.

NORTH LUANGWA NATIONAL PARK

Access and travel: The area is best visited with Shiwa Safaris, the safari company that operates in the park.

Mobility: No access during the rains.

Accommodation: None.

Other facilities: None.

Hazards: Malaria; bilharzia; tsetse fly.

For further information: National Parks and Wildlife Service.

Shiwa Safaris, P.O. Box 820024, Chisamba; tel. 05-222730.

Wilderness Trails Ltd, P.O. Box 35058, Lusaka; tel. 220112/3/4/5.

Chibembe Safari Lodge, P.O. Box 66, Mfuwe; tel. 062-45083.

Chapter 8

QUEEN ELIZABETH NATIONAL PARK

SPLENDID SOLITUDE

Oh, 'tis a glorious thing, I ween,
To be a regular Royal Queen!
No half-and-half-affair, I mean,
But a right-down regular Royal Queen!

W.S. Gilbert, *The Gondoliers*

At midday the air is heavy with the gathering thunderstorm. Great thrusting cloud-heads swirling thousands of metres above the lakes and their interlinking Kazinga Channel cast a gloomy but expectant air. With our backs to a tall tree euphorbia festooned with a red berry-bedecked creeper, we gaze down at the fishermen in their dugout canoes paddling for home, the day's catch ready for gutting and cleaning. Hippos honk and grunt from the water; those that had been lying on the sand-banks have taken to their liquid cocoon. Fish eagles are still calling. One flying past us throws back its head and proclaims its vocal

Above: Defassa waterbuck cows and yearling bull in the north of the park.

sovereignty over this stretch of the waterway. Toads and reed frogs begin their chorus in expectation of the rain drawing closer. They let out a mixture of duck-like quacking, shrill, ear-piercing whistles and "watch-winding" chirrups, and one sound that evokes memories of a cork being turned out of a bottle of fine Pinotage ... Dream on – only Bell's or Nile lager awaits to slake our thirst!

History

British explorer John Speke was the first European to penetrate the land we now know

as Uganda, in 1862, when searching for the source of the Nile. This was truly "darkest Africa" with its culturally and linguistically distinct peoples constantly at war with each other in conflicts over territory.

Stanley's second African expedition reached the escarpment to the east of Lake George in 1876 and looked down on what the expedition members believed to be a large lake, although its far shores were hidden by a haze. Stanley did not descend to the floor of the rift valley out of fear of the warlike tribes who lived there. However, he returned in 1889, approaching from the west of the Ruwenzori

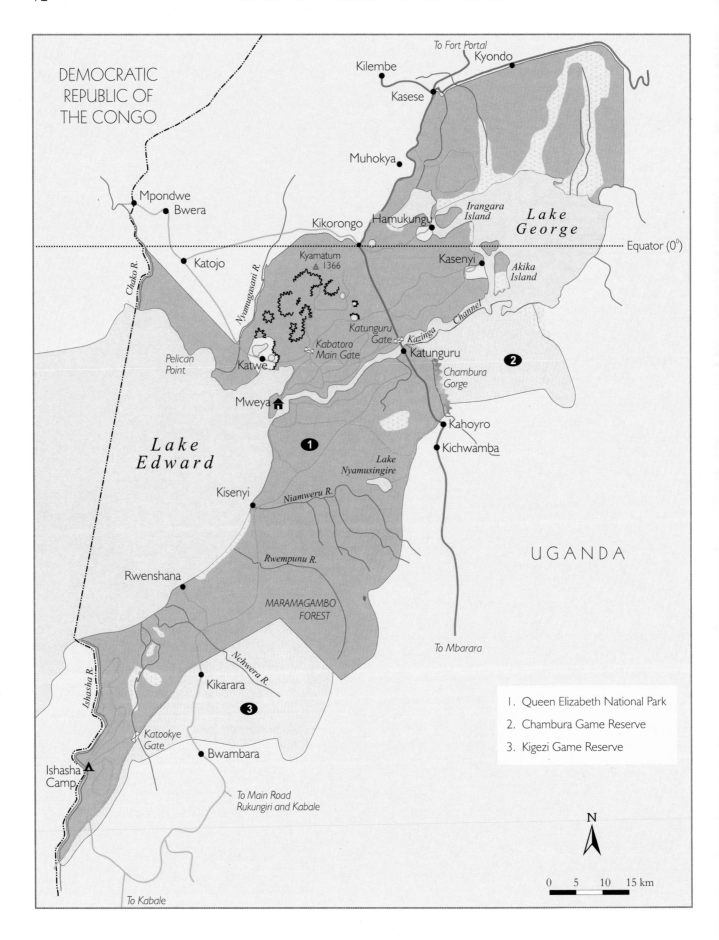

DEMOCRATIC
REPUBLIC OF
THE CONGO

To Fort Portal

Kilembe

Kyondo

Kasese

Muhokya

Mpondwe
Bwera

Kikorongo
Hamukungu

*Irangara
Island*

*Lake
George*

Katojo

Chako R.

Kyamatum
△ 1366

Kasenyi

*Akika
Island*

Equator (0°)

Nyamugasani R.

Katunguru
Gate

Kazinga Channel

*Pelican
Point*

Kabatoro
Main Gate

Katwe

Katunguru

②

*Chambura
Gorge*

Mweya

①

*Lake
Nyamusingire*

Kahoyro

Kichwamba

*Lake
Edward*

Kisenyi

Niamweru R.

U G A N D A

Rwempunu R.

Rwenshana

*MARAMAGAMBO
FOREST*

To Mbarara

Ishasha R.

Nchwera R.

Kikarara

③

Katookye
Gate

Bwambara

Ishasha
Camp

*To Main Road
Rukungiri and Kabale*

To Kabale

1. Queen Elizabeth National Park
2. Chambura Game Reserve
3. Kigezi Game Reserve

N

0   5   10   15 km

(also sometimes spelled Rwenzori) Mountains, down the Semuliki Valley and to the vicinity of Lake Edward. At the time of his visit the area was quite heavily populated, with a settlement of more than 2 000 people at Katwe and a thriving village at the site of the present park headquarters, at Mweya.

By 1894 the British had woven together a tenuous alliance between the different tribes, many being proud kingdoms such as those of the Banyankole, Batoro, Banyoro, Baganda and Basoga.

During the 1890s, however, the spread of rinderpest throughout East Africa, including western Uganda, decimated the once numerous cattle and game species such as buffalo. With the drastic reduction of cattle and certain game animals, there was an increase in the bush cover, providing ideal conditions for Africa's "greatest conservationist" the tsetse fly. The tsetse flies transmitted the parasite that causes sleeping sickness and by 1907 it had reached epidemic levels in the human population. Between 1912 and 1924 most people either left or were removed from the area.

At independence in October 1962 Uganda was one of Africa's "promised lands" but the first major trouble raised its ugly head in 1966 when Milton Obote drove the incumbent president into exile. He in turn was ousted in 1971 by Idi Amin, who would hold the reins of power until 1979 when an invading Tanzanian force drove him into exile and Obote was reinstated. There then followed, for five years, some of the worst mass slaughters East Africa had ever seen when Obote tried to destroy the guerilla forces of the current president, Yoweri Museveni.

The reason we mention this snippet of modern history is that during more than two decades of turmoil, slaughter and unrest, Uganda's conservation areas were largely left to their own devices and all parties in the different conflicts poached freely in its national parks and game reserves. What is most amazing is that any wildlife survived these repeated onslaughts; many surprisingly did, albeit in greatly reduced numbers. The Ugandan population of the northern white rhino was wiped out, primarily by the actions of Tanzania's poorly disciplined army, and the once healthy elephant stocks were greatly reduced.

Despite the troubled recent past the game populations are steadily increasing in the Queen Elizabeth Park and a few species, such

as the Uganda kob, are abundant. It is certainly one of our favourite East African conservation areas, partly because it is not overrun by tourists but primarily because of its great diversity of habitats and species.

The park covers 1 978 km² and was proclaimed as the Kazinga National Park in 1952. Following a visit by the British monarch in 1954 it was renamed in her honour but confusingly Amin renamed the park Ruwenzori and this name is still found on a number of maps. A park of this name has been recently proclaimed in the Ugandan sector of the cloud-bedecked Ruwenzori Mountains, the fabled *Mountains of the Moon*.

Initially the British had proclaimed two separate game reserves here, Lake George in 1925 and Lake Edward in 1930. Additional areas were proclaimed up to 1952, including the area south of the Kazinga Channel below the Kichwamba Escarpment.

Geography

Queen Elizabeth Park straddles the equator, lying in south-western Uganda and bordering on the Congo. In the south-west it shares a common border with *Parc National des Virungas* (originally named *Parc National Albert* at its proclamation in 1925), to the north with the Kibale Forest National Park and to the east with the Chambura and Kigezi game reserves. Part of Lake Edward is incorporated into the park in the west and it encompasses most of Lake George and its associated swamps in the north, both being linked by the 33 km long Kazinga Channel. Lake George drains its waters into Lake Edward, which in turn flows out through the Semuliki River to Lake Albert, eventually reaching the Nile.

Top: Elephant were greatly reduced in numbers by ivory poachers but they have started a slow but steady recovery. Most concentrate today in the crater region in the north of the park but are still difficult to approach – a legacy of Amin and Obote!
Above: *Although seldom seen, the swamp-loving sitatunga (Tragelaphus spekei) occurs in the dense reedbeds that fringe Lake George.*

One of the more prominent landscape features is the system of explosion craters located to the north of Katwe, now carpeted with grass and scattered trees, which were formed a mere 10 000 years before present.

One afternoon we were sitting on the Mweya Peninsula, and to the north we could make out the lower slopes of the *Mountains of the Moon*, their heads, as nearly always, buried

Top right: An agama (Agama sp.) photographed on the north bank of the Kazinga Channel, that links lakes George and Edward. Above: Butterflies extracting moisture from loosely dropped elephant dung.

in the clouds, and the Mitumba Mountains on the Congolese shore. Then within minutes heavily laden black clouds, with the most dramatic lightning flashes we had ever seen, rolled over the Mitumbas, turning the lake into a churning cauldron. In not much more than the blinking of an eye the rain was beating around us in torrents and the thunderclaps overruled all conversation. Every month delivers rain here but the periods March to May, and September to November, show distinct peaks. Depending on the area of the park, annual falls range from 750 mm to 1 250 mm.

Flora

There are several areas of forest, by far the largest being the Maramagombo, extending over 280 km², which is located in the south and not yet fully explored. It is defined as a medium altitude semi-deciduous forest and is the only one of its type that is protected in Uganda.

Over 50 vegetation communities have been recognised by botanists in the park, but the average visitor would note forest, open grassland, a thicket-grassland mix, and in some areas, such as the crater country and at Ishasha, *Acacia gerrardii* thickets.

Since the 1970s, with the great reduction in elephant numbers as a result of poaching, two changes have taken place in the vegetation structure: a dramatic increase in *Acacia* thickets – a favoured food of these gentle giants – and the extent of the bush thickets. The effect of the park's second largest mammal, the hippopotamus, still abundant in the lakes and along the Kazinga Channel, is clear to see in overgrazing and erosion close to the water.

Fauna

Apart from a recovering population of elephant, possibly as many as 10 000 hippos, thousands of buffalo, topi, defassa waterbuck with bulls carrying the longest horns of their species anywhere in Africa, bushbuck, bohor reedbuck and sitatunga, we had mainly come to Queen Elizabeth Park to see and photograph the courtship rituals of the Uganda kob. It is estimated that there are more than 20 000 of these handsome, open-grassland antelope in the park, and this is one of the few locations in East Africa where they occur in viable numbers; in fact its last stronghold.

During dry periods they congregate in mixed herds of up to 1 000 strong, but during breeding times the adult males adopt a unique and highly refined territorial, or lek, system. The rams use permanent traditional breeding grounds where tiny, roughly circular, defended areas lie very close to each other, and these breeding grounds are referred to as leks. Within each lek many rams are located and the individuals defend their territories in highly ritualised displays, with occasional brisk but short fights breaking out, each trying to unbalance or drive back the other. These displays involve a slow, deliberate walk,

SPECIES TO WATCH FOR

MAMMALS

Elephant	*Loxodonta africana*	Red-tailed guenon	*Cercopithecus ascanius*
Hippopotamus	*Hippopotamus amphibius*	Straw-coloured fruit-bat	*Eidolon helvum*
Giant forest hog	*Hylochoerus meinertzhageni*	Striped ground squirrel	*Xerus erythropus*
Uganda kob	*Kobus kob thomasi*	Giant forest squirrel	*Protoxerus stangeri*
Defassa waterbuck	*Kobus ellipsiprymnus defassa*	Lord Derby's flying squirrel	*Anomalurus derbianus*
Chimpanzee	*Pan troglodytes*		

BIRDS

Pink-backed pelican	*Pelecanus rufescens*	Chocolate-backed kingfisher	*Halcyon badia*
Rufous-bellied heron	*Ardeola rufiventis*	Black bee-eater	*Merops gularis*
Shoebill	*Balaeniceps rex*	Black and white casqued hornbill	*Ceratogymna subcylindricus*
African open-billed stork	*Anastomus lamelligerus*	Hairy-breasted barbet	*Tricholaema hirsuta*
Sooty falcon	*Falco concolor*	Green-breasted pitta	*Pitta reichenowi*
Long-crested eagle	*Lophaetus occipitalis*	Red-bellied paradise flycatcher	*Terpsiphone rufiventer*
Grasshopper buzzard	*Butastur rufipennis*	Snowy-crowned robin chat	*Cossypha niveicapilla*
African fish eagle	*Haliaeetus vocifer*	Uganda warbler	*Phylloscopus budongensis*
Scaly francolin	*Francolinus squamatus*	Black-headed gonolek	*Laniarius erythrogaster*
Brown-chested lapwing	*Vanellus superciliosus*	Piapiac	*Ptilostomus afer*
African skimmer	*Rhynchops flavirostris*	Stuhlmann's starling	*Poeoptera stuhlmanni*
Afep pigeon	*Columba unicincta*	Superb sunbird	*Nectarinia superba*
Blue-headed coucal	*Centropus monachus*	Orange weaver	*Ploceus aurantius*
Black-billed turaco	*Tauraco schuetti*	Slender-billed weaver	*Ploceus pelzelni*
Great blue turaco	*Corythaeola cristata*	Crested malimbe	*Malimbus malimbicus*
Red-headed lovebird	*Agapornis pullaria*	Red-headed malimbe	*Anaplectes rubriceps*
Blue-throated roller	*Eurystomus gularis*	Black-crowned waxbill	*Estrilda nonnula*
Blue-breasted kingfisher	*Halcyon malimbica*		

with ears depressed, head up and tail raised, and with the penis frequently erect, as they patrol the invisible territory boundary.

A territory is usually defended for only a few days because the rams have to vacate their "beat" to graze and drink, or if one is ousted by a stronger ram. During this time the ewes roam at will through the leks, apparently showing a preference for those rams that control the central territories. When ewes are present competition for mating rights is particularly brisk. If a ram loses his territory he will join one of several bachelor groups that circulate around the perimeter of the lek, and attempt to regain his territory at a later stage.

Some of these traditional lek sites have been in use for many years and can be easily distinguished, even if no animals are present, by the short grass that has been trampled by many kob hooves.

It is an unforgettable sight indeed when two dozen kob rams patrol their tiny territories, displaying and intermittently clashing horns, with the occasional ewe walking nonchalantly through this swirl of male activity, to be courted and occasionally mated, all against the backdrop of the *Mountains of the Moon*. If

anything, it was even more impressive than described in the books and scientific papers that we had read. The rams were so intent on their activities that our vehicle was totally ignored – a photographer's dream.

It is possible that four of Africa's five wild pig species occur in the park, but three are known to be definitely present, namely the giant forest hog, the bushpig and the warthog. The question mark hangs over the red river hog, once believed to be a subspecies of the bushpig but now considered to be distinct enough to warrant its own banner. If it does indeed occur its presence will most likely be confirmed by greater exploration of the Maramagambo Forest.

Queen Elizabeth is one of the best parks in Africa to observe the world's largest wild pig, the giant forest hog, with adult boars tipping the scales at as much as 275 kg, but usually averaging a "mere" 235 kg. If we look at that measure another way, we are talking about one quarter of a ton, quite a lot of pork sausage indeed! Although these porcine giants are usually associated with dense lowland and montane forest, in Queen Elizabeth National Park they occur in the dense thicket-grassland

Below: A candelabra tree (Euphorbia candelabrum) draped with a berry-carrying creeper. These trees occur mainly in association with thickets but many grow alone on the grassed plains.

Top: A fine Uganda kob ram resting within its territory before facing further threats from other rams, and mating with cooperative ewes.
Above: *Probably one of the greatest bird "twitches" in Africa is the bizarre shoebill, and in the park the best location to begin the search is in the vicinity of the papyrus beds around Lake George.*
Far right: *A wattled plover (Vanellus senegallus) sitting on eggs; this is one of but 540 bird species that have been recorded in the park.*

mosaic on the slopes and flats adjacent to the Kazinga Channel.

Although lions occur throughout the park, they are not common, in part as a result of poison baits being put out by villagers both within the park and around its fringes. This is mainly because there have been many recorded cases of man-eating in the park and its surrounds, principally of local people walking on the tracks at night.

The most famous population of lions occurring in the park lives in the extreme south in the vicinity of Ishasha, where they have taken to climbing tall trees and sleeping on large horizontal branches. Several possible reasons have been put forward for this behaviour – one is that it gives them a better vantage to look over the long grass for potential prey – but we feel the most plausible is that it is cooler and keeps them away from the biting flies which are abundant in the ground vegetation.

The leopard, like its larger cousin the lion, occurs throughout the park, including the dense forested areas. It is probably more common than the few sightings would indicate. On the southern bank of the Kazinga Channel there is a dirt road called Leopard Loop and lo and behold on our first visit a very large male leopard was lying within 2 m of our vehicle. He was certainly one of the largest leopards we had ever seen, with a very broad head and a weight we estimated at 80 kg or more. A magnificent cat! We couldn't help thinking that if this had been in the Masai Mara or Kruger this superb beast would have been surrounded by tourist vehicles and the whirring of cameras.

Of the smaller cats, the beautiful long-legged serval shows a marked preference for the grasslands, with the African wild cat only avoiding the dense forests. Although its presence is not yet proven there is a very good chance that the golden cat will be found to occur in the Maramagambo Forest.

It is known beyond doubt that nine species of primate are present in the park's forests, and almost certainly at least one more, the red colobus. The western Ugandan forests are East Africa's stronghold of the chimpanzee, and in Queen Elizabeth unknown but possibly substantial numbers occur in the Maramagambo Forest, with smaller populations in the riparian forest fringing the Ishasha River and in the Chambura River Gorge. At the latter location the authorities are habituating troops in order

that visitors can become better acquainted with these intelligent primates. The chimps in the gorge, apart from foraging in the forest, also range short distances into the adjacent wooded grassland, probably in much the same way that our early ancestors took their first tentative steps on a path that would lead them to conquer planet earth!

To the north the adjoining Kibale Forest is home to at least several hundred chimpanzees. The primates that the visitor is most likely to encounter are the savanna baboon and the vervet (grivet) monkey. Both these species show a strong preference for wooded and woodland savanna country, while the other species are much more closely tied to the true forests and not their margins.

Bird life

Queen Elizabeth National Park is one of Africa's premier bird-watching destinations, with influences from the eastern savannas and the tropical lowland forest of the Congo Basin and West Africa. More than 540 different species are known to occur but if one studies available habitats, and species distribution and requirements, it is almost certain that this total could eventually be pushed close to 600.

The elusive shoebill is probably resident in the papyrus swamps, particularly around Lake George, but despite our best efforts it did not deign to grace us with its presence. This is not the place for a listing of species, nor personal bird-spotting highlights, but we will just relate one incident that certainly astounded us. Given the park's tropical and relatively wet nature, insects occur in great abundance, not least the hordes of mosquitoes that emerge at night seemingly intent on sucking one dry of the last millilitre of blood. But there are also vast numbers, and I am sure we do not exaggerate if we talk of multiples of millions, of lake flies, members of the *Chironomid* family. The books we read or consulted while in the park still remind us of these tiny flies as hundreds have been pressed between their pages! The lake fly larvae are completely aquatic. All metamorphose at the same time and form such dense swarms that they give the impression of columns of smoke rising from the shores of the lakes and channel. While watching these columns and clouds of "lake smoke", we were amazed at the great flocks of swallows, martins and white-winged black terns feasting on this insect bounty.

QUEEN ELIZABETH NATIONAL PARK

Travel and access: The good tarred road that links Kampala with Fort Portal passes through the park (somewhat over 400 km, allow about six hours) and will present no difficulties for saloon cars. From Kampala travel to Mbarara (282 km), pass through the town, travel 2 km in a westerly direction and turn right before the bridge. At the turn-off there are signposts to Traveller's Inn, Lakeview Hotel and Sabena Club. Shortly after you cross the Kazinga Channel, the turn-off to Mweya park HQ is on your left, clearly signposted. It is 20 km from the first entrance gate to HQ, 8 km from the main entrance gate. Permits are obtained at the entrance gate. If you are travelling from the north, the distance from Kasese to the park entrance is about 30 km (on your right). If you intend visiting Ishasha in the south of the park there are two possibilities, but both are 4x4 territory. We advise that you use the route just to the south of the Kazinga Channel (9 km from the Mweya turn-off). The 100 km will take you at least four hours even under optimal conditions. We tried it after rain and it was very, very sticky. The alternative route from the south (we have not attempted it) leaves the main tarred road at Ishaka (just beyond Bushenyi), proceed on poor roads to Rukungiri and then westwards to Ishasha. If you are coming from Kampala you can travel to Mbarara, continuing in the direction of Kabale and turning off to Rukungiri from Ntungamo. Bear in mind that the southern accesses will be considerably longer in distance and time. If you decide to try a southern access route we suggest you check the state of the roads in advance.

The Chambura Gorge: if you are coming from Kampala, the gorge is on your right and 115 km from Mbarara. If you arrive at the signpost to Ishasha you have gone too far.

Queen Elizabeth NP is on the itinerary of several safari companies. *Note that this is the only national park or reserve in Uganda where fuel (petrol and diesel) is available.*

Mobility: Although a number of roads are suitable for ordinary vehicles in the northern sector when it is dry, for reasonable mobility we strongly suggest a 4x4. The area north of the Kazinga Channel is reasonably well served by fair dirt roads but the southern network is very limited. After even light rain the tracks become very slippery and cautious driving is called for; heavy rain makes most of the roads impassable. The road to Ishasha from the north is particularly bad after rain, as is the track along the southern bank of the channel. Access to the crater area and Baboon Cliffs is also by 4x4 only.

The only organised walking trail at present is in the Chambura Gorge, primarily established to observe chimpanzees, but it may be possible to organise walks in the Maramagambo Forest with the permission of the warden.

Accommodation: Mweya Safari Lodge is located at park HQ and is classed as one of Uganda's best tourist accommodations. The lodge offers full board, with clean rooms, bar and restaurant facilities. At the time of writing it was not necessary to book, but check with the Uganda Parks HQ in Kampala for the latest situation. The lodge is fantastically situated and offers views over Lake Edward, the Ruwenzoris (usually cloud covered) and the Democratic Republic of Congo. There is a private safari camp in the Chambura Game Reserve (Hot Ice Safaris) and reasonable hotel accommodation in Kasese and Mbarara.

For visitors on a tighter budget there is a hostel with basic facilities at Mweya. There is a campsite with basic showers and toilets at Mweya but this can be noisy and may be frequented by large numbers of hippo at night. At two locations (4 km and 6 km from Mweya) along the channel there are very basic campsites with pit toilets, and no water. The campsites are very muddy after rain but offer the advantage of peace and quiet.

The Ishasha Camp in the extreme south of the park offers very basic campsites, and you should supply your own tent, equipment and food. Water is available but should be boiled or treated. A basic campsite is located at the ranger post on the edge of the Maramagambo Forest – first enquire at Mweya HQ.

Other facilities: The Mweya Lodge is fully catered, with bar and restaurant. A canteen offering basic food is located near the hostel. There is a reasonable network of game drives to the north of the Kazinga Channel but these can be slippery (at best) during rain. The limited number of roads in the south are generally poor and can be impassable during rain. There is the possibility of undertaking a guided walk in the Chambura Gorge, notably to observe habituated chimpanzees. There are regular trips by boat on the Kazinga Channel which offer excellent views of hippos and aquatic birds (bookings can be made at the HQ).

Climate: Although rain can be expected at any time of the year, there are two peaks: March to May and September to November. Rainfall ranges from about 750 mm in the Mweya area to 1 250 mm in the south-east towards the Kichwamba Escarpment. Mean annual minimum temperature is 18 °C; maximum average 28 °C; there is little monthly or seasonal variation.

Best times to visit: The park is open throughout the year; mobility is most limited during the peak rainy periods. Usual parks regulations apply.

Main attractions: Probably Uganda's most accessible national park; good game-viewing – best location for kob – and bird-watching; launch trips on the Kazinga Channel; chimpanzee tracking in Chambura River Gorge.

Hazards: Although you are required to remain in your vehicle, visitors should be aware that none of the camps are fenced and they are frequented by potentially dangerous animals: hippopotamus, buffalo and on occasion lion. Should you walk along the edges of water bodies outside the park be alert for crocodiles. Malaria; bilharzia. Roads very slippery after rain.

For further information: Uganda National Parks HQ in Kampala; Warden-in-Charge, Queen Elizabeth National Park, P.O. Box 22, Lake Katwe.

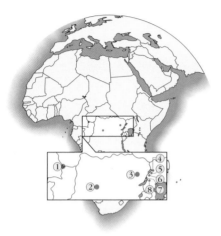

① *Ndoki National Park*　⑤ *Bugoma Forest Reserve*
② *Salonga National Park*　⑥ *Itwara Forest Reserve*
③ *Ituri Forest*　⑦ *Semuliki National Park*
④ *Budongo Forest*　⑧ *Kibale Forest National Park*

Chapter 9

TROPICAL RAIN FORESTS

LAND OF TWILIGHT

I have come to the borders of sleep,
The unfathomable deep
Forest where all must lose
Their way.

Edward Thomas, *Lights Out*

It is shortly after dawn and Kibale is beginning the shift change; creatures of the night are at rest but those of the day are starting to emerge. Turacos with their frog-like croaking – how can such beautiful birds have such unglamorous voices? – and noisy black and white casqued hornbills proclaim the filtered sunrise. The blue monkeys, red-tailed guenons and Uganda red colobus slowly begin to stir in the roadside trees, but the mangabeys are deeper in the forest. In the distance we can hear the faint pant-hoots of chimpanzees, but they remain well clear of the road traversing the forest. The nocturnal

moths are now being replaced by cohorts of brightly coloured butterflies. Some settle on damp roadside mud to extract water, others feed from flowering shrubs and several large swallowtails search the forest canopy high above our heads. A troop of red-tailed guenons, one by one, launch themselves across the tree-bridge spanning the road: dark silhouettes, the bright red of the tail and pale nose spot not visible in the dim forest light.

The tropical lowland rain forests hold some of Africa's last truly wild places, but there are those, particularly in West Africa, to the west of the Dahomey Gap, that are by and large destroyed, modified or on the verge of ruin. So here we look at those of the Congolean basin, the "armpit of Africa" – or more politely those forests that extend inland from the Bight of Biafra – and the forest pockets of western Uganda. Here lie some of the world's largest and most unspoiled rain forests, and some of its most important conservation areas, although many exist only on paper.

Approximately 1 million km² of the Democratic Republic of Congo are covered by tropical rain forest, and the Congo Republic and Gabon have a further 420 000 km² between them – a lot of potential wild places!

Above: The okapi, sometimes called the "forest giraffe", because of its dense forest habitat, was only discovered by the scientific community in 1900!

PHOTO: KLAUS RUDLOFF

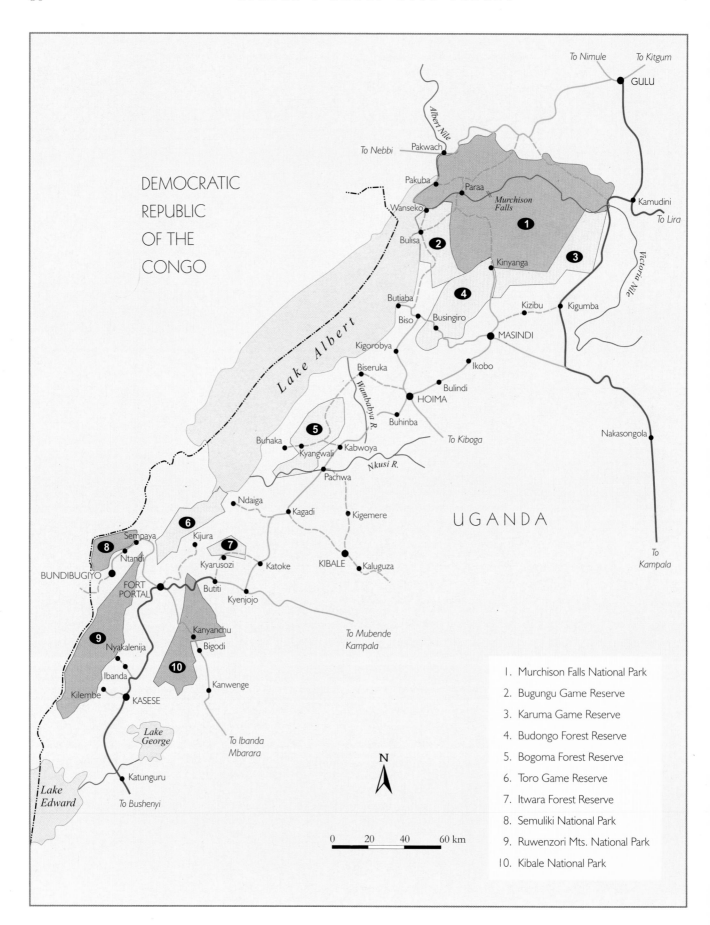

DEMOCRATIC
REPUBLIC
OF THE
CONGO

To Nimule　To Kitgum

GULU

Albert Nile

To Nebbi　Pakwach

Pakuba

Paraa

Murchison
Falls

1

Kamudini

To Lira

Wanseko

2

Bulisa

Kinyanga

3

Victoria Nile

Butiaba

4

Kizibu

Kigumba

Biso　Busingiro

MASINDI

Kigorobya

Biseruka

Wambabya R.

Bulindi

HOIMA

Ikobo

Buhinba

Nakasongola

5

Buhaka

Kyangwali　Kabwoya

To Kiboga

Pachwa

Nkusi R.

Ndaiga

Kagadi

Kigemere

U G A N D A

6

Kijura

Sempaya

8

7

Ntandi

Kyarusozi　Katoke

KIBALE

Kaluguza

BUNDIBUGIYO

FORT
PORTAL

Butiti

Kyenjojo

To Mubende
Kampala

To
Kampala

Kanyanchu

9

Nyakalenija

Bigodi

10

Ibanda

Kanwenge

Kilembe

KASESE

Lake
George

To Ibanda
Mbarara

Katunguru

Lake
Edward

To Bushenyi

Lake Albert

N

0　　20　　40　　60 km

1. Murchison Falls National Park

2. Bugungu Game Reserve

3. Karuma Game Reserve

4. Budongo Forest Reserve

5. Bogoma Forest Reserve

6. Toro Game Reserve

7. Itwara Forest Reserve

8. Semuliki National Park

9. Ruwenzori Mts. National Park

10. Kibale National Park

A tropical rain forest is by far the richest environment on the earth's land surface – this is the Great Barrier Reef of dry land. Although it is true that Africa's rain forest diversity is not as great as that found in the Amazon of South America or those rapidly dwindling forests of southeast Asia, this does not in any way diminish their interest or value. The lesser diversity is in large part explained by the fact that the continent's rain forests are relatively young, being perhaps little more than 10 000 years old.

There are also permanent and seasonal swamp forests, areas hostile to humans because of their blood-sucking leeches, mosquitoes, stinging and stingless bees… so many of them that they threaten to block every exposed orifice as they relish the salts secreted in human perspiration.

Throughout the rain forests one is always hot to mighty-sticky hot. In many areas, particularly those associated with riparian woodlands, lurk our old friends the tsetse flies, just waiting to take advantage of exposed skin. There are ants that seem to inject fire into your body, ticks that penetrate the smallest skin fold, and flies that lay their eggs under your skin. There are plants that cause rashes and mind-shattering itching if you are foolish enough to come into contact with them. The difficulty of access and all these "nasties" will ensure that the rain forests and in particular the conservation areas *never* attract the mass tourist trade. Although in some areas logging companies (legal and illegal) have cut roads into the forests, there are still vast tracts where access is only possible along river courses or on foot.

Prehistory

Prior to the last Ice Age tropical rain forests covered a much more extensive area than they do today. When the glacial advance reached its peak some 18 000 years ago the rain forests were largely displaced by temperate, deciduous tree species tolerant of cool temperatures. The rain forests, retreating from the now unsuitable climate, only survived in a number of isolated pockets, but with the retreat of the northern glaciers and rising global temperatures these forest "islands" once again were able to recolonise vast tracts of land. The fact that these Pleistocene climatic changes were more severe in Africa than in South America and southeast Asia also explains this "poorer" diversity.

Little is known about the prehistory of humans in the great central African rain forest region. Only two fossil sites are known from its present fringes: Chambuage Mine in the south and Matupi close to the western shore of Lake Kivu. The southern remains have been designated as archaic *Homo sapiens* and those at Matupi as being modern anatomically, but more than 50 000 years old.

Although the Portuguese seafarers had reached the estuary of the mighty Congo River by 1482, and made contact with two so-called Sudanic States, actual exploration of the interior of the great rain forests had to wait until the late 19th century. When the Portuguese arrived in the Gulf of Guinea the Kingdom of Bakongo occupied parts of the coastal plain and adjacent interior of what we know today as Gabon, Congo Republic and the Democratic Republic of Congo. At that time the king, Manicongo, had his capital at Mbanzacongo, the present-day San Salvadora of northern Angola. It is believed that the Bakongo kingdom was founded in the late 14th or early 15th century by invading Bantu-speaking peoples from the south-east who are believed to have been related to the Luba civilisation of Katanga. Three additional kingdoms, Nyoyo, Kakongo and Loango, were located northwards along the coast and at least nominally they acknowledged the supremacy

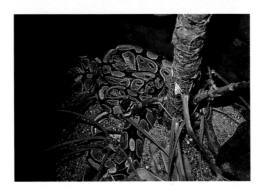

Above: *Long believed to be a subspecies of the bushpig, the red river hog is now recognised as a full species. With its red coat, white vertebral stripe and long ear-tufts, this pig is, in our opinion, the world's most handsome porcine.*

Below left: *Ants occupy virtually every available habitat within the forest and its fringes, and there are many species, including the remarkable tailor ant (Oecophylla longinoda). Adult workers pull the edges of adjacent leaves together and silk-spinning larvae, held by workers, bind the leaves together.*

Bottom left: *The royal python (Python regius) is restricted to the African rain forests, its skin patterning blending in with the leaf-litter of the forest floor.*

Below right: If there is one group
of antelope that has "conquered"
the African forests it has to be the
duikers. The smallest, the blue
duiker (Cephalophus monti-
cola) is known to occur at very
high densities in some regions.
Below middle: Although usually
associated with rivers and streams
in savanna woodland, the flat-
backed toad (Bufo maculatus)
also occurs in association with
some rain forest fringes.
Below: Pottos, a primitive primate, are only found in Africa's
tropical forests, where they feed on
a wide range of animal
and plant foods.

of Manicongo. From the little evidence that is available, settlement by the Bantu-speaking peoples was largely restricted to the periphery of the main forest blocks, although there were forays in search of such commodities as ivory by certain tribes.

History

Within these forests the first explorations by Europeans only occurred between about 1873 and 1900, a little over 100 years ago. Considerable areas of rain forest were only explored after the 1920s, and even today some areas are virtually unknown. Good old Henry Stanley, a busy man indeed, was the first to travel the length of the Congo River, from Lake Tanganyika to the mouth, in 1877.

Various European powers had established coastal "colonies" but it was King Leopold II of Belgium who laid claim to the entire

a result of intermarriage with Bantu tribes. Although some pygmies still continue with their hunter-gatherer lifestyle, most have settled on the forest edge and cultivate basic crops such as bananas and cassava.

Geography

The Congo River and its great number of large tributaries, such as the Cuango, Kasai, Lufira, Lubefu, Luapula, Lomami, Lualaba and Oubangui, dominate the second largest rain forest on earth, second only to the Amazon of South America. Most of the area covered by the rain forest is flat to gently undulating, but in the east it comes up against the mountain ranges of the western Great Rift, with now isolated forest pockets located in western Uganda. The forests adjacent to the "armpit" are traversed by numerous rivers that rise in the rain forests and pour their waters into the

Left: L'Hoest's
guenons are fre-
quently seen in the
company of other
guenon and colobus
monkey species.

Congo Basin and its vast rain forests – and of course its suspected mineral wealth. He sent two exploratory expeditions, in 1878 and again in 1879, under the cover of the African International Association. His intention, however, was to develop his colossal colony as a close-fisted personal commercial monopoly.

Although today there is more extensive settlement in parts of the rain forests, human populations are still generally low, except along major watercourses. However, there is one group of people that has successfully come to terms with living in the deep forests, the so-called pygmies. Different pygmy groups live in a belt some five degrees north and south of the equator, from Gabon in the west to western Uganda in the east. They include the Akka, Tiki-Tiki, Efe, Bambuti and Batwa, but to a large extent their racial purity has been lost as

Bight of Biafra and the Gulf of Guinea.

This region receives Africa's highest rainfall: in places more than 10 000 mm each year. Because of continuous leaching of the thin soils by the copious rainfall, and contrary to popular belief, tropical rain forest substrates are poor in nutrients. It is actually the thin layer of humus, which is rapidly processed by a host of micro-organisms, invertebrates and fungi for re-use as nutrients by the forest plants, that ensures this mighty botanical diversity.

Flora

The multi-faceted "botanical high-rise" of tropical climax forest is made up of not one vegetation component but a broad base of five different layers or strata. The first layer of green plants consists of herbs and tree seedlings, followed by the shrub layer that averages 3 m above the forest floor. Then there is a layer of short trees with long and narrow crowns that claw towards the little light that manages to filter its way through the contiguous, closed canopy of tall trees that have their crowns exposed to the sky. This canopy is the power house of rain forests and some 90% of all photosynthesis takes place here.

Below the canopy, growing on the mighty branches of the forest giants, are veritable gardens of epiphytic plants. These are not parasitic species and include a host of mosses, lichens, orchids and ferns. These epiphytes make a massive contribution to the productivity of the forest by ensnaring solar energy and increasing photosynthesis levels, filtering nutrients out of the atmosphere, contributing to the humus layer on the forest floor and providing micro-habitats for a vast and complex array of invertebrates and small vertebrates.

The forests are by no means uniform as far as plant species composition is concerned, with some areas having very high tree diversity, such as the 138 species identified on 0,64 ha at Korup in south-western Cameroon. In other areas the forest may be dominated by a handful, or even one, tree species. In these places animal diversity is at its lowest.

Within the forests are numerous clearings, ranging in size from a few hundred square metres to a couple of square kilometres, many having been opened originally by the activities of forest elephants, which have created these important feeding grounds for many species.

Fauna

Tropical rain forests are not the easiest of habitats in which to view wildlife but rich they are! This is the haunt of forest elephants, considerably smaller than their savanna-dwelling cousins, with neater, rounded ears and tusks that point groundwards; giant forest hogs, the world's largest wild pigs; red forest hogs; the deep red-chestnut bongo with its distinctive white markings; and the "forest giraffe", the okapi. The chevrotain is more closely related to deer and pigs than to antelope, and its nearest relatives live in Asia. Neither sex carries horns or antlers but the male is equipped with long, sharp canines that are used to good effect in conflicts over females. These forests are home to eight species of *cephalophine*, or forest, duikers, that

range in size from the diminutive 4 kg blue duiker to the 80 kg yellow-backed duiker. Even smaller is Bates's pygmy antelope at only 2-3 kg. In many parts of the rain forests these small antelope occur at very high densities, a further indication, if one is needed, that these wild areas are biologically very rich indeed.

Then there are the primates, and what an assemblage it is, ranging from gorillas, common chimpanzees and their close relative the bonobo to a staggering array of true monkeys and guenons, mangabeys and colobuses, galagos, pottos and angwantibos. In the forests of the "armpit" live the baboon-sized, black-faced drill and the rainbow-faced mandrill, which crow like cockerels and have the misfortune of being on Africa's long list of threatened species. Some species are widespread throughout the forests. In contrast the sun-tailed guenon, only discovered in the early 1980s, occurs in an area of less than 9 000 km^2 in central Gabon. Another species, the Salongo guenon, was also first described very recently and lives only, as far as we know, in the Wamba Forest of the western Democratic Republic of Congo. Virtually nothing is known about it.

We have only mentioned the larger mammals, and new species are still being discovered. What waits in the forests to excite our imaginations further? It is even rumoured, and the locals swear it is true, that a rhino-like "dinosaur", *mokélé-mbembé*, the elephant killer, roams the rain and swamp forests of part of the Congo Republic. It has been suggested that these creatures might be black rhinos that became isolated as the forests expanded with the retreat of the northern glaciers.

The rain forests are also home to scaly pangolins, with their long prehensile tails to grasp branches and elongated tongues to probe the nests of tree ants and termites; squirrels with wing-like membranes that enable them to glide from tree to tree, and fruit-eating bats that sing singly and in chorus. There are leopards that prowl the forest floor and stalk the understorey, golden cats and aquatic genets, giant genets and otter shrews.

Bird life

For the ornithologist, bird-watcher and fanatical twitcher the bird life is second to none, if you can see them. Hear them you certainly do, but it is not easy to identify the individual

Top: *The largest of the forest raptors is the mighty crowned eagle, large enough to kill and carry monkeys, small antelope, hyrax and guineafowl.*

PHOTO: JOHN CARLYON

Above: *The world's largest wild pig, the giant forest hog occupies many forest types and in some areas has adapted to living in mixed thicket and grassland.*

PHOTO: ROLAND VAN BOCKSTAELE

S P E C I E S   T O   W A T C H   F O R

M A M M A L S

(NOTE: This applies to lowland tropical forest as a whole and not a specific reserve.)

Forest elephant	*Loxodonta africana cyclotis*	Tree civet	*Nandinia binotata*
Red forest buffalo	*Syncerus caffer nanus*	African linsang	*Poiana richardsoni*
Okapi	*Okapia johnstoni*	Ansorge's cusimanse	*Crossarchus ansorgei*
Water chevrotain	*Hyemoschus aquaticus*	Gorilla	*Gorilla gorilla gorilla* and *graueri*
Giant forest hog	*Hylochoerus meinertzhageni*	Chimpanzee	*Pan troglodytes*
Red river hog	*Potamochoerus porcus*	Bonobo	*Pan paniscus*
Bongo	*Tragelaphus (Boocercus) euryceros*	Potto	*Perodicticus potto*
Bay duiker	*Cephalophus dorsalis*	De Brazza's monkey	*Cercopithecus neglectus*
Yellow-backed duiker	*Cephalophus silvicultor*	Mona monkey	*Cercopithecus mona*
Peters' duiker	*Cephalophus callipygus*	Red-tailed guenon	*Cercopithecus ascanius*
Black-fronted duiker	*Cephalophus nigrifrons*	L'Hoest's guenon	*Cercopithecus l'hoesti*
Bates's pygmy antelope	*Neotragus batesi*	Tree hyrax	*Dendrohyrax dorsalis*
Golden cat	*Profelis aurata*	Long-tailed tree pangolin	*Manis tetradactyla*
Giant genet	*Genetta victoriae*	African brush-tailed porcupine	*Atherurus africanus*

B I R D S

White-crested bittern	*Tigriornis leucolophus*	Red-headed lovebird	*Agapornis pullaria*
Spot-breasted ibis	*Bostrychia rara*	Shining-blue kingfisher	*Alcedo quadribrachys*
Hartlaub's duck	*Pteronetta hartlaubi*	Blue-breasted bee-eater	*Merops variegatus*
Crowned eagle	*Stephanoaetus coronatus*	Blue-headed bee-eater	*Merops mülleri*
Congo serpent eagle	*Dryotriorchis spectabilis*	Black-headed bee-eater	*Merops breweri*
Chestnut-flanked goshawk	*Accipiter castanilius*	Piping hornbill	*Ceratogymna fistulator*
Forest francolin	*Francolinus lathami*	White-thighed hornbill	*Ceratogymna cylindricus*
Black guineafowl	*Agelastes niger*	White-crested hornbill	*Tockus albocristatus*
Congo peacock	*Afropavo congensis*	Black-casqued hornbill	*Ceratogymna atrata*
Nkulengu rail	*Himantornis haematopus*	Pied hornbill	*Tockus fasciatus*
Afep pigeon	*Columba unicincta*	Red-chested owlet	*Glaucidium tephronotum*
Western bronze-naped pigeon	*Columba iriditorques*	Akun eagle-owl	*Bubo leucostictus*
Blue-headed wood dove	*Turtur brehmeri*	Fraser's eagle-owl	*Bubo poensis*
Gabon coucal	*Centropus anselli*	Bare-cheeked trogon	*Apaloderma aequatoriale*
Black-billed turaco	*Tauraco schütti*	Yellow-billed barbet	*Trachyphonus purpuratus*
Great blue turaco	*Corythaeola cristata*	Lyre-tailed honey-guide	*Melichneutes robustus*
Grey parrot	*Psittacus erithacus*	Yellow-crested woodpecker	*Dendropicos xantholophus*

***Above:** The strangler figs (*Ficus sp.*) of which there are many species associated with forests, do not in fact "strangle" the unwilling host tree.*

species from this cacophony of sound. To further sow confusion one encounters multi-species flocks of birds, with each benefiting from the foraging behaviour of the others.

The eastern rain forests are home to the Congo peacock, whose nearest relations live in Asia, and this is the stronghold of a plethora of hornbills and turacos, greenbuls (if you can identify them!) and weavers – what else awaits us in this sticky, dark green world? Here there are many species of feathered beasties that are known only from a specimen or two reclining in dusty, musty museum drawers, or descriptions of their primaries and secondaries in journals that are sagging the shelves of libraries.

The rain forest reserves

As is common to many regions of Africa, the countries with tropical rain forests have numerous designated national parks, game reserves and forest reserves but alas, most exist on paper alone. Many have not even been visited by scientists, never mind adequately surveyed and inventories of their plant and animal life compiled! Most boundaries are ill defined. But in many cases these reserves' very isolation is their best protection; none will ever appear on the mass-tourism trail.

At this stage the only forest reserves that are reasonably accessible to visitors are Budongo, Bwindi, Kibale and Semuliki in Uganda, but only the latter can be classified as true lowland rain forest. Kahuzi–Biega National Park in eastern Democratic Republic of Congo is reasonably reachable, with its main attraction being habituated troops of the eastern lowland gorilla, but the turmoil that has enveloped the Great Lakes region in recent times no longer makes this an attractive destination. In fact fears have been expressed that the hundreds of thousands of refugees who have been roaming the rain forests of the eastern Democratic Republic of Congo, living of necessity off the land, have had a major impact on the fauna and flora of the region.

As we write this section, we have a map in front of us that depicts every national park, nature and forest reserve located in the lowland rain forests, and an impressive coverage it appears to be. However, there are three that deserve individual mention, each for its own reason that we shall make clear, namely Ituri Forest, Salonga North and South, and possibly the most fascinating of all, the Nouabalé-Ndoki National Park in the Congo Republic.

Nouabalé-Ndoki

Nouabalé-Ndoki was proclaimed in 1993. The first explorations of this park have only taken place over the past 10 years, and there are still areas that have not been penetrated, apparently not even by the Babenzélé pygmies who live on its fringes. The park covers approximately 4 000 km² and is surrounded by what are referred to as managed forest reserves. The park and forests are located in northern Congo Republic, sharing the western boundary with the Central African Republic, where it adjoins the Dzanga-Ndoki National Park and the Dzanga-Sangha Dense Forest Reserve. According to author Douglas Chadwick, who visited Ndoki, it "is like being passed through the guts of the forest and being slowly digested." Living within this "difficult" environment are large numbers of forest elephant and red forest buffalo, and densities of lowland gorillas and chimpanzees that have rarely been encountered elsewhere. The most amazing fact about these populations of the two large primates is that they have never encountered humans, and hostile approaches are therefore unknown to them. This is very unlike other areas of their distribution, where they are hunted for their meat and flee at the first sign or sound of *Homo sapiens*. There are also hosts of guenons, monkeys, mangabeys and colobuses, equally unafraid of their naked relatives.

Salonga (North and South)

Although limited tourist access into the periphery of Ndoki forest complex is a possibility in the future, getting into the Salonga national parks is a totally different issue. Salonga North and Salonga South national

parks are located in west-central Democratic Republic of Congo and the only way to get to them is on foot or by canoe. This giant conservation complex covers some 36 000 km², making it one of Africa's largest national parks. Although it receives no control or management input, its very isolation is its best protection. It has never been fully surveyed and our knowledge is still very limited. It is flat country, with an average altitude above sea-level of only 350 m. It has a particularly rich diversity of primates, carnivores and ungulates. Although current lists for such groups as bats and rodents are small, when (if) more comprehensive surveys are undertaken they will probably be found to be some of the most extensive in Africa. There are forest elephants, red forest buffalo, okapi (these reports still need to be confirmed) and bongo, six duiker species, sitatunga (the swamp antelope), red forest hog and giant forest hog, with hippos in the rivers and swamps. The primates range in size from the diminutive Demidov's bushbaby to the bonobo, believed by many to be man's closest relative. Fourteen species of carnivore are known to occur, sev-

Below: *The turacos, here a race of the green turaco (Tauraco persa), are predominantly forest-dwellers, although several species have adapted to life in woodland savanna.*
Middle: *Many species of hornbill call the rain forests home, including the large black and white casqued hornbill (Ceratogymna subcylindricus).*
Bottom: *Fraser's eagle-owl, also known as the nduk eagle-owl, is restricted to forest but little is known of its behaviour.*

eral of which have never been studied in the wild, such as the African linsang, servaline genet and two species of cusimanse – small, long-snouted and coarse-haired forest mongooses. As far as we are aware no survey, no matter how minimal, has been undertaken on the bird, reptile and amphibian life but it is almost certainly incredibly rich.

Epulu

Epulu National Park, covering 13 800 km² and proclaimed in 1987, is located in the Ituri Forest of north-eastern Democratic Republic of Congo. It is intended as a primary sanctuary for the "forest giraffe", the okapi, which is believed to be fairly common, occuring in fairly high densities in some areas. However, it also protects large tracts of rain forest and the organisms that depend on it for their survival. Ranging in altitude from 500 m to about 1 000 m above sea-level, it lies somewhat higher than most of the tropical lowland rain forest but its vegetation is largely similar. The okapi was only discovered by the scientific world in 1900, after vague reports began filtering out of a large and mysterious mammal living in the rain forests of the Congo. The first comprehensive study of this unusual ungulate started only in 1986, but only in a small part of the forest.

Semuliki

At present Semuliki National Park in western Uganda is the only realistic possibility for the visitor wanting to visit a tropical lowland rain forest. This small park was proclaimed in 1993 and conserves some 220 km² which forms part of the more extensive, although exploited, Bwamba Forest. It offers a glimpse of the east-ernmost extension of the great Congolean rain forest and averages less than 750 m above sea-level. This forest has one of the richest faunal communities in East Africa.

It includes 15 different primates, small numbers of forest elephant and buffalo, hippos in the Semuliki River, as well as several duiker species. This is also the only location in East Africa where the chevrotain occurs, but the okapi was wiped out by poachers before the proclamation of the park.

The future

As we have mentioned earlier, Africa's tropical forests are, in general, poorly explored by scientists and naturalists and inventories of their biodiversity are largely incomplete. In the Democratic Republic of Congo, with the continent's largest tropical rain forest holdings, only an estimated 0,2% of forests are destroyed annually, and there is considerable hope that a balance between conservation needs and sustainable exploitation can be achieved. Forest loss in the Congo Republic and Gabon is even lower at just 0,1%. However, those conservation areas that do exist in the rain forests are by and large "paper parks" and their only protection lies in their isolation. With ever-growing human populations and increased demands for timber and "bush-meat", pressures will certainly increase.

Below: Many species of frog are associated with forest wetlands, and the Hyperolius *genus is particularly well represented. These small reed and tree frogs come in an amazing array of colours and patterns, this particularly handsome one was photographed in the Kibale forest of western Uganda.*

SEMULIKI NATIONAL PARK

Travel and access: Access is from Fort Portal, which lies on the main road from Kampala (the southern loop route via Mbarara and Kasese is good tar), along the dirt road to Bundibugyo. The road to the park, in the direction of Bundibugyo, is rough and in poor condition, particularly after rain. We recommend 4x4 vehicles, although you will encounter other transport. You should set aside up to three hours to reach the park HQ at Ntandi; you first encounter the park boundary at the Sempaya hot springs, where there is also an office. The drive is rough but more than compensated for by some of the finest scenery in East Africa.

Mobility: There are no internal roads but there are trails and more are being developed. There is a short self-guided trail (about two hours) at Sempaya; other routes of up to six days can be taken but you will be required to take a guide. This is important because trails are not clearly marked and in places vegetation has to be cut.

Accommodation: Camping only in the park. The campsite is located at Ntandi HQ and has pit toilets, water and charcoal. A second campsite is located just outside the park at Sempaya, with small shelters under which you can do your cooking. You must bring all your own camping gear, as well as food.

Other facilities: Apart from trails, guides and campsites, nothing.

Climate: Very wet and rain can be expected at any time of the year, although June-July and December-February are the driest months. Generally warm and humid.

Best times to visit: June-July; December-February.

Main attractions: Equatorial lowland forest; abundant bird life, as well as other organisms; the Sempaya hot springs; Mungilo Falls (outside park); very scenic access road.

Hazards: Potentially dangerous animals; abundance of biting and stinging insects, particularly during principal rain months.

For further information: Uganda National Parks HQ; Warden-in-Charge, Semuliki National Park, P.O. Box 1153, Bundibugyo.

BUDONGO FOREST

Lying just south of Murchison Falls National Park, and bisected by the Masindi-Bulisa road, Budongo Forest is well worth a stay of two or three days. It is the largest mahogany forest in East Africa and is home to more than 600 chimpanzees, as well as six other primate species. It is also exceptionally rich in other mammals, birds and butterflies. There are two basic campsites, with thatch shelters, pit toilets, water and an area for fires, located just off the road at Kaniyo Pabidi (29 km north of Masindi on the direct route to Paraa) and Busingiro (40 km west of Masindi on the route to Paraa via Lake Albert). Guides live close by to collect fees (very reasonable) and take you on the network of forest trails. The attractions are primate tracking, including habituated troops of chimpanzees, and learning some of the workings of the forest biota from knowledgeable guides. At night you will hear the distinctive calls of the tree hyrax, as well as many other species. The roads are reasonable dirt but can become sticky and unpleasant after rain.

For further information: Budongo Forest Ecotourism Project, Nyabyeye Forestry College, Private Bag, Masindi; fax (256 41) 259536.

ITWARA AND BUGOMA

Two other forest reserves, Itwara and Bugoma, lie to the west of the Kyenjojo-Hoima road and are worth exploring. Although there are no facilities you can probably camp without too much trouble. The best approach to Bugoma is west from Kabwoya, which lies about halfway between Kyenjojo and Masindi, on the track to Kyangwali and Buhaka. An alternative is to take the Biseruka road just north of Hoima. These roads are not in good shape and can be difficult after rain. We suggest you make enquiries at Fort Portal or Kyenjojo for Itwara, and at Hoima or Pachwa for Bugoma. Bugoma in particular is a good birding destination. Remember that it is surprisingly easy to get lost in forests, so enquire for a suitable local guide.

KIBALE FOREST NATIONAL PARK

Travel and access: The road from Kampala via Masaka, Mbarara and Kasese to Fort Portal is tarred, but the stretch from Kasese to Fort Portal (105 km) is deteriorating with some bad potholes. The road from Kampala to Fort Portal is considerably shorter (about 320 km) but is in a very poor state. If you are in your own transport set aside at least six hours for the drive. We do not recommend that you use the Mbarara-Fort Portal, via Ibanda, route. In Fort Portal, on the south side of the river, there is a sign to Kibale National Park (reasonable dirt but we suggest 4x4), and at the first village there is a sign to the education centre. Total distance from Fort Portal to Kanyanchu visitor centre is 35 km. No permit is required if you stick to the road from Fort Portal to Ibanda that passes through the park; if you intend walking in the forest (only with a guide) permits are obtained at Kanyanchu; park entrance is about $12.

Mobility: Apart from the public Fort Portal-Ibanda road, all movement is restricted to a network of trails in the vicinity of Kanyanchu. Visitors do not require permits to walk on the public road (well worth while). If you don't have your own transport, there are taxis that run from Fort Portal past Kanyanchu, but don't expect luxurious travel. After rain the road can be very slippery.

Accommodation: At Kanyanchu there are two private campsites, each with a tent equipped with two beds, bedding and paraffin lamp. There are three additional sites where you may pitch your own tent; there is also a communal camping area. All are pleasant but the advantage of the individual sites is that you are isolated. There are pit toilets and cooking sites; firewood is available but bring all your "kitchen kit" and food. Snacks and drinks are usually available but don't rely on it. Alternatives are basic but cheap accommodation in the villages of Nkingo and Bigodi, both short distances south of the park. For those without transport these two settlements are an easy walk from the visitor centre. Just outside the western park boundary is the Crater Valley Beach Resort where visitors can camp overlooking a superb crater lake; snacks, beers and cold drinks are usually available. This site is also a good place to encounter the abundant frog life. Some people prefer to base themselves in Fort Portal; there are several options, ranging from the Mountains of the Moon Hotel to the Wooden Hotel, Ruwenzori Tea Hotel and a number of budget options.

Other facilities: The possibility of chimpanzee tracking; network of forest trails and knowledgeable guides. At the time of writing forest walks leave at 07h30 and 15h30 each day, last two to three hours and are limited to six people per guide.

Climate: Rain can be expected at any time of the year, so come prepared. Temperatures are generally mild but high humidity can make things uncomfortable; evenings may be cool.

Best times to visit: Open throughout the year.

Main attractions: Great diversity and numbers of primates; guided forest walks; low tourist levels.

Hazards: It is forbidden to enter the forest without a guide; this is for a number of good reasons, not least that it is extremely easy to get lost in this type of forest and there are potentially dangerous animals.

For further information: Uganda National Parks HQ or Warden-in-Charge, P.O. Box 699, Fort Portal.

①   *Ruwenzori Mountains*
②   *Mount Kenya*
③   *Mount Kilimanjaro*

Chapter 10

KILIMANJARO, MT KENYA & THE RUWENZORIS

EQUATORIAL SNOW PEAKS

I live not in myself, but I become
Portion of that around me, and to me
High mountains are a feeling, but the hum
Of human cities torture.

Lord Byron, *Childe Harold's Pilgrimage*

Dawn in the lower cloud forest; it is clear with no hint of mist, and there, grazing in a large open glade, are a trio of massively horned buffalo bulls, even at this early hour accompanied by cattle egrets. Somewhere close at hand the sound of branches snapping is the only indication that an elephant is here, and the sharp bark of a bushbuck carries over the forest, whether alarmed by a leopard or warning off rival rams we do not know. Then the guerezas give vent to their loud gobble-like calls, first the members of one group, then the next, until at least five troops are letting the new day know that they are still here

and proclaiming their dominance over their few hectares of feeding space. The "jack" calls of the Sykes's monkeys and the barking of the olive baboons add to the cacophony of sound. As the morning progresses the tendrils of cloud begin to enshroud the forest and the glade is hidden from view. Another day is well under way.

We never like to make the choice as to which this or that is our favourite but in the case of the snow peaks we prefer to see Kilimanjaro from the air, Mount Kenya along the Sirimon trail and the Ruwenzoris (sometimes spelled Rwenzoris) with a break in the

mists and rain clouds, viewed from the kob-dotted plains around Lake George. Each has its own appeal but the wrong way to approach all of the snow peaks is with the single idea in mind of just getting to the top; so much is missed in this way.

Unfortunately, it is only the higher altitudes of the three equatorial "snow mountains" that are protected in national parks. The lower forests, or rather what's left of them, having been severely degraded by many decades of settlement by people, are unprotected. The degradation is most obvious in the Ruwen-zoris, where much of the lower-lying forest

Above: Mount Kenya is Africa's second highest mountain, but offers little challenge to serious climbers.

PHOTO: COLIN MONTEATH

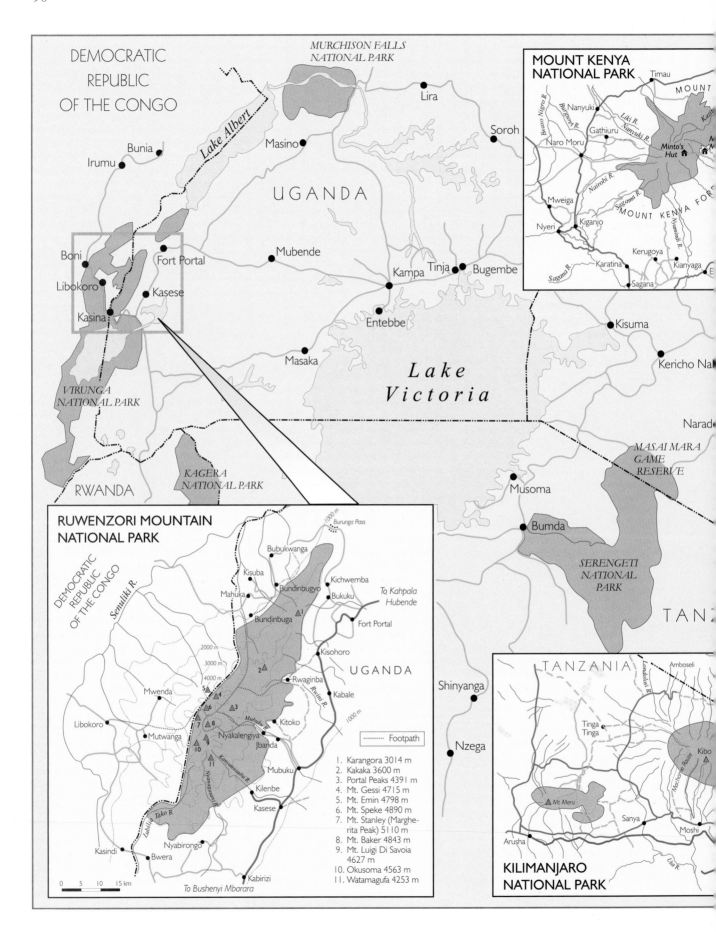

DEMOCRATIC REPUBLIC OF THE CONGO

MURCHISON FALLS NATIONAL PARK

Lira

Masino

Bunia

Irumu

Lake Albert

UGANDA

Boni

Fort Portal

Libokoro

Kasese

Kasina

VIRUNGA NATIONAL PARK

RWANDA

KAGERA NATIONAL PARK

Mubende

Kampa

Tinja

Bugembe

Entebbe

Masaka

Lake Victoria

Kisuma

Kericho Na

Narad

MASAI MARA GAME RESERVE

Musoma

Bumda

SERENGETI NATIONAL PARK

TAN

MOUNT KENYA NATIONAL PARK

Timau

MOUNT

Bwaso Nigro R.

Burguret R.

Nanyuki

Liki R.

Naro Moru

Gathiuru

Nanyuki R.

Kazit

Minto's Hut

M

Nairobi R.

Mweiga

Sagana R.

MOUNT KENYA FOREST

Nyeri

Kiganjo

Nyamali R.

Sagana R.

Kerugoya

Karatina

Kianyaga

Sagana

E

RUWENZORI MOUNTAIN NATIONAL PARK

DEMOCRATIC REPUBLIC OF THE CONGO

Semliki R.

1000 m   Burunga Pass

Bubukwanga

Kisuba

Kichwemba

Mahuka

Bundinbugyo

Bukuku

Bundinbuga

1

To Kahpala Hubende

Fort Portal

2000 m

Kisohoro

3000 m

4000 m

2

Rwaginba

UGANDA

Mwenda

5

4

6

3

Kabale

Mubuku R.

Kitoko

Rwini R.

Libokoro

7

8

Nyakalengiya

Mutwanga

9

Jbanda

10

1000 m

Kanyanwanha R.

11

Mubuku

Shinyanga

Nyamagami R.

Kilenbe

.... Footpath

Nzega

Zubilia Tako R.

Kasese

1. Karangora 3014 m
2. Kakaka 3600 m
3. Portal Peaks 4391 m
4. Mt. Gessi 4715 m
5. Mt. Emin 4798 m
6. Mt. Speke 4890 m
7. Mt. Stanley (Margherita Peak) 5110 m
8. Mt. Baker 4843 m
9. Mt. Luigi Di Savoia 4627 m
10. Okusoma 4563 m
11. Watamagufa 4253 m

Kasindi

Nyabirongo

Bwera

0   5   10   15 km

Kabirizi

To Bushenyi Mbarara

TANZANIA

Amboseli

Londolosi B.

Tinga Tinga

Kibo

Machame Route

Mt Meru

Sanya

Moshi

Arusha

Lisa R.

KILIMANJARO NATIONAL PARK

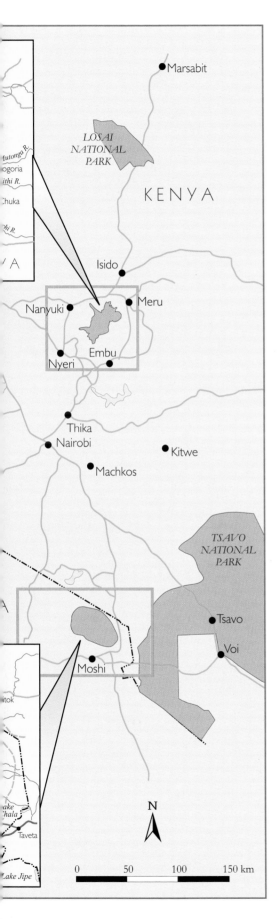

has been cut and cleared and replaced by small cultivated patches that are often on slopes so steep that it seems almost impossible that they could be worked. Encroachment into the protected forest belt is not as bad as it was a few years ago but poaching and wood removal is an ever-present problem for the conservation authorities. Tourist hikers, particularly on the most popular routes up mounts Kenya and Kilimanjaro, pose a threat in the form of too much disturbance, trampling, rubbish dumping and noise pollution.

Initially we were going to cover each of the equatorial snow mountains separately, but reviewing our visits we came to the conclusion that although each differs in some respect from the others, there are in fact enough similarities to justify an "amalgamation".

History

When the missionaries Johann Rebmann and J. Krapf regaled Europe in 1849 with their account of a high, snow-capped mountain close to the equator, their tale was greeted with disbelief. It seemed to many that these odd fellows had obviously spent too much time under the African sun! This was Kilimanjaro, Africa's tallest mountain and one of the highest free-standing peaks in the world.

The origins of the name Kilimanjaro have been obscured by time, with various translations referring to it as "white mountain", "water mountain" and even "little hill". The latter is very puzzling and certainly not logical but it may have its root in the Kiswahili word *mlima*, with the addition of the diminutive *ki*, therefore *kilima*, and it has been suggested that this is meant as an extension of affection for this African colossus. The meaning of *njaro* is equally obscure. It has been variously suggested that it is the Kichagga word for caravan (the mountain was presumably used as a landmark by the trading and slaving caravans that traversed the area) and that it was the name of a demon that created cold weather. These names seem likely to remain a puzzle.

Although not an explanation for the origins of the name Ruwenzori it is generally believed that this range is the fabled *Mountains of the Moon*, considered to be the source of the Nile River and recorded as such by Ptolemy in AD 150. Ruwenzori weather is that of near perpetual mists, rain and snow and hence its local name, meaning "rain maker".

Above: The melting snows of Kilimanjaro feed into small marshes on the surrounding plains, that form extremely important habitats for a wide range of biota.
Below: The large rameron, or olive, pigeon (Columba arquatrix) occurs in dense woodland and montane forests.

Although the first European reference to the existence of Kilimanjaro only came in 1849, it is believed that Chinese traders were familiar with "a great mountain" to the west of Zanzibar in the 6th and 7th centuries, and it is certain that Arab traders were familiar with its snow-capped peak but no references appear in their writings.

The first successful, recorded ascent of this mountain was made by the German scientists H. Meyer and L. Purtscheller on 6 October 1889. The first successful ascent of the second highest of the three peaks, Mawensi, was only made 23 years later by the geographer F. Klute. It was also the missionary Krapf who discovered for the Western world Mount Kenya in 1848, but the first attempt to climb this, Africa's second highest peak, had to wait until 1887 when Count Teleki reached an altitude of 4 700 m, 499 m short of the summit. The next attempt was in 1893 by the Englishman J.W. Gregory, but he had to turn back just short of the highest point. G. Kolb tried the following year, but only gained the crater rim.

summits of any of the high peaks. Several other scientists and naturalists explored the range but only in 1906 were first ascents made of most of the highest summits. In that year Prince Luigi Amadeo di Savoia, the Duke of Abruzzi, undertook the most extensive survey of the Mountains of the Moon, climbing most of the principal peaks and producing the first good map of the range.

But long before this "discovery" Ptolemy had referred to the snows of the "Mountains of the Moon" that fed the waters of the Nile. We think we know so much!

Geography

Those mountains that carry permanent, although diminishing, snow caps are Kilimanjaro, Kenya and the Ruwenzori range, with the latter two lying on the equator and Kilimanjaro just 330 km south of that invisible line that divides our planet into the northern and southern hemispheres. All owe their origins to one of Africa's greatest landscape features, that most massive of all dry land divides, the Great Rift Valley. Kilimanjaro lies in north-eastern Tanzania, bordering on Kenya's Amboseli National Park; Mount Kenya is in the country of the same name and the Ruwenzoris share their mist-shrouded heights between Uganda in the east and the Democratic Republic of Congo in the west.

Kilimanjaro is what is known as a layer volcano, with its origins in the Tertiary Era, and consists of three volcanic cones, namely Kibo (5 895 m), Mawensi (5 149 m) and the lowest, Shira (3 962 m). Shira is the oldest of the three cones and as a consequence is the most heavily eroded. It is estimated to have originally topped 5 000 m, but a powerful eruption collapsed the entire summit and all that remained was a caldera with a diameter of 3 km. From the bottom of this caldera further volcanic activity took place, which gave rise to a cone of lava, the present-day Mawensi. But then the mightiest of all, Kibo, thrust up between Shira and Mawensi, and its highest point, Uhuru (or Kaiser Wilhelm Peak, as it used to be called) is the highest that one can go skywards on the African continent while keeping one's feet firmly planted on *terra firma*. Its lava flows were so great that they reached the flanks of Shira and Mawensi and partly buried them. Until about 450 000 years before present Kibo continued to grow but then stabilised,

Success had to wait until 1899 when H. Mackinder was the first to reach the summit.

Sir Henry Stanley, he of "Dr Livingstone, I presume" fame, was the first European to sight the Ruwenzoris in 1876, but the peaks were shrouded in mist. However, on his return in 1888 their snow-capped crowns were visible. He returned yet again the following year, and one of his expedition members, W.G. Stairs, ascended to the 3 000 m contour. Dr Franz Stuhlman led an expedition deep into the Ruwenzoris in 1891 but did not reach the although volcanic activity continued with numerous satellite vents erupting, leaving a belt of distinctive cones and craters scattered across the slopes of Kilimanjaro.

Kibo's crater is 2 km across and is surrounded by a circle of cliffs that average 300 m above its floor. It is believed that the inner cone floor, known as the Reusch crater, was formed within the past few hundred years. Vulcanologists classify Kilimanjaro, and more particularly Kibo, as a dormant rather than an extinct volcano, as there are still active fumaroles within the inner crater and large recent deposits of sulphur, both apparent indicators of subsurface heat. Although the summit area is blanketed by an ice-cap from which hanging glaciers descend to about 5 000 m above sea-level, this is now in retreat. It has been predicted that with current climatic trends the glaciers will disappear, possibly within the next 10 years.

Mount Kenya, Africa's second highest mountain, is a complex of three distinct peaks: Batian (5 199 m) the tallest, Nelion (5 188 m) and Lenana (4 985 m). This, unlike Kilimanjaro, is an extinct volcano that was formed between 2,6 and 3,1 million years before present. It is estimated that its original height might have exceeded a whopping 7 000 m. However, erosion, to a large extent the work of glaciers, has exacted a severe toll, a whole 2 000 m! All volcanic activity in the central vent probably ceased more than two million years ago but some activity continued until 100 000 years before present in the vicinity of the mountain.

As with Kilimanjaro, Mount Kenya's glaciers are in rapid retreat. Eight of the original 18 glaciers described at the end of the last century by Gregory have since melted, and it is unlikely that the remainder will survive far into the 21st century.

The Ruwenzori range, approximately 120 km from north to south and 48 km at its widest, was formed by major uplifting of the earth's crust during the same period that the Great Rift Valley was born. It rises to its maximum altitude above sea-level of 5 120 m on Mount Margherita, with other major peaks such as Alexandria, Speke, Emin and Gessi soaring above 4 700 m. Most of the rocks in the Ruwenzoris are either of an igneous or metamorphic origin, consisting mainly of gneisses and amphibolite that form a central spine which extends from Mount Stanley to the Portal Peaks. As with Kilimanjaro and Mount Kenya, there are many landscape features in the range that owe their existence to long periods of glaciation, such as several deep valleys and heavy deposits of glacial debris in the form of lateral moraines. But the glaciers here are also in rapid retreat and it is unlikely that they will survive many more years; so if you want to see them don't waste time but expect a very hard climb if you want to get close.

Climate

High mountains produce the most bewildering contrasts in living conditions for animals and plants found anywhere on earth. Each of the equatorial snow peaks has a climate that bears little resemblance to that on the surrounding lowlands and each is banded into horizontal layers exhibiting different vegetation and animal components. Diversity is at its greatest at the lowest levels, decreasing with rising altitude as conditions become harsher, with greater contrasts in temperature, high solar radiation and strong winds. Weather at the bases of tropical mountains is usually very warm without drastic night and daytime contrasts, but closer to the summits, days can be hot and the hours of darkness glacially cold. A typical day starts with a crystal clear sky. As the ground begins to warm up, heated air starts to rise up the mountain and by midmorning the cloud layer is at about 3 000 m. By midday the entire mountain is shrouded in dense cloud. In the afternoon rain, sleet, hail or snow, depending on the altitude, are common, but as the rising air begins to cool in the evening the cloud descends, leaving only the stars and planets to commune with the peaks.

On a climb up the northern Sirimon track of Mount Kenya, we left the forest in warm, humid weather but as we entered the moorland the cloud soon enveloped us; we kept a wary lookout for elephant as a little lower we had encountered very fresh tracks; an hour later we were pelted by stinging sleet and hailstones the size of marbles – praise be to the giant heath plants under which we took shelter.

Rainfall is not evenly distributed on Kilimanjaro, Mount Kenya and the Ruwenzoris. Each receives its heaviest falls on the eastern slopes which face the dominant, prevailing winds. So, for example, the Ruwenzoris receive their highest falls on the

Top: High precipitation in the form of rain and mist in the cloud forest encourages a proliferation of plant growth, with even tree branches being bedecked with thick carpets of mosses, ferns and lichens. **Above:** Large ground orchids are a feature of the moister areas on the moorland and Afro-alpine.

SPECIES TO WATCH FOR

MAMMALS

Giant forest hog	*Hylochoerus meinertzhageni*		Guereza	*Colobus guereza*
Bongo	*Tragelaphus (Boocercus) euryceros*		Sykes's monkey	*Cercopithecus mitis*
Bushbuck	*Tragelaphus scriptus*		Olive baboon	*Papio cynocephalus (anubis)*
Black-fronted duiker	*Cephalophus nigrifrons*		Tree hyrax	*Dendrohyrax arboreus*
Abbot's duiker	*Cephalophus spadix*		Rock hyrax	*Procavia capensis*

BIRDS

Green ibis	*Bostrychia olivacea*		Alpine chat	*Cercomela sordida*
African cuckoo hawk	*Aviceda cuculoides*		White-starred robin	*Pogonocichla stellata*
Bearded vulture	*Gypaetus barbatus*		Archer's robin-chat	*Cossypha archeri*
Mountain buzzard	*Buteo oreophilus*		Prigogene's ground-thrush	*Zoothera kibalensis*
Verreaux's eagle	*Aquila verreauxi*		Cinnamon bracken warbler	*Bradypterus cinnamomeus*
Crowned eagle	*Stephanoaetus coronatus*		Mountain yellow warbler	*Chloropeta similis*
Scaly francolin	*Francolinus squamatus*		Wing-snapping cisticola	*Cisticola ayresii*
Jackson's francolin	*Francolinus jacksoni*		Chestnut-throated apalis	*Apalis porphyrolaema*
Red-fronted parrot	*Poicephalus gulielmi*		Mountain illadopsis	*Illadopsis pyrrhopterum*
Ruwenzori turaco	*Musophaga johnstoni*		African hill-babbler	*Illadopsis abyssinica*
Hartlaub's turaco	*Tauraco hartlaubi*		Stuhlmann's double-	
Cape eagle-owl	*Bubo capensis*		collared sunbird	*Nectarinia stuhlmanni*
Alpine swift	*Tachymarptis melba*		Tacazze sunbird	*Nectarinia tecazze*
Bar-tailed trogon	*Apaloderma vittatum*		Scarlet-tufted malachite sunbird	*Nectarinia johnstoni*
Silvery-cheeked hornbill	*Ceratogymna brevis*		White-necked raven	*Corvus albicollis*
Mountain wagtail	*Motacilla clara*		Brown-capped weaver	*Ploceus insignis*
Olive mountain greenbul	*Phyllastrephus placidus*		Yellow-crowned canary	*Serinus canicollis*
Northern anteater chat	*Myrmecocichla aethiops*		African citril	*Serinus citrinelloides*

Top: *The tussock grasses, mainly of the Afro-alpine zone, are particularly abundant on the drier mountain slopes.*
Above: *Lichens are common on the snow peaks, even at the highest levels where few other organisms can survive the harsh climatic conditions.*

Ugandan slopes. Even though the western side of the range is drier, it is certainly not dry. The combination of high to relatively high rainfall and rich soils on the slopes and surroundings has a strong influence on the associated vegetation. But this richness has one very serious drawback: it attracts large numbers of cultivators to these bountiful slopes, with resultant destruction of the natural vegetation, increased erosion as the soils are exposed and exploitation of the natural resources above the cultivation line.

Flora

The vegetation belts that encircle these mountains differ in composition at different altitudes and are rarely uniform and evenly spaced because of the effect of rainfall and the "rain-shadow". The vegetation of mounts Kenya and Kilimanjaro and the Ruwenzoris is particularly rich and diverse, and although they share many genera, a great number of the species and subspecies are endemic to each. The lowest zone consists of mixed forest, with mainly evergreen trees on the wetter slopes

and semi-deciduous species on the drier side of the mountain. There are extensive stands of junipers and podocarps, commonly known as yellowwoods, particularly on the drier slopes; the northern slopes of Mount Kenya have magnificent stands of these species.

Towards the upper reaches one moves into montane or cloud forest, consisting mainly of a low and dense canopy of smaller trees than are found at lower levels. Because of the high precipitation at this level the branches are thickly festooned with "gardens" of ferns, bryophytes, epiphytic orchids and lichens.

Mount Kenya and the Ruwenzoris differ in their vegetation structure from Kilimanjaro in one major way: they have extensive belts and patches of tall bamboo (*Arundinaria* spp.) but Africa's tallest mountain has none. The bamboo belts are located within the montane forest zone, or closely associated with it, and pose formidable barriers to human passage. When exploring areas of bamboo thicket on Mount Kenya, our only means of entry was along the tunnels created by elephants and buffalo, always keeping a wary eye, and ear, out for these animals. The passageways are used by many other species apart from their creators. We found signs of giant forest hog, bushpig, an unidentified duiker and olive baboons. White-collared Sykes's monkeys allowed us to approach within 2 m while they busied themselves with the harvesting of that delicacy, bamboo shoots. Below us, at the edge of the montane forest, a chorus of "gobble-whoops" of the guerezas, or black and white colobus monkeys, echoed around the mountain, each troop proclaiming its right to its patch of forest. Unlike the Sykes's monkeys and olive baboons, the guerezas seldom descend to the ground but partake of their leafy diet in the canopy, and occasionally in the understorey.

Beyond the bamboo and montane forest belts one encounters a zone of ericaceous scrub, or heathland, which includes low scrub and taller heath species such as the giant *Erica arborea*. Although relatively well developed on mounts Kilimanjaro and Kenya, it is on the Ruwenzoris between 3 000 m and 3 500 m that this vegetation type is particularly well developed, forming dense and almost impenetrable thickets.

In the next vegetation zone, the Afro-alpine, one finds those plants that are best adapted to withstand the rigours of high-altitude living, including extremely low and high temperatures, strong winds and other extremes. Our first experience of this high-altitude vegetation was on Mount Kenya; shall we ever forget struggling through near-vertical bogs and stumbling over meadows of tussock grass? But the first sight of stands of giant senecios (*Dendrosenicio* spp.) and giant lobelias (*Lobelia* spp.) made it all well worth while. At lower altitudes members of these genera are generally small and not particularly eye-catching, but species on the upper slopes may reach several metres in height; for example the blue bog lobelia *Lobelia deckenii* on Kilimanjaro reaches 4 m. On Kenya and Kilimanjaro they occur in small scattered patches but in the Ruwenzoris the lobelias and senecios form dense stands spread over extensive areas.

These plants grow slowly and some of the giant senecios may only flower at 10 to 20 year intervals, but when they do their tall flower spikes, each spike containing many individual flowers, are an imposing sight. In order to survive freezing the leaves provide insulation for developing buds and some even produce a thick, sticky substance that serves as a very effective anti-freeze, preventing frost and ice damage to the plant's growth core.

The highest point of the Afro-alpine belt has very little vegetation and what there is, is short and ground-hugging. This has been likened to a high-altitude desert; precipitation falls primarily in the form of snow on and near the peaks, and any form of animal life is scarce, in sharp contrast to the situation at lower levels.

Fauna

Elephant and buffalo not infrequently feed on the grasslands of the Afro-alpine zone, and black-fronted duikers are present on the moorlands. Occasional high-altitude visitors on Kilimanjaro have included a leopard that was frozen in one of the glaciers. These big cats frequent the moorland and their tracks are on occasion seen in the snow. There have been sightings of a wild dog pack on the snowy peaks and lions sometimes hunt on the Shira Plateau. The forests of Mount Kenya are probably the last stronghold in East Africa of that boldly striped chestnut antelope, the bongo. Previously considered to be common in the Aberdares to the west, the bongo has been greatly reduced in numbers there as a result of predation by lions that come mainly from an ill-advised restocking programme.

Mount Kenya has the greatest diversity of large game species but even here signs of their passing are more frequently seen than the ani-

Below: Giant lobelias (Lobelia spp.) are a prominent feature on the moorland and Afro-alpine, with particular abundance of these and giant senecios on the Ruwenzori range.
Bottom: Buffalo (Syncerus caffer) grazing in a forest clearing on the northern slope of Mount Kenya.

Above: Protea kilimandscharica, *unlike many of its southern protea relatives, does not have particularly showy blossoms. They grow in the altitudinal belt between 2 700 m and 3 400 m above sea-level.*

Middle: *The distribution of Verreaux's, or black, eagle is largely dictated by where its principal prey, the hyrax, occurs. As these mammals occur commonly on the snowpeaks, the eagles are also in residence.*

PHOTO: JOHN CARLYON

Right: *As one ascends above the giant heath* (Erica arborea) *zone, you enter the moorland, or Afro-alpine, which consists mainly of tussock grassland and as pictured here numerous large-leaved giant senecios* (Senecio *and* Dendro-senecio *species*).

mals themselves. Eland move across the heath and moorlands, with bushbuck common in the forested and bamboo areas and waterbuck at the lower levels. In forest clearings, along tracks and on the heathlands there are numerous piles of loose earth – these are the creations of one of the most abundant snow mountain mammals, the root rat. Living a largely fossorial existence like moles, root rats create extensive networks of tunnels as they move to the best root "pastures". In one such clearing on the Naro Moru trail we were sitting photographing a troop of Sykes's monkeys when clumps of grass close to us started shaking. When we listened carefully we could hear the sound of teeth grinding soil. This was followed by a waving of the grass clump and then it disappeared underground, the roots to be enjoyed as an underground feast.

A mammal that has been able to adapt to near desert environments as well as the freezing alpine heights is that primitive ungulate, the hyrax. In these equatorial snow mountains at higher altitudes hyraxes grow long, shaggy coats. Tree hyraxes in the Ruwenzoris have expanded their range well into the treeless Afro-alpine zone, joining their cousins as rock-dwellers. One of our most exciting experiences on the East African snow mountains was at our camp at the lower edge of the montane forest on Mount Kenya. As the sun disappeared below the horizon and the darkness settled quickly, as it does close to the equator, the spine-chilling African equivalent of the Hounds of the Baskervilles let loose with a chorus of ratchet-rattle croaks. The tree hyraxes, on their traditional perches, were announcing their intention to begin the night's feeding session – the uninitiated could be for-

given for thinking that an army of trolls were hell-bent on an orgy of horrific enormity!

Like the mammals, birds are most abundant in the forest belt, which is not always the easiest of habitats to observe the beasties creating that cacophony in the canopy and the undergrowth. Families that are well represented in these high-altitude forests include hornbills, fruit-eating turacos, parrots, doves, pigeons and sunbirds. We have found that the only way to really observe forest birds is to find a clearing or glade, a pool with low scrub around it, or a wild fig or other fruiting tree with an abundance of ripe fruits, and then wait for the action. A source of frustration are those small birds that forage in mixed feeding parties, flitting through the undergrowth and high in the canopies. A larger bird that frequents the open glades and streamside clearings, the green ibis, has continued to frustrate us by giving vent to its somewhat goose-like honkings, sometimes within a few metres, or so it seems in the forest, and yet remain elusive.

The bamboo zone is fairly uniform in structure and the bird life is poor in diversity. As one moves higher up the mountain conditions become harsher and bird numbers and diversity decrease. In the Afro-alpine and heath belts the scarlet-tufted malachite sunbird feeds from the flowers of the protea bushes and giant lobelias. During the breeding season the male has an elaborate courtship display, flashing his red shoulder patches and spreading his wings. It is an impressive and shimmering performance as he runs and shakes his way up and down a long lobelia flower head. It is also in these higher altitudes that the mighty Verreaux's eagle hunts the hyraxes that make up more than 90% of its diet.

MOUNT KENYA NATIONAL PARK AND FOREST RESERVE

Travel and access: The Mount Kenya ring road links the towns of Nyeri, Nanyuki, Meru and Embu. Access from Nairobi is via Thika; it is about 100 km on good tar to the southern sector of the ring road. There are three principal access routes (all are clearly signposted): Chogoria gate in the south-east lies 30 km from the village of the same name, with a further 10 km to the road-head; Naro Moru gate lies 18 km from Naro Moru village, with about another 8 km to the end of the road. The access point we prefer, Sirimon, enters from the north and the turnoff lies 16 km beyond Nanyuki. It is 29 km from the turnoff to the entrance gate, and one can drive a further 10 km to the moorland. This entrance is much less utilised than the other routes, hence its appeal. There are a number of minor access routes but if you intend tackling any of these you must first go to park HQ at the Naro Moru gate.

Mobility: Apart from the drivable tracks through the forest reserve and to the road-heads, it is all footwork. Walking is allowed, with a minimum of two people, but if you intend going to the peaks it is best to hire porters and a guide, or even wiser to book an organised hike with one of the specialist companies. During heavy rain it can become extremely slippery.

Accommodation: Within the national park there are campsites at each of the three gates and you can camp at the road-heads (pit toilets, water at some). At the Met Station (road-head Naro Moru) there are bandas (huts) and a campsite (book through Naro Moru River Lodge); Mackinder's Camp, 6 hours further, has a bunkhouse and several permanent tents. At Chogoria, near the gate, are the reasonably priced and nicely located Meru Mount Kenya Lodge (Let's Go Travel) bandas (huts). On this route lies Minto's hut, which has seen better days; it takes about 6 hours to reach from the road-head. There are a number of other huts (about 12 plus suitable caves) in the surrounding area, usually used by hotels and lodges, so it is advisable to check with them. Outside the park there are different accommodation options, at several of which climbs, porters and guides can be arranged (for your own safety only use those registered with Kenya Wildlife Service or KWS). The very upmarket Mount Kenya Safari Club (Lonrho Hotels, P.O. Box 58581, Nairobi; tel. 02-216940; fax 02-216796), located 10 km out of Nanyuki, has many accommodation options, the usual hotel facilities, good views of Mount Kenya and a waterhole with a viewing platform that offers the best chance of seeing bongo in Kenya. The Naro Moru River Lodge (P.O. Box 18, Naro Moru; tel. 0176-62023/62201; fax 0176-62211; an Alliance Hotel) offers different accommodation options (including camping) and is one of the most experienced at organising mountain climbs and short trips in the area; trout-fishing. Mountain Rock Hotel (P.O. Box 333, Nanyuki; tel. 0176-62625) is similar to Naro Moru and lies on the Naro Moru-Nanyuki road; it also organises mountain climbs on the Sirimon route. Chogoria Transit Inn (P.O. Box 114, Chogoria; tel. 0161-22096) is said to be reliable in organising climbs.

Other facilities: There is a mountain rescue facility operated by KWS; guides and porters can be hired but we suggest you do this through one of the hotels mentioned, or one of the reputable tour operators.

Climate: Two rain peaks: late October to end-December; mid-March to mid-June. Drier months (note we don't say dry) usually January to mid-March and July to mid-October. Rainfall per annum ranges from about 1 000 mm to 2 500 mm, with the northern slopes being the driest. Temperatures decrease with rising altitude and you can expect nights to be cold to bitterly cold. Strong winds blow, particularly in the early morning and late afternoon.

Best times to visit: Open throughout the year, although after heavy rain access roads can provide difficult going. If you intend going for the peaks it is best to stick to the driest months.

Main attractions: Scenic beauty; great diversity of animal and plant species.

Hazards: Potentially dangerous animals, such as elephant and buffalo; be alert for mountain sickness, hypothermia; don't take foolish risks as this mountain has killed many people; if you are in dense cloud or mist do not move around, wait till it lifts or clears.

For further information: Kenya Wildlife Service HQ in Nairobi, or the park HQ at Naro Moru gate. *The Walker's Guide and Map to Mount Kenya* is available in Nairobi, otherwise try Savage Wilderness Safaris (P.O. Box 44827, Nairobi; tel. and fax 02-521590).

Below: Mount Kilimanjaro, Africa's highest mountain, rising above the plains of the Nyiri Desert of southern Kenya.

KILIMANJARO NATIONAL PARK

Travel and access: The main town in the area, Moshi, lies on the road linking Arusha with Dar es Salaam (at the time of writing this road was in pretty bad shape and most shuttle-bus services running between Nairobi and Arusha no longer make the run to Moshi, but link-ups can be made by local taxi). At the village of Himo (26 km from Moshi in the direction of Dar) turn onto the tarred road to Marangu; it is a steady 11 km climb from the turn-off and a further 7 km to the park entrance. Even if you intend ascending by any of the other routes you must first go to this park gate to purchase your permit and hire guides and porters. Although some prospective climbers arrange their own climb at the gate, most people use the services of local companies, notably the Marangu and Kibo hotels. Other routes start from the villages of Mweka, Umbwe and Machame; the only drivable road (4x4 only) turns off from the Moshi-Arusha road at Boma la Ng'ombe (Hai), with 23 km of tar followed by 20 km of murram or dirt (no go during the rains). Where the track forks go right for 13 km to the Londorossi Glades gate. The drivable track continues for a further 25 km. Because of the rapid ascent, you are strongly advised to spend at least two days acclimatising should you plan to go further on foot. Remember that you must first obtain your permits at Marangu. There is plenty of cheap public transport that goes to Moshi and Marangu if you do not have your own vehicle or are independent of a safari company. Apart from the two hotels listed under Accommodation, many safari outfits offer organised Kilimanjaro climbs. We suggest that you ask around as several offer low rates, but you will probably also get a lower level of service.

Mobility: Apart from the motorable track to Londorossi gate in the west, all access to the park is on foot. Marangu route is by far the most popular and the one most heavily used by hikers, the round trip taking five to six days. In all cases the relatively slow ascents on all routes are to allow for acclimatising and obviating serious occurrences of altitude sickness. The Mweka route leaves from Mweka, the location of the College of Wildlife Management. The Umbwe route is very steep and most authorities suggest this as a descent only, after ascending the Mweke or Machame routes. Machame route is considered by some to be the nicest ascent and descent. In general you should get good route advice before an ascent and ensure that you are properly equipped and fit. An excellent Tanzania National Parks booklet is available with route details. Some track sections are muddy and slippery, particularly after rain.

Accommodation: There are two hotel options in Marangu. The Marangu Hotel (P.O. Box 40, Moshi; tel. and fax 055-50369; tel. local exchange Marangu 11) has reasonable rates and a campsite (very cheap); campers may use all the hotel's facilities. The hotel staff also

arrange climbs of Kilimanjaro; there are "fully equipped" and the "hard way" options: the former means that all you have to do is pay and walk! The 5-day Marangu route costs approximately US $530 per person at the time of writing; the Machame route US $800 per person if three or more. These rates include all park fees, which consume a fair percentage of the total. Although we have not personally used these services we have had very good feedback from people who have.

The Kibo Hotel (P.O. Box 102, Marangu; tel. local exchange Marangu 4; fax 055-52687) also has reasonable rates (also camping) and organises climbs on the Marangu and Machame routes, at similar rates. We have also heard positive reports about this establishment so we suggest you enquire from both. The two hotels also offer safari packages to other areas of Tanzania. Keys Hotel (also takes campers) in Moshi is also highly rated for organising climbs.

There are two basic hostels close to the park gate and bookings should be made with the Warden (Kilimanjaro National Park, P.O. Box 96, Marangu; tel. Marangu 50). In the park itself, along the climbing routes, there are 11 mountain huts of different standards. If you are on an organised climb they will be booked for you, but if you are climbing independently you should book in advance through the warden's office. Some huts have pit toilets, others do not; water is collected from streams at varying distances from the huts. Alternatively, you can camp near the huts but you must obtain permission and you pay the same fee.

Other facilities: Apart from the trails and huts, climbers must be accompanied by registered guides and porters who can be hired; a rescue service is on call in emergencies (you will pay for it); packages offered by Marangu and Kibo Hotels, as well as other operators, for climbs – this is by far the best option; fuel and supplies in Moshi; although it is possible to rent equipment it is best to bring your own basic gear.

Climate: Expect equatorial to polar conditions; generally the higher you are the colder it will be. Although rain falls during every month of the year, the highest rainfall period is March to June, and cloud cover is fairly constant. Late June to July is fairly dry; nights are usually cold but the advantage is that this period is usually fairly cloud free. August and September are also cool months but cloud cover at forest level is common, with October to December having thunderstorms, but nights and mornings are often clear. January and February are also generally favourable for climbing.

Best times to visit: January, February and September are considered to be the best climbing months, with July-August and November-December close runners-up. However, always remember that weather conditions are notoriously unpredictable.

Main attractions: Africa's highest mountain.

Hazards: Altitude sickness; hypothermia; accidents – see introductory chapter. Potentially dangerous animals, such as buffalo. Many potential problems are obviated by ensuring that your trip is organised by a competent operator.

For further information: Tanzania National Parks HQ in Arusha; The Warden, Kilimanjaro National Park, P.O. Box 96, Marangu; tel. Marangu 50 (it's easier to work through Arusha). See the accommodation accounts and Useful addresses at the back of this book.

RUWENZORI MOUNTAINS NATIONAL PARK

Travel and access: The road from Kampala via Mbarara to Kasese (433 km) is good quality tar, as is the following 10 km in the direction of Fort Portal, where you turn off to park HQ at Nyakalengija. If you come from Fort Portal in the north the turn-off to the park is after 54 km. The 15 km stretch to HQ is in fairly poor shape and although it can be negotiated by ordinary vehicles when dry, we suggest a 4x4. For hikers, small pick-up truck taxis operate from Kasese to Ibanda, which is 3 km from HQ. Within the park all movement is on foot, with the most popular hike taking 6-7 days. Longer is required for peak climbing. Park fees are payable at Nyakalengija and no visitor may venture into the mountains without a guide hired from Rwenzori Mountain Services (US $250 to $350 per person for 7-9 day hike; this also includes porters). If you intend to hike the main circuit it is essential to book in advance with RMS, and it is advisable to do so for all hikes to avoid being disappointed. We suggest that you make enquiries about possibilities with one of the tour operators listed under Useful addresses. Although the possibility exists of climbing the range from the Democratic Republic of Congo side, within Parc National des Virunga, this is infinitely more complicated. You will have to be prepared to put up with appalling access roads (if such they can be called), poorly trained guides and other difficulties…! During the Ugandan upheavals of the 1970s and 1980s the Virunga access was more frequently used. Park headquarters are located at Mutwanga.

Mobility: All internal movement is on hiking trails, the most popular being the main circuit, which takes 6-7 days; more time is required if you intend to tackle any of the peaks. The visitor should be aware that hiking in the Ruwenzoris is not for the faint-hearted or unfit. It is difficult and arduous, and no matter what precautions you take you will get wet and muddy.

There are a number of shorter routes and combinations, but none can be classified as strolling and none will take you to the highest reaches. RMS will design routes according to the visitor's interests, for example primates or vegetation. One of the best accounts of the different trails, including detailed directions, maps and descriptions of the hazards is the *Map and Guide to the Ruwenzori*. Mobility is severely restricted and movement can be decidedly unpleasant during the peak rain months.

Accommodation: There are a number of huts along the trails, each sleeping up to 15 people. However, during the drier months the main circuit trail, and consequently the huts, can be relatively crowded; there are places to pitch tents adjacent to the huts and we advise you to take a tent along. You can hire equipment through RMS or bring your own. In any case you have to bring your own basic utensils and food for the full length of your stay. The park authorities prefer that you bring your own stove. There is a basic hostel, run by RMS, at Nyakalengija. Kasese, where the office of RMS is located and where you need to make arrangements, has a number of accommodation options ranging from the upmarket Margherita Hotel, through the moderately priced and popular Saad Hotel, to numerous good budget options.

Other facilities: Apart from the trail network, huts (pit toilets and water), guides and porters, nothing in the park. At Nyakalengija simple meals and drinks are available at the Mubuku Valley Restaurant. All litter must be taken out of the park, no firewood may be collected and you must stay on the trails.

Above: Although species diversity is small, a number of plant species are unique to the equatorial snow peaks.
Far left: Because of the frequent rains and moisture-laden low clouds, moss "gardens" flourish on the slopes of the snow mountains.

Climate: In one word, wet! The driest months are July and August, and December to February, but even then rain falls copiously. During the months of heaviest rain trails may be impossible to negotiate. At higher altitudes it can be very cold and you will need to make adequate provision for this. Cloud cover and mist only rarely open up to allow views of the peaks and surrounding country.

Best times to visit: Although the park is open throughout the year, July-August and December-February have the least rainfall.

Main attractions: Climbing and hiking in Africa's highest, and probably wettest, mountain range; unusual vegetation, particularly in the Afro-alpine zone; primates. One really worthwhile detour, the Kilembe Copper Mine, to see the colony of thousands of tree-roosting fruit bats. Kilembe lies 11 km from Kasese; at the gate you will be charged a small fee. The colony lives in several large eucalyptus trees.

Hazards: The usual problems associated with high altitude and wet, cold conditions. You are unlikely to encounter potentially dangerous animals, but small numbers of elephant and buffalo are present. We only recommend a trip to Ruwenzori if you are fit and healthy! Always exercise caution, as a major accident can pose severe rescue problems, particularly should this happen on one of the high climbs.

For further information: Uganda National Parks HQ in Kampala; Warden-in-Charge, Ruwenzori Mountains National Park, P.O. Box 188, Kasese; Rwenzori Mountain Services, P.O. Box 33, Kasese: tel. 0493-4115; fax 0493-4410. Note that park HQ has radio contact only with Kampala.

①   *Lake Bogoria*
②   *Lake Nakuru*
③   *Lake Magadi*
④   *Lake Natron*

Chapter 11

THE SODA LAKES

THE PRIMORDIAL SOUP

Nor shall this peace sleep with her; but as when
The bird of wonder dies, the maiden phoenix,
Her ashes new-create another heir
As great in admiration as herself.

William Shakespeare, *Henry VIII*

As the sun's first rays fall on the leaden waters of Bogoria, the fish eagles ready themselves for the day's hunt. Sharp eyes are not watching for tell-tale ripples on the surface or movement below, they are focusing on more exotic, non-piscine prey. One bird launches itself from a small acacia tree, branches whipping as they are relieved of its weight, and flies strongly at some 30 m above the lake. The "Phoenix" birds begin to stir, an awkward run accelerating in alarm and then in sheer panic. Long legs flailing at the water surface, pink and white wings flashing, long necks stretched out – which one will provide the eagle with

its first meal of the day? The fish raptor that has turned to eating flamingos selects its victim ... a powerful stoop, a flurry of wings and this Phoenix is no more.

The ancient Egyptians revered the Nile River, the carrier of life-giving waters and silt, which permitted survival while surrounded by desert. Its bounty came from the Great Rift Valley and the ancients believed that the symbol of resurrection, Benu, the bird brought out of the ashes by the god Osiris, had its origin here. Benu was the Phoenix! But was the flamingo the mythical Phoenix, as some believe, or was it something we do not know?

Along a stretch of the eastern arm of the Great Rift Valley, and sandwiched between its walls, lies a necklace of small to medium-sized lakes. A few of the beads in the necklace, such as Baringo and Naivasha, are filled with sweet waters, but the majority are fed by volcanic springs. It is those lakes, filled with their caustic brew, that concern us here: from the north Bogoria, Nakuru, Elementeita, Magadi and the largest of all, Natron. Why, you may ask, do we include these lakes in this book? There are several reasons: these soda lakes are true wildernesses, their waters totally hostile to humans; they are home to the world's greatest

Above: Lake Nakuru from Baboon Cliffs with its pink fringing of flamingos, is one of the world's greatest wildlife sights.

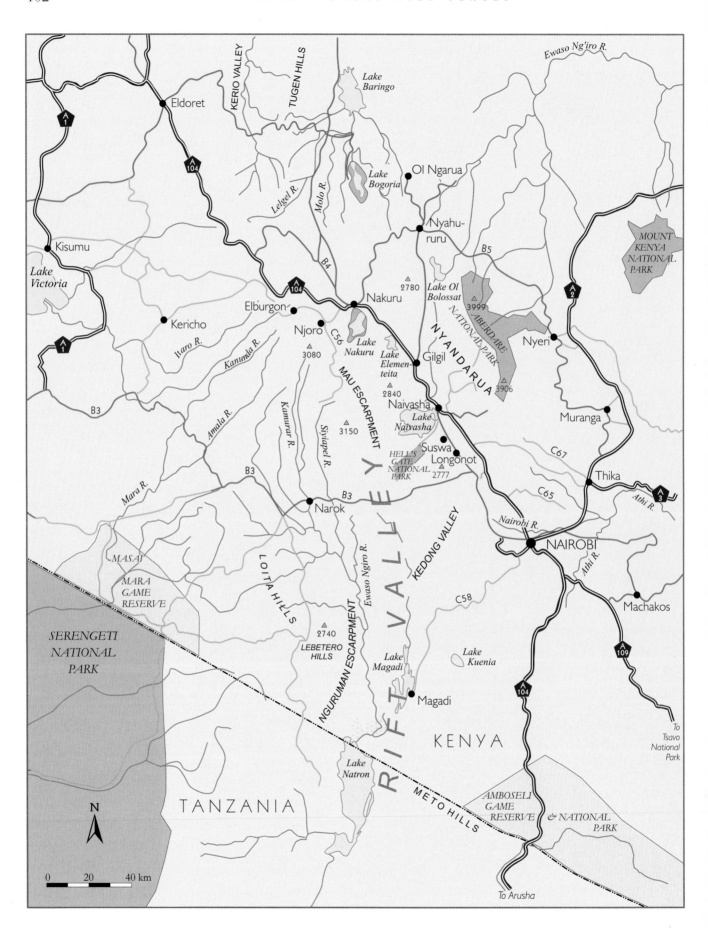

gatherings of flamingos, and are among our favourite African destinations.

Geography

The lakes were formed as the layers below the earth's crust moved, causing the surface to crack and the two plateaux to move slowly but steadily apart. Along the eastern arm of the rift are, besides the alkaline lakes, Africa's two highest mountains, the volcanoes of Kilimanjaro and Kenya. Some life remains deep in the belly of Mount Kilimanjaro but Mount Kenya is dead. There are other volcanoes, some that still steam and rumble with the threat of eruption, interspersed between the beads in the necklace. Menengai keeps watch over Lake Nakuru; the great volcanic cone of Longonot stands guard over the fresh waters of Naivasha, with Suswa just to the south. The most active is Ol Donyo Lengai (Mountain of God), which feeds its heated, soda-saturated waters into Lake Natron. Was this the home of the fabled Phoenix?

The flamingos

These waters, with their toxic brew, can scald and sear the flesh on the feet and legs of all species but the greater flamingo *Phoenicopterus ruber* and lesser flamingo *Phoeniconaias minor*.

These strange, long-legged and long-necked birds, feeding with head upside down and frequently congregating in feeding and breeding flocks that may number in the millions, find their principal strongholds in the beads of the necklace. One of the greatest natural wonders on earth, and certainly the most glorious of avian phenomena, has to be these massed flocks of white-and-pink-plumaged birds.

The most accessible of the flamingo lakes is Nakuru, and for this reason it is on the tourist route, but even this could not prevent our visiting the area more than once. As one enters the park one has no sight of the flamingos and only brief glimpses of the lake itself, but as one drives through the fever tree woodland and emerges on the shore ... the entire rim of the shallow lake is tinged with pink, too distant at first to distinguish individual birds, but on closer approach the ribbon of colour takes on life. At times well over a million flamingos may be feeding on the rich primordial soup. From the road to the top of Baboon Cliff one has the entire lake in sight, and what a sight it is!

Africa is the stronghold of the lesser flamingo, with the vast majority – probably three million but possibly as many as five million – feeding and breeding on the alkaline lakes that form the beads of the rift necklace. An estimated three million lesser flamingos at a time have been seen on Lake Magadi, two million

Below left: The yellow-barked acacia, or fever tree (Acacia xanthophloea), is a common feature around the fringes of both soda and sweet-water lakes.
Below right: An amazing feature of these hot, toxic water geysers is the thick crust of algae that grows in this seemingly inhospitable medium.

on Lake Bogoria and more than a million on Nakuru, Naivasha and others. The numbers of flamingos on the lakes fluctuate and the mobility of the birds makes accurate counting extremely difficult.

In contrast, the numbers of greater flamingo on the soda lakes are not so significant. Probably only about 7% of the Old World population is present here; the majority of the estimated 800 000 live in the Indian Rann of Kutch. In East Africa the only regular breeding sites of the greater flamingo are at lakes Natron and Elementeita.

The necks and legs of flamingos are longer in proportion to their bodies than those of any other bird – can anyone remember the scene in *Alice in Wonderland* where the Queen of Hearts uses an upside-down flamingo as a successful substitute for a croquet mallet? Although there is some controversy as to their position in avian classification, it is known that their origins are ancient and can be traced back to before the dawn of the Tertiary Era. The fossil *Scaniornis* from Swedish deposits is a primitive flamingo that dates from the Upper Cretaceous period. Adult birds, in particular lesser flamingos, have a considerable area of the plumage, principally on the wings, pinky-red in colour. This coloration comes from the carotenoid pigments that are abundant in their food. The carotenoids are converted into absorbable pigments through the action of enzymes produced in the bird's liver. This

Above: *Grey-headed gulls can be seen at most of the soda lakes.*
Right: *Lake Magadi in Kenya, a millpond from hell!*

SPECIES TO WATCH FOR

MAMMALS

(NOTE: The following mammals are only easily seen at Nakuru.)

Rothschild's giraffe	*Giraffa camelopardalis rothschildi*	Bohor reedbuck	*Redunca redunca*
Defassa waterbuck	*Kobus ellipsiprymnus defassa*	Warthog	*Phacochoerus africanus*
Chanler's mountain reedbuck	*Redunca fulvorufula*	Guereza	*Colobus guereza*

BIRDS

Great white pelican	*Pelecanus onocrotalus*	African marsh-harrier	*Circus ranivorus*
Pink-backed pelican	*Pelecanus rufescens*	Augur buzzard	*Buteo rufofuscus*
Marabou	*Leptoptilos crumeniferus*	Water thicknee	*Burhinus vermiculatus*
Yellow-billed stork	*Mycteria ibis*	Grey-headed gull	*Larus cirrocephalus*
Lesser flamingo	*Phoeniconaias minor*	White-winged black tern	*Chlidonias leucopterus*
Greater flamingo	*Phoenicopterus ruber*	Tropical boubou	*Laniarius ferrugineus*
Egyptian goose	*Alopochen aegyptiacus*	Bristle-crowned starling	*Onychognathus salvadorii*
Cape teal	*Anas capensis*	Vitelline masked weaver	*Ploceus velatus*
Black kite	*Milvus migrans*	Baglafecht weaver	*Ploceus baglafecht*
African fish eagle	*Haliaeetus vocifer*		

bright coloration is essential to stimulate breeding, and the elaborate wing flashing of thousands of flamingos has to be one of nature's greatest cabaret shows.

Lake Natron is the only location in the world where large numbers of lesser flamingos regularly breed with considerable success. They establish their colonies and build their nests in what is hardly water but rather a slushy mixture of soda. From the air it has the appearance of shattered glass. The location of the principal breeding site of these flamingos remained a mystery until one of the greatest ornithologists to tread African soil, Leslie Brown, discovered their mass breeding by flying in a light aircraft over Natron in the early 1950s. He located nesting mounds and "herds" of grey youngsters. In a subsequent attempt to reach the colonies he nearly died. Some of the difficulties of his lonely journey can be gauged from his own words:

On the far side of the water the soda was not flat and hard as it was near the Gelai shore, but had formed polygonal plates with raised edges rather like giant waterlily leaves… The mud beneath the crust, partially dry as it was but yet gelatinous in texture and extremely sticky, gripped my feet in their protective boots with a tenacity I had never before encountered… The frightful passage I had just completed was barely two hundred yards across and it had cost me the uttermost effort I could produce.

He spent many weeks in hospital recovering from severely burnt feet. Yet here the flamingos breed, feed and obviously thrive. The only predators that dare to venture here are the occasional Egyptian vulture and marabou stork.

The flamingos usually breed in large colonies, with pairs mating for life. They construct raised mounds of mud and soda sludge so that the eggs and newly hatched chicks are out of reach of the occasional flash flood. The

Above: Lesser flamingos greatly outnumber their larger cousins, the greater flamingo, on the soda lakes of the Great Rift Valley.

extra height of the mound also ensures a slightly lower ambient temperature for the vulnerable chicks. The chicks leave the nest mound on about the third day after hatching and gather in highly mobile herds. They are fed by the parents with crop milk, a product of their own food that has been desalted. As the chicks get older they are moved about by the adults in great ash-coloured creches, which pose a hazard to eggs and very young chicks still on the nest mounds. Any chick younger than three days knocked off the nest mound can die within minutes from heat exhaustion.

Although it would seem unlikely that any aquatic organisms could survive in the alkaline lakes of the Great Rift Valley, they do and in unbelievable numbers. The feeding behaviour and diet of the two species of flamingo occurring in Africa differ considerably. Lesser flamingos feed mainly on or close to the sur-

face, and frequently swim in deeper water. On one visit to Lake Naivasha, in the early, clear post-dawn light we were treated to the sight of more than a million lesser flamingos swimming over the millpond-like surface, filtering blue-green algae *Spirulina platensis* and diatoms through the special structures in their beaks.

Both flamingos feed with their heads hanging upside down, looking backwards between their legs. The two halves of the beak are held together, the lower mandible fitting neatly into the upper, then the head is swung from side to side in the water. At the same time the tongue is moved back and forth, pumping water and silt in and out of the beak. In this way food organisms are caught in platelet-like filters that lie inside the beak. They are then swallowed.

Greater flamingos feed mainly on larger organisms, such as small molluscs and crustaceans, but also on blue-green algae and diatoms, more frequently feeding with head immersed than lesser flamingos. The nature of the greater flamingo's principal foods means that it also does much bottom-feeding.

Despite the minute size of much of the food that they eat, the sheer numbers of flamingos at the main feeding lakes ensures that vast, almost unbelievable, quantities of aquatic organisms are ingested. It has been estimated that in just one day, a million lesser flamingos consume about 180 tons of blue-green algae. If one extrapolates that over a year's feeding we have 65 000 tons of blue-green algae being

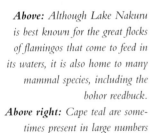

Above: Although Lake Nakuru is best known for the great flocks of flamingos that come to feed in its waters, it is also home to many mammal species, including the bohor reedbuck.
Above right: Cape teal are sometimes present in large numbers on Lake Bogoria.
Right: Reliant on fish, the white pelican frequently breeds on islands in the soda lakes, but they have to fly to fresh waters to feed.

converted into flamingo-survival fodder. An estimated 5-8 tons of blue-green algae per acre of soda lake are cropped annually, and this does not make a dent in the population. It is astounding that these foul-smelling and hostile waters house some of the most productive "pastures" on earth. The nutrition must be good as flamingos not infrequently reach the ripe old age of 50 years!

Bogoria, previously known as Hannington, is a long and narrow soda lake dominated on its eastern shore by the Ngendalel Escarpment, a steep section of the rift valley that rises some 600 m. The green water of the lake has an oily consistency and when the mud is disturbed it gives off a distinctly unpleasant smell. All around the edge of the lake hot steam and water escape from fissures and vents, giving one the eerie feeling that this could be a foretaste of hell! As with all the soda lakes, vast numbers of flamingos are not always present but we have been lucky, with these pink and white birds dominating the shoreline on our visits.

Although the flamingos feed in these lakes, they have to find fresh water elsewhere. The numerous hot springs that release their waters at the edge of Lake Bogoria are therefore frequented by dense clusters of flamingos bathing and drinking, even though the water may be as hot as 50 °C. To sit in the reeds just 10 m away from several thousand flamingos beautifying themselves and slaking their thirst is not only awe-inspiring but also deafening. The backdrop of steam rising from vents beyond the flamingos creates the impression that they are walking on air.

Other fauna

Where cooler fresh water is available greater kudu, crowned cranes and countless doves mingle with the flamingos.

At Lake Bogoria several pairs of fish eagle breed and feed. Nothing unusual in that, you say, but there is: there are no fish in this lake! Here the eagles hunt and eat flamingos. To the north of Bogoria is the fresh-water lake of Baringo. It is well populated with fish and fish eagles, and presumably there are no vacant territories, so young birds dispersing in search of their own territories may have settled on the lake without fish. Although fish eagles will on occasion include birds in their diet, this is not the norm, but if you are hungry a snack of

flamingo flesh would probably not go amiss. It is probably in this way that the "flamingo eagles" of Bogoria came to be. Motto: If your normally preferred food is not available then you adapt your menu accordingly.

It is not only blue-green algae and flamingos that thrive in the primordial soup. In Lake Magadi a small cichlid *Oreochromis alcalicus* has evolved to survive in a very narrow range between the boiling hot water emerging from springs and the caustic waters that would eat its flesh. These tiny fish dash into the hot waters to snatch mouthfuls of the algae that thrive there and return rapidly to the safe haven of the cooler waters. Too long a delay and they perish! As the saying goes, where there is something to eat there will always be something to eat it.

There are no crocodiles to fear, although swimming in the soda lakes is definitely not a very attractive prospect.

Marabou storks have been increasing in number, partly as a result of greater availability of food from rubbish dumps, abattoirs and fish factories. This resulted in great mortality and nest abandonment by the greater flamingos at Lake Elementeita in the 1970s. Apart from eating eggs and chicks, the marabous' mere presence in large numbers serves to intimidate and drive the flamingos away. An increase in the number of white pelicans at breeding locations is also known to result in flamingos abandoning traditional nesting sites. Natural mass die-

Top: The flamingo-speckled waters of Lake Nakuru are viewed to best advantage from the Baboon Cliffs. At times more than one million flamingos gather here to feed but most of these long-legged birds travel to Natron in the south to breed.

Above left: *One of the sources of Lake Bogoria's primordial soup, continuously pushing super-heated water from the fractured and volatile crust.*

Above right: *Water rising from hot springs flows into Lake Bogoria; no fish survive in these waters but vast quantities of blue-green algae flourish, attracting hundreds of thousands of flamingos to these floating pastures.*

offs of flamingos are occasionally recorded, such as when an estimated 25 000 lesser flamingos perished at Lake Bogoria in 1993. In this particular case they died of septicaemia induced by bacterial infections.

The future

One would think that humans pose little threat to the soda lakes, but they do. Some of these threats are of a direct nature and others are indirect. Lake Nakuru, protected as a national park, is threatened by pollution from the rapidly growing town of Nakuru, and although efforts have been made to reduce effluent flowing into the lake, general disturbance is sure to escalate. Another problem faced by the soda lakes is the commercial extraction of such products as hydrous sodium carbonate, in particular from Magadi in Kenya and Natron in Tanzania. The Kenyan government is investigating the feasibility of developing a hydroelectric power scheme on the Ewaso Ngiro River, the main feeder of water into Lake Natron. This could change the entire hydrological regime, which could threaten the world's largest and most secure breeding site of the lesser flamingo.

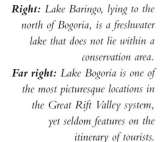

Right: *Lake Baringo, lying to the north of Bogoria, is a freshwater lake that does not lie within a conservation area.*
Far right: *Lake Bogoria is one of the most picturesque locations in the Great Rift Valley system, yet seldom features on the itinerary of tourists.*

LAKE NATRON GAME CONTROLLED AREA

Hunting companies operate in the area but there is nothing to stop the adventurous from exploring.

There are three access possibilities but all are rough going. We suggest that at least two vehicles together should attempt such a venture, fully equipped with water, fuel and food, as nothing is available in the area. From Mto Wa Mbu, head due north at the foot of the rift escarpment in the direction of Sonjo to the west of the lake.

Alternatively head north past the Gol Mountains in the Ngorongoro Conservation Area (first secure permission to do so). The third and best option is to follow the eastern arm to Malambo and Sonjo. We emphasise again that these tracks are in poor condition, so travel with caution. Some stretches can be confusing so carry a compass or GPS. The advantage of such an area is that no entrance or overnighting fees are payable but of course there are no facilities whatsoever. There are safari outfits operating in this area; enquire from your travel agent.

LAKE MAGADI

Lake Magadi receives no formal protection and a commercial soda extraction company operates here, yet it is one of Kenya's best birding locations. It is about 100 km from central Nairobi to Magadi settlement and soda works, on a good tarred road. If you have a 4x4 vehicle it is well worth while driving westwards to the Nguruman game post (about 30 km) which lies on the forest-lined Ewaso Ng'iro River. There are several other jeep tracks in the area but most cannot be traversed after heavy rain. If you intend exploring the area, particularly in the vicinity of the soda works, it is probably good policy to introduce yourself; in any case the locals can give you some tips on good destinations. However, remember it is a private enterprise and not an information centre! The diversity of habitats in the area, including the harsh soda and mud flats, open grassland, thickets and riparian forest, ensures good bird-watching. This is also good game country, with a wide spectrum of antelope species, as well as lion. Should you go strolling around (as it is not a formally conserved area there are no restrictions) be aware of the presence of potentially dangerous species. Large numbers of flamingo, mainly lesser, usually gather in the south of the lake. There is no accommodation and no facilities for tourists, so go fully equipped for camping if you intend overnighting.

LAKE BOGORIA NATIONAL RESERVE

Travel and access: The quickest route is to take the tarred road from Nakuru (B4) in the direction of Lake Baringo. Nakuru to the Loboi gate is just over 100 km. About 5 km south of the village of Marigat turn right (signposted); it is a further 20 km to Loboi. The road is tarred to the gate, as well as a further 11 km to the main hot spring and geyser. An alternative signposted route, rough and only suitable for a 4x4, turns right from the village of Mogotio (38 km from Nakuru). It is well worth the effort for the scenery (43 km from turn-off to Emsos gate). Be alert for the signpost at the point where the track forks – take the one marked Bogoria/Maji ya Moto. Unlike at most other park and reserve entrances, payment may only be made in Kenyan shillings.

Mobility: The road is tarred between Loboi and Maji ya Moto but the continuation is fairly rough, with loose stones, and areas towards Fig Tree Camp could be difficult after rain. There is only a single road down the western and southern edge of the lake. Loboi to Emsos gate is 26 km; we would suggest a 4x4 vehicle or one with high clearance. One is free to walk anywhere in the park.

Accommodation: Near the Loboi gate lies Lake Bogoria Hotel (P.O. Box 208, Menegai West; tel. 037-42696; fax 037-40896; or through African Tours and Hotels bookings in Nairobi). Full board rates are reasonable; usual hotel facilities including conference room and swimming pool; staff can arrange tours of reserve. The garden is good for bird-watching. At Loboi gate, Papyrus Inn Hotel has a restaurant and bar but the accommodation, we think, would make

camping preferable. It is not likely that booking would be necessary. There are three public campsites, Acacia, Riverside and Fig Tree, all at the southern end of the lake. Acacia has pit toilets, is open to the lake shore and has some tree shade; Riverside has no toilet but good shade, and is away from the shore; Fig Tree has lots of good shade, disintegrating pit toilets and fresh water from a stream (boil or treat it). For us Acacia had the nicest atmosphere and view.

Other facilities: There is a picnic site at Maji ya Moto; no toilets. Nearest fuel Kabarnet and Lake Baringo.

Climate: Usual rain months for this region; generally semi-arid and it can get very hot – if you go walking carry adequate water.

Best times to visit: Open throughout the year; access to Fig Tree Camp could be difficult after rain.

Main attractions: Impressive scenery; large numbers of flamingos may be present; good for birds; hot water springs and geysers; one of best locations in Kenya to see greater kudu; ease of access.

Hazards: Watch for buffalo; at certain times mosquitoes are bad, particularly at Fig Tree Camp; tsetse flies present in parts; don't be tempted to swim.

For further information: Although Bogoria is not a national park, the best bet is probably Kenya Wildlife Service HQ in Nairobi.

LAKE NAKURU NATIONAL PARK

Travel and access: Nairobi to Nakuru town (156 km) is a good tarred road, although there are a few potholed sections. There are three access roads to the park, the main gate lies 4 km south of the town and is signposted; as you enter town turn into Moi Road, which runs into Flamingo Road to park HQ. The Lanet gate turn-off lies on the Nairobi side of Nakuru, close to the Stem Hotel, and about 1 km from the main road. Nderit gate turn-off: take same road as for Lanet gate but continue for 11 km in the direction of Elementeita. All gates are signposted.

Mobility: Internal roads are generally good and most vehicles should experience few problems. However, after rain some of the side tracks can become slippery.

Accommodation: Two upmarket lodges are located in the park, both pleasant but the older Lake Nakuru Lodge has more character. Lake Nakuru Lodge (P.O. Box 70559, Nairobi; tel. 02-226778; fax 02-230962; or Nakuru 037-85446) has 120 beds in family rooms and cottages, and full hotel facilities. Sarova Lion Hill Lodge (P.O. Box 30680, Nairobi; tel. 02-333248; fax 02-211472) has 132 beds and full hotel facilities. Most lodges offer lower out-of-season rates, so this is worth checking. There is a camp at the main gate set in yellow-bark acacia woodland, with water, showers and toilets, but whenever we have been there facilities were overworked. The baboon troop that associates with the camp is very pushy, as are the vervet monkeys, so leave no food for them to grab. The only other public campsite is at the southern tip of the park; it is much quieter than the main gate

camp and has water and pit toilets. There are several special camp-sites, which for a higher fee you can have to yourself. At the main gate you can enquire about the dormitory beds and bandas (huts) belonging to the Wildlife Club of Kenya but they are not too special. There are a number of different options in Nakuru town.

Other facilities: There are several picnic sites; the one on Baboon Cliff offers good views over the park; all have pit toilets but no water. Although there are two education centres in the park, there is little information available to the general visitor. Fuel and supermarkets in Nakuru town, nothing in the park.

Climate: The usual rainfall pattern, with "short" and "long" rains; it can get hot during the day but evenings can be cool.

Best times to visit: Open throughout the year; mobility may be restricted after heavy rain, particularly on tracks.

Main attractions: Easy access; 1,5 to 2 million flamingos; great bird and mammal diversity; one of Kenya's black rhino populations (although not easily seen).

Hazards: Camps and picnic sites are not fenced so you need to be aware of the presence of potentially dangerous animals, such as buffaloes and rhinos.

For further information: Kenya Wildlife Service HQ in Nairobi.

① Masai Mara National Reserve
② Serengeti National Park
③ Ngorongoro Conservation Area
④ Lake Manyara National Park
⚫ Approximate extent of Serengeti ecosystem

Chapter 12

THE SERENGETI ECOSYSTEM

GRASSLAND SPLENDOUR

And how the silence surged softly backward,
When the plunging hoofs were gone.

Walter de la Mare, *The Listeners*

Bewilderment! Serengeti is a place of such plenty that it seems almost impossible to comprehend all that one sees. It is an ecosystem that one can only begin to appreciate if one has the time to observe, and not just to look but actually to see. Just sit and gaze out over the vast grass plain and think about the millions of mammals these grasslands sustain. In the foreground are the diminutive Thomson's gazelles, short tails constantly flicking, and just off to the right the much larger, long-horned Grant's gazelles. In characteristic pose, standing atop that large termite mound, is a topi ram; certainly the elevation improves his visual cover-

age but does it also enhance his status? The main wildebeest migration has already moved beyond this point but a few stragglers are still feeding in the company of some plains zebra just behind where we are seated. And there is a lone giraffe bull striding across the open grassy plain, travelling between *Acacia* thickets in the Olduvai Gorge and the eastern craters of Ngorongoro. But here at our feet, cutting and gathering pieces of grass stalks and blades, are the most prolific of all the Serengeti herbivores: termites numbering in their billions. Each termite colony, and there are millions here, is a miniature Serengeti in its own right.

Serengeti, Ngorongoro and Masai Mara are without doubt three of Africa's best-known conservation areas, and home to the continent's greatest herds of hoofed game animals. This vast ecosystem is largely defined by the migration route of the white-bearded wildebeest, which sweeps over an area of more than 25 000 km² in an annual cycle, leading the animals to new grazing grounds and drinking water.

The question we always ask ourselves after visiting a new location: Would we want to come again? Despite their rich diversity and interest to us as naturalists, the Masai Mara and the Ngorongoro Crater would probably not

Above: *The steep sides of the Ngorongoro Crater are no hindrance to the movement of game animals but the year-round abundance of food and water obviates the need to migrate.*

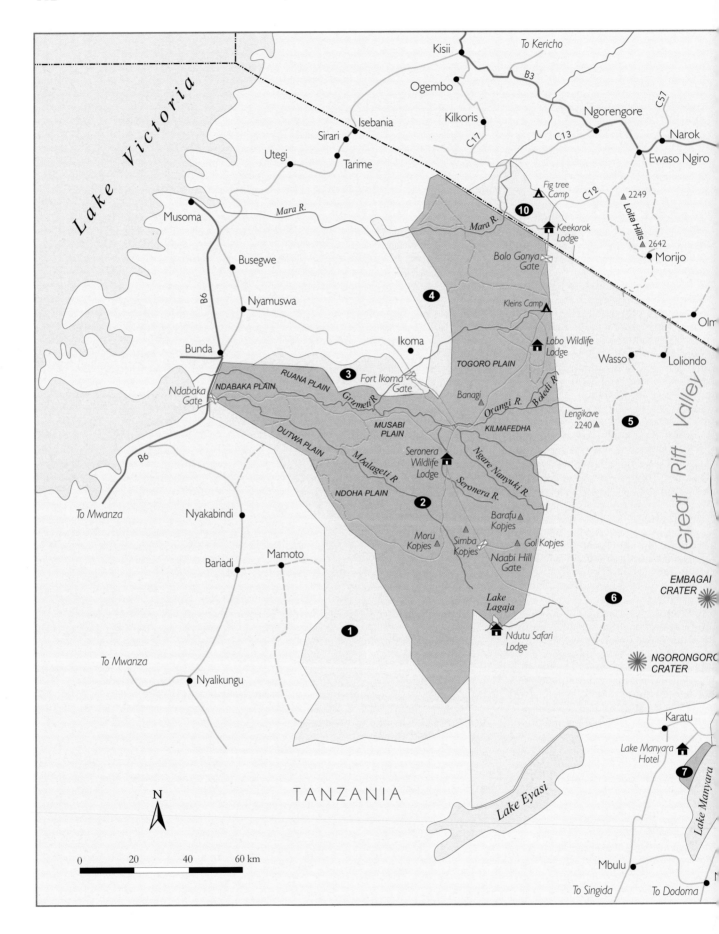

N

0　　　20　　　40　　　60 km

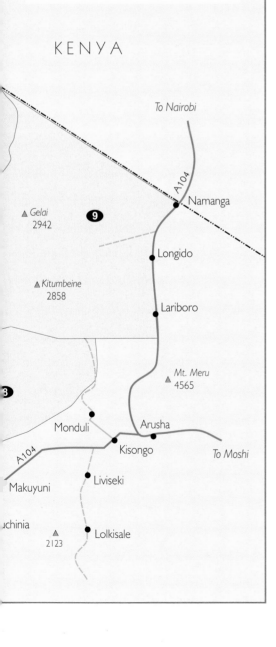

appear high on our list of priorities. Part of our problem is that we have seen many great parks and wild places that have been spoilt by ecotourism spinning out of control.

In the Masai Mara we were left cold by tourist vehicles jockeying for prime positions at the wildebeest river-crossing sites, with little feeling for the animals they came to see, and the harassing of predators, in particular the cheetah, for a better view. Another negative factor is the proliferation of tourist lodges and camps, with in some cases little thought given to aesthetics and blending the artificial structures into the environment. But we did enjoy the matriarchal elephant herd that entered our camp at night, gently feeling our tent with their sensitive trunk tips. And despite the tourist hordes, we will never forget the noise and dust of the river crossing by the wildebeest.

The vast expanses of the Serengeti will definitely see us again. It is truly one of Africa's great unspoilt game parks. Likewise the Ngorongoro Conservation Area, but we probably will not descend to the crater floor, with its cobweb of vehicle tracks and disregard for the rights of the wildlife. The rest of Ngorongoro is really true wilderness and a place to spend time; shall we ever forget the sight of a lioness in hot pursuit of a young giraffe in the arid western hills – and not having to share the moment with 30 or more other vehicles.

Geography

We have chosen not to separate the Serengeti, Ngorongoro and Masai Mara but to treat the three parks as the ecological unit that they are; after all it is humans who created the artificial boundaries.

This ecosystem qualifies as both Africa's greatest game area and one of its finest wild lands. Of course certain areas attract the tourist masses and the safari vehicle brigade but vast tracts of this landscape see few visitors, the exceptions being the Masai Mara and the Ngorongoro Crater. If we begin our journey in the Ngorongoro Conservation Area in the south-east, first climbing the western wall of the Great Rift Valley, we find ourselves in the heart of the Tanzanian crater highlands.

The landscapes of Ngorongoro, in geological terms, are of both ancient and modern origins, with the western Gol Mountains and

Above: White-bearded wildebeest in the crater do not participate in the great migration that takes place to the west, as there is sufficient grass and water to sustain them throughout the year.
Below: The double-banded courser (Rhinoptilus africanus) is one of four courser species that live within Serengeti.

granitic outcroppings on the Serengeti Plains originating several hundred million years before present. But it is the volcanic features dominating the east that are the first to attract the visitor's attention. About 20 million years ago the eastern side of the African land mass started a powerful process of cracking and faulting, causing the land in the principal rifts to subside. With the weakening and thinning of the earth's crust on the floor of the rift, vast quantities of molten materials thrust to the surface to form lava beds and volcanoes. The oldest volcanoes formed along the Eyasi Rift and bear the names Sadiman, Lemagrut, Oldeani, Olmoti, Sirua, Ngorongoro, Lolmalasin and Empakaai. The largest of these was Ngorongoro and it is believed to have once rivalled Mount Kilimanjaro, Africa's highest mountain, in height. The lava that once filled this massive volcano was capped with a solid lid, which subsequently collapsed as the molten rock subsided and left in its place one of the largest and best-known calderas on earth. Two volcanoes of more recent origin were formed to the south of Lake Natron, along the Gregory Rift. They are Kerimasi and Ol Doinyo Lengai, which last erupted in 1983. Ol Doinyo Lengai is of great religious significance to the local Maasai pastoralists; its name means *Mountain of God*.

The combination of fertile volcanic soil and the moisture-laden winds that sweep in from the distant Indian Ocean makes this one of the most productive regions, in terms of biomass, in Africa. However, although this mix sustains lush forest in the eastern highlands, the western plains fall directly within the rain shadow and during the dry season the shrubs and grasses turn brown and become brittle, most of the surface water dries up and the great herds are forced to resume their never-ending migration. Above all else volcanic ash plus water equals grass, and grass means life for the multitude of herbivores, and food for the predators who feed on them. The German explorer, hunter and naturalist Jaeger summed it all up: "And all this a sea of grass, grass, grass, grass and sky."

Prehistory

It is the products of these volcanoes in the crater highlands, those great billowing clouds of fertile ash and dust that settled over thousands of square kilometres, that today maintain the rich savanna grasslands which in their turn support the vast ungulate herds. This thick ash deposit has also contributed to the preservation of the signs of the passing of some of our earliest ancestors. It was here that the large and heavily built *Australopithecus robustus* entered the human fossil record about 1,2 million years before present. The smaller but larger-brained *Homo habilis*, or "handy man", is believed to have evolved into the more advanced "upright man" *Homo erectus*; the remains of both these ancestors of ours were found in the strata of Olduvai. (We prefer the spelling Oldupai. Oldupai is the Maasai name for the wild sisal plant *Sansevieria ehrenbergiana*, which grows in abundance in the region, and Olduvai is merely a corruption of the word. We have however retained Olduvai because it is still the generally accepted name at present.) It was only in the uppermost deposit, dated at some 17 000 years before present, that "modern man" *Homo sapiens,* our good (sometimes not so good!) selves, was discovered. Some 3,5 million years ago a small group of our ancient human ancestors walked across the rain-dampened volcanic ash blanketing the Laetoli Plain. Alongside their tracks were those of guineafowl, giraffe and the three-toed

Top: *The savanna (olive race) baboon (Papio cynocephalus) occurs widely in the Serengeti ecosystem but it avoids the treeless grass expanses.*
Above: *Topi live in small herds but larger numbers may mix with other antelope and zebra on favoured feeding grounds.*
Right: *The kongoni, or Coke's hartebeest, occurs widely throughout Serengeti but in fairly low numbers. This race of the hartebeest has the bulk of its population living within the ecosystem.*

Hipparion, an extinct species of horse. Shortly after these tracks were imprinted, fresh deposits of ash drifted over the plains from the deep bellies of the volcanoes, covering and preserving them until their discovery in 1978, when erosion exposed them for the first time.

Local place names

One aspect that is of great interest to us is the origins of the local African names given to reserves and landscape features, some of which are simple and straightforward whereas others require much more investigation. The Il-Masai (also spelled Maasai) clans have a common language, namely Maa. *Mara* means spotted, and in the name Masai (Maasai) Mara this is a reference to the isolated bush and tree clumps that are scattered over the grassland plains. Several decades ago, however, this

landscape was very different to what we see today. There were more extensive woodlands, referred to by the Maasai as *Osere*, meaning thick bush. A combination of fires and increased numbers of elephant has greatly expanded the areas of grassland, to the benefit of the grazers but to the detriment of such browsers and mixed feeders as black rhino, impala and Kirk's dik-dik.

The origin of *Ngorongoro* is a little more difficult to explain. The most romantic etymology is that it was the name of a very brave unit of Datoga warriors who showed great valour in a battle lost to the Maasai some 150 years ago. Less romantic versions are that it was the name of a Maasai bell maker who lived on the crater floor, or the name for a grain grinding stone, which the caldera resembles. It is one of those mysteries for which we are never likely to find a solution.

Serengeti is a Maasai word that means "endless plains", a very apt name indeed.

The migration

The grasslands, supporting as they do an enormous biomass and diversity of herbivores, have evolved over many thousands of years to cope with grazing and fires. What is particularly amazing is that so many different species are able to feed on the grasslands, co-existing on what is seemingly a homogenous plant community. They are able to avoid excessive competition because each species has evolved a unique feeding strategy. The plains zebras, with their ability to digest coarse, relatively unpalatable grass stems, are often the first grazers to enter long grass areas. With the long grass stems removed the protein-rich grass blades are exposed and eaten by the broad-mouthed wildebeest, in this way exposing the new-growth grass shoots and small herbaceous plants favoured by the Thomson's gazelles. The less numerous topi and kongoni, with their long muzzles and

Above: The great wildebeest migration that takes place each year within the Serengeti ecosystem presents its most dramatic face with the crossing of the muddy waters of the Mara River.
Left: The Serengeti ecosystem probably has Africa's largest lion population, even though possibly one third have died of disease in recent years.
Far left: During the course of the great wildebeest migration, hundreds of thousands of these antelope must cross the Mara River, within the Masai Mara National Reserve. Substantial numbers of wildebeest drown during the crossing and their bodies provide a feast for vultures and marabou storks (Leptoptilos crumeniferus).

SPECIES TO WATCH FOR

MAMMALS

Giraffe	*Giraffa camelopardalis tippelskirchi*	Serval	*Felis serval*
Plains zebra	*Equus burchellii*	Spotted hyaena	*Crocuta crocuta*
Blue wildebeest (white-bearded)	*Connochaetes taurinus*	Dwarf mongoose	*Helogale parvula*
Coke's hartebeest (kongoni)	*Alcelaphus buselaphus cokei*	Banded mongoose	*Mungos mungo*
Topi	*Damaliscus lunatus jimela*	Golden (common) jackal	*Canis aureus*
Grant's gazelle	*Gazella granti*	Bat-eared fox	*Otocyon megalotis*
Thomson's gazelle	*Gazella thomsoni*	Honey badger	*Mellivora capensis*
Kirk's dik-dik	*Madoqua kirki*	Patas monkey	*Erythrocebus patas*
Lion	*Panthera leo*	Blue monkey	*Cercopithecus mitis*
Leopard	*Panthera pardus*	Yellow-spot hyrax	*Heterohyrax brucei*
Cheetah	*Acinonyx jubatus*		

BIRDS

Ostrich	*Struthio camelus*	Rufous-crowned roller	*Coracias naevia*
Palmnut vulture	*Gypohierax angolensis*	Yellow-billed barbet	*Trachyphonus purpuratus*
Egyptian vulture	*Neophron percnopterus*	D'Arnaud's barbet	*Trachyphonus darnaudii*
Bateleur	*Terathopius ecaudatus*	Nubian woodpecker	*Campethera nubica*
Rüppell's griffon	*Gyps rueppellii*	Fawn-coloured lark	*Mirafra africanoides*
White-headed vulture	*Aegypius occipitalis*	Pied wheatear	*Oenanthe pleschanka*
Augur buzzard	*Buteo rufofuscus*	Red-faced cisticola	*Cisticola erythrops*
Grey kestrel	*Falco ardosiaceus*	Northern black flycatcher	*Melaeornis edolioides*
Scaly francolin	*Francolinus squamatus*	Silverbird	*Bradornis semipartitus*
Coqui francolin	*Francolinus coqui*	Red-throated tit	*Parus fringillinus*
Temminck's courser	*Cursorius temminckii*	Scarlet-chested sunbird	*Nectarinia senegalensis*
Long-toed lapwing	*Vanellus crassirostris*	Magpie shrike	*Corvinella melanoleuca*
Dusky turtle-dove	*Streptopelia lugens*	Hildebrandt's starling	*Spreo hildebrandti*
Fischer's lovebird	*Agopornis fischeri*	Superb starling	*Spreo superbus*
Ross's turaco	*Musophaga rossae*	Grey-headed social weaver	*Pseudonigrita arnaudi*
Pearl-spotted owlet	*Glaucidium perlatum*	Brimstone serin	*Serinus sulphuratus*

Above: *The grass owl (Tyto capensis) is resident only in the northern part of the Serengeti ecosystem; it only occurs at low densities throughout its range.*

small mouths, are highly selective feeders and pick out only the most nutritious grasses. Of course the large mammalian plant-eaters have to share this grassland bounty with the much more numerous smaller creatures: the uncountable numbers of rodents, the densely populated harvester termite communities and the great swarms of grasshoppers and locusts.

This bounty is, however, transient, and areas that can play host to the great hordes of grazers at one time of the year can only carry comparatively few at other times. We shall follow the wildebeest, plains zebra, Thomson's gazelles and others on one of the world's greatest natural wonders, their migration for survival. The biomass, or number of animals, is truly astonishing, with some 1,5 million wildebeest, more than 250 000 plains zebra and 500 000 "Tommies". More than three million ungulates – 12 million hoofs – trample this piece of Africa's landscape!

During the rainy season, between November and April, the great herds gather on the short-grass plains that straddle the invisible boundary between the Serengeti National Park and the Ngorongoro Conservation Area. It is during this time of plenty that the wildebeest cows and females of other species give birth. But at the onset of the dry season most of the grass is gone and the rain-filled depressions are dry, forcing millions of hoofs to churn the powdery soils as they move to the north-west, mainly to what is known as the Western Corridor, remaining there for only a short period during May and June. Then they swing further westwards and northwards into the northern Serengeti woodlands and to the end of their journey in the Masai Mara. Although the Tommies also follow the annual migration they always stay on the open grasslands, avoiding the woodlands.

None of the migrants follow exactly the same route, or timing, each year, but the general pattern stays the same. Once the herds have entered the woodlands they tend to disperse, but they continue to move in response to rainfall and the availability of grass, with large numbers reaching the Masai Mara by

June and July, and remaining there until late October or early November.

In the Masai Mara rain falls throughout the year, although the highest falls are usually in December-January and April, with up to 1 200 mm sustaining the grass that ensures the survival of the grazers and the predators that feed on them. When the rains start falling again on the short-grass plains to the south the migrants move to close the circle, leaving the Masai Mara and north-western Serengeti in a steady stream.

Other than in most antelope species, the wildebeest mating season, or rut, takes place during the migration. The bulls hold small mobile territories, at densities of as much as 280 per square kilometre, in which they try to retain cows for as long as it takes to mate with them, at the same time driving off bachelor bulls and keeping neighbouring bulls holding territory at a respectable distance. All of this activity takes place in a space of but three weeks. After a gestation period of about 250 days the calves are dropped on the southern short-grass plains and within a few minutes of birth they can stand and suckle for the first time. They can soon run with the mother, but nevertheless large numbers are killed by predators, particularly in the first week of life.

Few people are aware that the "Mara leg" of the migration, which brings Serengeti wildebeest into the Masai Mara, is a fairly recent phenomenon and followed a massive increase in wildebeest numbers in the 1960s and 1970s. Up to this time outbreaks of rinderpest and other influences held population growth back, but vaccination of cattle greatly reduced the risk of mass die-offs of wildebeest and other species. Prior to this some 100 000 wildebeest spent the dry season

in the Masai Mara but these came from a population that spent the rainy season on the Loita Plains to the north-east, with only a few animals crossing from Serengeti. This wildebeest population explosion benefited, among others, the Thomson's gazelles. These small gazelles feed on short, close-cropped grass, now present in great abundance courtesy of the wildebeest. This enabled the gazelles to more than double their previous numbers.

In order to reach the Masai Mara vast numbers of wildebeest make the hazardous crossing of the Mara River. When the river is in flood many animals drown and others fall victim to crocodiles·waiting at the few suitable crossing places. The land-based predators, such as lion and wild dog, are also out in force, making the most of what has sometimes been referred to as a mobile feast. Seemingly as if building up communal courage, the wildebeest gather in vast, bawling, dust-enshrouded herds on the river bank, waiting for "someone" to literally take the plunge. At some crossing points they have to jump from the steep bank into the water and then scrabble and slide up the opposite bank along gouged troughs that have been carved by the hoofs of generations of wildebeest. Some groups land where the bank is too steep to climb out and are forced to swim further to try again. Young animals that crossed before their mothers stand in tight groups calling for their dams and, becoming impatient, leap back into the river. Many, young and old, drown.

When the river is low, those unfortunates that drowned from exhaustion or trampling float downstream for a few kilometres to a rapid where the carcasses get caught up among the boulders. Here the feathered undertakers, white-backed vultures, Rüppell's

Above: The Masai race of the giraffe has a wide range in Kenya and Tanzania, and it is common in the Serengeti.
Below: Although no longer allowed to graze their cattle in the Serengeti National Park, the Maasai people do live in the Ngorongoro Conservation Area. It is not uncommon to see cattle, wildebeest and plains zebra sharing the same natural pastures.

Above: *There are estimated to be more than 500 000 Thomson's gazelles within Serengeti, but the larger Grant's gazelle, here a ewe, occurs in smaller numbers.*

griffons and marabou storks, gather to feast. The scavengers stand drowsing, with bloated crops and an air of satisfaction, on the banks and rocks.

Ngorongoro Crater

Within this vast ecosystem there is one area of but 264 km², the Ngorongoro Crater, that is a microcosm of Africa. Here the normally migratory wildebeest, plains zebras and Tommies remain throughout the year, food and water being present in abundance. Elsewhere in the ecosystem migration is essential to survival, but on the crater floor the abundance of long and short grasslands, forests, wetlands and wooded slopes obviate the tiresome need to move.

This giant caldera has a diameter of about 14,5 km and ranges in depth from floor to rim

from 610 m to 760 m. Although the caldera walls are not particularly steep and present no real barrier to the animals living there, the abundance of food and water throughout the year gives them little cause to leave. There are some grazers and browsers that occur widely within the ecosystem but do not live on the caldera floor, including giraffe, topi and impala. Why these species should be absent is not known, nor is it clear why it is usually only bull elephants that enter the caldera, with matriarchal herds remaining on the forested rim.

In this reserve within a reserve, predators benefit from having a resident source of prey, and Ngorongoro Crater can lay claim to having the densest lion population anywhere, with numbers fluctuating between 80 and 100 individuals. However, for this easy life the lions have had to pay a price. Very few lions enter the crater from the outside and those already

Conservation issues

The vast Serengeti ecosystem may hold as many as 3 000 lions, one of Africa's greatest concentrations, but in recent months this population has been particularly hard hit by disease. One estimate puts the mortality as high as 1 000 individuals, a third of the presumed population. Many have died from distemper transmitted by the ever-growing population of domestic and feral dogs which roam the outer limits of the ecosystem.

Another predator that has undergone near catastrophic declines here is the wild dog. Throughout much of its former range it was heavily persecuted by humans; it has been extirpated in many regions and brought to the brink of extinction in others. Apart from direct persecution these dogs seem to be increasingly falling victim to a number of different diseases, and as with the lions, contact with domestic dogs could well be exacerbating the problem. Twenty members of a pack of 22 wild dogs died of rabies in the Masai Mara in 1989, and others have died from canine distemper and anthrax.

The wildebeest and other herding species are also being affected by the activities of humans, including agricultural developments, particularly in the north, and poaching by Wakamba tribesmen in the area surrounding the Western Corridor. Even here in one of Africa's largest conservation areas not all is secure.

Humans are an integral part of this ecosystem and cannot be disregarded. Within the 8 280 km² of the Ngorongoro Conservation Area the authorities are attempting a delicate experiment in balancing the needs of wildlife, Maasai pastoralists and tourism. The elements that allow the great game herds to survive here – fertile but shallow soils and abundant seasonal grass – are also an attraction to nomadic tribes with their herds of cattle and flocks of goats and sheep. It is believed that the first pastoralists entered this area about 10 000 years ago. The last people to lay claim to the vast tracts of grazing were the Maasai, a proud Nilo-Hamitic tribe.

In Ngorongoro the Maasai continue to graze their herds and flocks among the wild game and water them at the same springs and seeps, but this relationship is gradually losing its harmony. The Maasai and their livestock are becoming more numerous and increasingly they are settling to produce crops.

Left: Small numbers of hippopotamus (Hippopotamus amphibius) *live in the Gorigor and Mandusi swamps on the floor of the Ngorongoro Crater.*
Below: The whistling thorn (Acacia drepanolobium) *is a small tree, or shrub, common within the Serengeti ecosystem. It is easy to recognise by the round, black galls at the base of the larger thorns, which are hollow and inhabited by ants.*
Bottom: The sausage tree (Kigelia africana), *with its large showy flowers and distinctive grey, cylindrical fruits, occurs sparsely throughout the Serengeti ecosystem.*

there have little reason to leave. This causes a high level of inbreeding, which has resulted in an increased incidence of sperm abnormalities and the loss of about 10% of the genetic diversity of the population. In 1962 this lion population was reduced to just 10 animals by a particularly severe and prolonged outbreak of *Stomoxys calcitrons*, a small biting fly. This "fly explosion" was a result of an unusually long rainy season, which presented the flies with the opportunity to proliferate for six months. However, within 10 years the lion population reached its former numbers. Although lion numbers are now stable and cub mortality is not particularly high, there is still the danger that any epidemic could virtually wipe out these crater-dwelling cats. But it is almost certain that the ideal conditions in Ngorongoro would then cause lions to invade the region from the hills and plains to the west.

MASAI MARA NATIONAL RESERVE

Travel and access: Many tour companies operate between Masai Mara and Nairobi, and there are regular flights to several of the lodges, but if you are driving yourself be prepared for some rough roads (we suggest 4x4 even in the dry season, although ordinary vehicles such as minibuses regularly use the access and internal roads). The main access route is from the Nairobi-Nakuru road, via Naivasha, signposted to Narok. When we last travelled the stretch to Narok it was "tar" but in a terrible state, with some stretches having more potholes than tar. There were some road works going on, so perhaps you might be pleasantly surprised, but don't count on it. The following 54 km are also on "tar", and the next stretch of gravel road is badly corrugated, with lots of loose rock and occasional washaways. From Narok there are four routes to different gates. Although there are a few signposts, many confusing jeep tracks crisscross the plains. If you choose to follow one of these routes check directions; a GPS and map would be useful. The only track coming in from the west, from Kisii and Migorii, was badly washed out, with some stretches boulder-strewn, when we were last there. The Sand River gate, on the border with Serengeti, is not in use at present. Apart from the main route to Sekenani gate, none of the other access routes should be tackled after heavy rain.

Mobility: Although for the main roads an ordinary high-clearance vehicle should be adequate, for full mobility you would be better off with a 4x4. During the rains many of the minor tracks are closed, and even some of the all-weather roads could be hard going. Some of the lodges outside the park offer walking options.

Accommodation: This is the most heavily "lodged and tented" reserve in Kenya, and virtually everything is in the upmarket bracket. Many cater for tour operators, package tour groups and private groups. Many do not take casual guests, so booking is advisable; as this is Kenya's busiest park, particularly during the migration months, it is in any case advisable to make bookings. You are not likely to get away with anything less than US $100 per person per day, and a number go much higher. Package tours are generally less expensive but you have little or no flexibility. Because of the great number of options we can do little more than give you the lodge and camp names and their contact details. Some we prefer to others, but this is a matter of personal choice and it would not be fair to the reader, nor the company, if we selected those we favour. In the areas beyond the boundaries of the reserve there are also several tented camps. In general, if you intend staying in a lodge or tented camp, make enquiries through a travel agent. Let's Go Travel in Nairobi is probably a good starting point.

KEEKOROK LODGE (Block Hotels)
OLKURRUK MARA LODGE (AT & H)
SIANI SPRINGS CAMP (Windsor Hotels)
KICHWA TEMBO CAMP (Windsor Hotels)
MARA INTREPID'S CAMP (Prestige Hotels)
MARA SAFARI CLUB (Lonrho Hotels Kenya)
MARA SERENA LODGE (Serena Hotels)
MARA SAROVA LODGE (Sarova Hotels)
GOVERNOR'S CAMP (P.O. Box 48217, Nairobi; tel. 02-331871; fax 02-726427). They also operate Governor's Paradise, Private and Little Governor's camps.
OUT OF AFRICA CAMP (P.O. Box 67449, Nairobi; tel. 02-212975; fax 02-218735)
MASAI MARA RIVER Camp (P.O. Box 48019, Nairobi; tel. 02-331191; fax 02-216528)

MARA SOPA LODGE (P.O. Box 72630, Nairobi; tel. 02-336088)
FIG TREE CAMP (P.O. Box 40683, Nairobi; tel. 02-220592)
MPATA SAFARI LODGE (P.O. Box 58992, Nairobi; tel. 02-217015)
TALEK RIVER CAMP (P.O. Box 74888, Nairobi; tel. 02-338084)

As we mentioned earlier, there are other operators in the area, so make enquiries and shop around for what best meets your needs. Standards are generally high because of the level of competition for a piece of the lucrative tourist cake.

Camping possibilities are rather limited (campers don't usually spend as much as lodge and tented-camp customers). Camping is permitted at the gates but you have to be totally self-sufficient as in most cases there are no facilities. Musiara gate camp in the north is our favourite, and an excellent location for watching elephant and lion which are usually very active there. There are community-run campsites near the Telek gate.

Other facilities: A number of the lodges and tented camps offer short (1–2 hour) hot-air balloon flights (expect to pay US $250-400 but check prices); these can be booked through the lodges and camps. Campers can have meals and drinks at some lodges but a number do not look kindly on casual visitors. If you are self-drive visitors it is possible to arrange a ranger-guide to accompany you but this is not compulsory.

Climate: Rain can fall during any month (annual average fall 1 200 mm) but the heaviest falls are usually in December-January and April. There is no great seasonal temperature fluctuation but the days can be very hot, with nights cooler and even cold on occasion.

Best times to visit: Open throughout the year; if you are most interested in seeing the migration the great herds are generally there from July to October, but to be safe plan for August to mid-October. Always remember that there is usually some variation. During the wettest periods mobility can be severely restricted.

Main attractions: The migration months; great diversity of species; open terrain ensures good sightings; diversity of accommodation.

Hazards: No lodge or campsite fenced so be aware of potentially dangerous animals: elephant and lion regularly enter. During and after rain stay off the black soil, the chances are very good that you will get stuck.

For further information: Kenya Wildlife Service HQ in Nairobi for general enquiries; for accommodation see individual addresses given above, or Useful addresses at the back of the book.

Above: The Ngorongoro Crater floor viewed from the road that ascends to its rim.

SERENGETI NATIONAL PARK

Travel and access: The vast majority of visitors travel from Arusha via Ngorongoro, entering Serengeti at the Naabi Hill gate. From Arusha take the good tarred road for 80 km in the direction of Tarangire National Park and Dodoma, then turn right at Makuyuni, onto a badly corrugated but "all-weather" gravel road, passing through the village of Mto Wa Mbu (petrol and diesel, basic supplies and over-priced curios), past Lake Manyara National Park and up the rift wall (watch for the interesting tree euphorbias). You then pass through densely populated farmland to the Lodware entrance gate of the Ngorongoro Conservation Area. When we travelled this road it was in a poor state of repair, and as far as we could ascertain it is rarely treat-ed to a grading. The total distance from Arusha to the Serengeti park HQ at Seronera is 325 km. Some stretches of road in Ngorongoro were badly corrugated but at the time of our last visit to Serengeti, the road from Naabi Hill gate to Seronera was in the process of being upgraded, and the road to Lobo Lodge was also reasonable.

Access from Masai Mara (Kenya) to Keekorok across the Sand River to Bologonja gate was closed when we were last there, so check current situation at the warden's office. Although we did not travel on it, we were told that the road linking Fort Ikoma gate with Nyamuswa near Lake Victoria was in very bad shape. The road to the gate at the end of the Western Corridor, Ndabaka, was in good con-dition (dry season) but being black-cotton soil becomes impossible to negotiate during the rains. Even light rain makes for heavy going. Although not essential on the stretches of all-weather road, we strongly recommend 4x4 vehicles. The Ndabaka gate opens on the Mwanza, Musoma, Kenya border road, the first stretch of which is tarred but then becomes all-weather gravel. This was rough but road construction was underway and we were told that it was to be resur-faced to the Kenyan border.

To pass through Ngorongoro Conservation Area one has to pay full entrance fees, and at the time of writing they were payable in US dollars. Permits to enter Serengeti are payable at any of the entrance gates. Remember, in all Tanzanian national parks you pay for each 24-hour period you are in the park! Distance from Ndabaka gate to Seronera is 145 km; Naabi Hill gate to Seronera 48 km and Ngorongoro HQ to Seronera 152 km. Some safari operators fly vis-itors in to Seronera and Lobo airstrips.

Mobility: During the dry season mobility within the park presents no problems but during the rains movement is greatly restricted. The black-cotton soils, notably in the Western corridor, turn into a glue-like substance when wet. If you intend visiting during the rainy peri-od stick to the all-weather roads and do not drive off the roads. Remember that rain may fall at other times of year, particularly close to Lake Victoria.

Accommodation: This ranges from formal lodge accommodation to tented camps and camping. Seronera Wildlife Lodge is located at the centre of the park, Lobo Lodge in the northern sector of the park. Both offer full board (we have had very mixed reports on the quality of the food), and each has 150 beds, each bedroom with own bathroom. Both lodges are owned and managed by Tanzania Hotels Investments, P.O. Box 877, Arusha; tel. 057-2711/12; fax 057-8221, but if you are an independent traveller, bookings are through Seronera Wildlife Lodge/Lobo Wildlife Lodge, P.O. Box 3100, Arusha; tel. 057-3842. These are modest establishments but clean and quite adequate when we visited them, and Lobo in particular is in a very impressive setting. The luxury Serengeti Sopa Lodge, located to the south-west of Seronera, is not a particularly attractive structure in our view, but it is generally highly rated by tour operators for service. Sopa Lodge, P.O. Box 1823, Arusha; tel. 057-6886.

Two tented camps are located just outside the park: Kijereshi near Ndabaka gate in the Western Corridor, and Ikoma Camp, just 1 km from Ikoma gate. Ikoma has nine safari tents, each with its own bucket shower, wash basin and chemical toilet. There is a communal dining area, with meals prepared by the staff. This camp is run by Sengo Safaris, P.O. Box 207, Arusha; tel. 057-8424 or 3935; fax 057-8272, in conjunction with the local community. The rates are very reasonable compared with the lodges. For the Kijireshi Camp contact P.O. Box 190, Mwanza; tel. 068-40139. For the budget traveller there are public campsites at Seronera and Lobo (we were told that public camps at Bologonja and Kirawira were not available). There are pit toilets at some sites but water was not available at any site. There are several special campsites that can be booked by one party (in most cases taken by safari companies) and cost double (US $40 per person per night) the public campsites. They have the advantage of complete privacy. Such camps are located at Lobo, Seronera, Naabi Hill, Lake Ndutu, Moru Kopjes and western Grumeti River. Special camps must be booked through the wardens; check at the gates, or Seronera. We were told that there are plans for additional lodges, tented camps and special campsites but could not establish specifics and suggest you enquire about new possibilities. A number of small operators offer low-key, exclusive and well-organised tented safaris (at a price).

Other facilities: Fairly extensive network of game-viewing roads but many become difficult during the rains, although access to Seronera and Lobo is on all-weather roads from the south. The lodges have restaurants and bars, and these may be used by campers as well as residents. Airstrips at Seronera and Lobo lodges. Serengeti Balloon Safaris operated two hot-air balloons from Seronera at the time of writing; this is the only such service operating in Tanzania. Petrol and diesel are available at Seronera (whether fuel is available at Lobo is a matter of luck), as well as limited garage facilities (punc-tures, etc). A new visitor information centre has been built (judging by the way the hyraxes and birds had left evidence of their presence it has been ready for some time!) but there are no displays or infor-mation. A small information centre is located at the Naabi gate. If you intend to drive to the Gol and Barafu Kopjes or the Moru Kopjes in the south, you must arrange to be accompanied by a park guide. Guides can also be hired for general game drives but this is not oblig-atory. You are allowed to get out of your vehicle but only in areas where you have clear vision. Be constantly alert and remain close together.

Climate: The main rains fall between November and May, with the driest months from June to October. Although temperatures are gen-erally mild, mid-year evenings can be cool.

Best times to visit: Much depends on what you want to see. The great herds gather on the short-grass plains from November/December to May and then trek westwards and northwards: around Lobo June, July and August are good; for Western Corridor June to October is best – note that during the rains this area is virtually impossible to access. Although the Seronera Valley is good through-out the year, the dry season of June to October is best for game-viewing. The park is open throughout the year but movement is lim-ited to the few all-weather roads during heavy rains and some areas remain waterlogged for long periods. It is during the rains that many species drop their young and large numbers of migrant birds arrive.

SERENGETI NATIONAL PARK CONTINUED

Main attractions: Relatively low tourism pressure compared with some of the Kenyan parks; the world's largest herds of game species; the spectacular migration; some of the best large carnivore viewing in East Africa; great diversity of bird species. Close proximity to several other wildlife destinations such as Ngorongoro, Lake Manyara, Natron, Tarangire and mounts Meru and Kilimanjaro. One of the true wonders of the world!

Hazards: As for all East Africa, malaria; be aware that the camps and lodges are not fenced and potentially dangerous animals may wander through from time to time. If you must leave your tent at night, first check the area with a torch and never wander far from your camp. Sleeping under the stars may be a romantic notion but where there is an abundance of lions, as in Serengeti, we don't recommend it! Wet black-cotton soil is among the worst substrates in which to get your vehicle stuck – do not be tempted to drive on it. Drink only bottled water, otherwise boil or treat water before drinking.

For further information: Tanzania National Parks, Tourism Office, P.O. Box 3134, Arusha. Also see under Accommodation above

Left: Serengeti is dominated by vast expanses of grassland and open woodland.

LAKE MANYARA NATIONAL PARK

Travel and access: As for the previous two parks; take the Arusha–Dodoma tarred road for about 80 km, turning off onto a corrugated all-weather gravel road at the village of Mukunyuni. After some 40 km you arrive at the village of Mto Wa Mbu, a short distance further and on your right are the park HQ and on the left the entrance to Manyara. Permits are obtained at the gate.

Mobility: The internal track network was in fair condition at our last visit but many tracks are closed, or difficult to negotiate, during the rains. The driest months are usually June-September and January-February. Guides are available at a small fee; this is particularly useful if you have limited time, as they know the best observation localities. No walking is permitted.

Accommodation: The upmarket Lake Manyara Hotel (see Ngorongoro above) is located on the edge of the rift wall, with excellent views over the area. Just inside the park are 10 bandas (huts), with a central kitchen and dining area; these are basic but clean and situated in the forest. Gas (when available) and firewood are provided, as is water (boil or treat it). Basic ablution facilities. Book through the head office in Arusha or through the park warden. There are two public campsites just inside the park, in the forest, with pit toilets and water. A special campsite, with no facilities, is located closer to the lake and must be booked through the warden (fees are higher than at the public campsites).

Hoopoe Safaris operate a basic tented camp, located on the top of the escarpment, at reasonable rates. There are possibilities in Mto Wa Mbu but it is a generally noisy and crowded settlement. A basic hostel to sleep 48 people, with toilet and kitchen facilities, is located at park HQ and can be booked for large groups. A private tented safari camp is located in the far south of the park, near Maji Moto, which is used by UTC, one of East Africa's largest safari companies.

Other facilities: The possibility of being accompanied by a guide in the park; basic supplies and fuel can be obtained in Mto Wa Mbu. Although first aid is offered at the hotel and at a clinic in the village, it is always a good idea to carry your own basic kit. There is a small museum and information centre at the park gate.

Climate: Distinct wet and dry seasons: rainy months mainly October-December and March-May. Temperatures are generally mild but be prepared for cool evenings, particularly in mid-year.

Best times to visit: Open throughout the year but mobility can be greatly reduced during the wet months.

Main attractions: Easy access; great diversity of habitats and species; spectacular backdrop of the rift wall; not heavily utilised by tourist traffic. Good overnight stop between Arusha and Serengeti.

Hazards: Camps not fenced and potentially dangerous animals present: hippo, elephant, buffalo and lion. Baboons and vervet monkeys can be a nuisance – do not feed them or leave edibles exposed or accessible to them; they may look cute but they can inflict extremely nasty bites.

For further information: Tanzania National Parks HQ, Arusha; Chief Park Warden, Lake Manyara National Park, P.O. Box 12, Mto Wa Mbu. Lake Manyara Hotel, P.O. Box 3100, Arusha; tel. Mto Wa Mbu 10 (or contact Tanzania Hotels Investment in Arusha); Kiriruma Tented Camp run by Hoopoe Safaris, P.O. Box 2047, Arusha; tel. 057-7011; fax 057-8226.

Travel and access: If you are coming from Arusha, the directions are the same as given for the Naabi Hill gate into Serengeti National Park; likewise if you are entering from the west and Seronera. Lodware gate in the south (from Arusha) and Naabi Hill gate (from Serengeti) are the only official entry and exit points. There are access roads in the vicinity of the Gol Mountains in the north but these are extremely rough and you will need special permission to use them. Although the main through road (Lodware to Seronera) is all-weather gravel, it is fairly heavily used and badly corrugated in parts. To descend into the crater or travel on side roads, you will need a 4x4. Distance from Arusha to Ngorongoro HQ is 175 km, of which the first 80 km is tarred. Permits must be obtained at Lodware or Naabi Hill, and a guide booked to descend into the crater.

Mobility: There is an all-weather gravel road from Lodware gate into Serengeti, but if you intend to descend into the crater (you are obliged to take a guide with you at a small fee), or explore other areas, you will need a 4x4 vehicle. Access to the lodges and public camp ground should present no problem. Roads are generally rough and corrugated (the short stretch of all-weather road to Olduvai information centre can be a real bone-shaker), and there are soft patches on side tracks. During the rains most tracks are difficult to impassable. Remember that even in the dry season the going can be very difficult on some tracks; we suggest that if you are unsure ask about hiring a guide to accompany you.

Accommodation: This is the most densely "lodged" conservation area in Tanzania, with four lodges around the crater rim (a fifth is planned) and one in the west against the invisible border with Serengeti. Ngorongoro Wildlife Lodge is owned by the Tanzanian government and has magnificent views of the crater floor; 150 beds with full board, restaurant and bar (campers may also use these facilities). Contact Tanzania Hotels Investment, P.O. Box 877, Arusha; tel. 057-2711/2; fax 057-8221.

Ngorongoro Crater Lodge has a capacity of 60 beds, located in separate wooden cabins and rooms, with a central dining and bar building (open also to campers). Although a relatively modest establishment this would be our first choice. Contact Windsor International Hotels, P.O. Box 751, Arusha; tel. 057-3530. Rhino Lodge is located in a beautiful patch of forest just off the main rim road and has 46 beds, communal lounge, dining area and bar. Reasonably priced and good for bird-watching. Contact Rhino Lodge, P.O. Box 792, Arusha.

Ngorongoro Sopa Lodge is located on the eastern rim of the caldera and has 96 beds, all rooms with en-suite facilities, dining room, lounge and bar. Contact Ngorongoro Sopa Lodge, P.O. Box 1823, Arusha; tel. 057-6896/6886; fax 057-8245. Ndutu Safari Lodge, situated on the lake of the same name, is an excellent destination during the wet season when the great herds are concentrated on the short-grass plains. It lies in *Acacia* woodland at the edge of the open grassland and offers 32 double rooms (separate cottages) and 6 double tents, each with its own shower and toilet. Contact Ndutu Safari Lodge, P.O. Box 6084, Arusha; tel. 057-6702/8930; fax 057-8310.

There is a public campsite, Simba, located on the crater rim close to headquarters; it has pit toilets, cold showers that are generally overworked and very little shade, and when overlander lorries are present it can be very noisy. From the campsite you are permitted to move after dark to eat and drink at the lodge bars and restaurants. No camping is permitted on the crater floor but camping is allowed at other locations within the conservation area, with permits available from HQ, but at a higher fee than that payable for the public camp-site; in addition you may be obliged to employ a guide. Several small, exclusive safari companies offer personalised camping trips in Ngorongoro Conservation Area and Serengeti National Park.

En route to Ngorongoro from Arusha there are several accommodation possibilities, including bandas (huts) at Lake Manyara National Park, at the foot of the rift wall (see below). Lake Manyara Hotel (Tanzania Hotels Investment, P.O. Box 877, Arusha; tel. 057-2711/2; fax 057-8221) is modern with excellent views over Lake Manyara and surrounds (full board about US $200 per person per day). Gibb's Farm (P.O. Box 6084, Arusha; tel. 057-6702; fax 057-8310), an upmarket and highly rated establishment, offers 30 beds with full board in pleasant surroundings, and is clearly signposted on your right coming from Arusha. It also offers several safari-camping options into Ngorongoro and Serengeti (as well as Lake Manyara and Ruaha in the south). Just outside the village of Karatu, the Safari Junction Campsite offers huts, tents and camping space at reasonable rates; there is a bar and restaurant.

Other facilities: There is a reasonable road network, although most are for dry-weather use. One is allowed to get out of one's vehicle (not in the crater except at designated toilet and picnic stops) but always be aware that potentially dangerous mammals occur, including lion, elephant and buffalo. *Never* wander far from your vehicle! At Olduvai information centre you can go on a guided walk to get a better feel of the area, and walk in the footsteps of your ancestors who strode these plains some 2,5 million years ago. Guides can (must!) be hired for more adventurous explorations. Should you intend to go further afield, ensure that you are well equipped and self-sufficient (this includes fuel, food and water). Fuel (diesel and petrol) is available at park HQ, Mto Wa Mbu (at the foot of the rift wall) and Seronera (Serengeti).

Climate: The area has distinct dry and wet seasons; the latter lasts from November to May but bear in mind that there is always some variation. Although temperatures are generally mild, dry season evenings can be cool.

Best times to visit: During the rainy season (November/December to May) the great migratory herds are concentrated on the Serengeti and Salei plains, but at this time your movement may be limited.

Main attractions: Vast herds of plains game during the rains; the biological wealth of the Ngorongoro Crater and relative ease of access. The Olduvai Gorge is an internationally important archaeological centre; guided tours of the area can be arranged. Very large cliff-breeding site of Rüppell's griffon in the Olkarien Gorge. Freedom to leave one's vehicle (except in the crater) but with caution and care! Presence of Maasai pastoralists appeals to some visitors – permission must be asked before you take photographs and you will be expected to pay.

Hazards: Camps and lodges are not fenced and potentially dangerous species such as buffalo, elephant and lion can be expected to wander through. Side tracks can be sandy.

For further information: Apart from the addresses given for the various accommodation options, see Useful addresses at the back of the book. The postal address (we never received any response) is Ngorongoro Conservation Area Authority, P.O. Box 1, Ngorongoro (or P.O. Box 776, Arusha).

Chapter 13

TSAVO

THE PLACE OF NDOVU

Here with a loaf of Bread beneath the Bough,
A flask of Wine, a Book of Verse – and Thou
Beside me singing in the Wilderness
And Wilderness is Paradise enow.

Edward Fitzgerald, *The Rubáiyát of Omar Khayyám*

Tsavo evokes images of large elephant herds, lions stalking their prey and a multitude of game animals, and indeed all those are there, but one incident that stands out in our minds involves none of these. Termite alates on their nuptial flight were emerging in their millions and the birds were moving in. The first to arrive were the fork-tailed drongos, abandoning their normal aerial hunting for more productive ground attacks; then a pair of Von der Decken's hornbills, he with red and white beak, she with black, hopped clumsily in pursuit of the slowly emerging insects. A white-browed coucal joined the fray, to be followed

by a more elegant act – a striped kingfisher selected its perch and proceeded to prepare for dinner. A splash of colour was then added by a flight of carmine bee-eaters, swirling and wheeling as they plucked the termites from the air. This was the avian version of a shark feeding frenzy…

Tsavo, place of *ndovu*, the elephant, is Kenya's Serengeti and Selous. With only a relatively small area feeling the impact of tourists, this is a true wilderness. A place where one can really follow the advice of Omar Khayyám, that is if you can afford the price of wine in Kenya!

We have visited Tsavo several times and it is the eastern sector that will continue to draw us back again and again – it is one of those great conservation areas that one never tires of. Tsavo has had its share of problems in recent decades: drought, poachers and great herds of cattle and flocks of sheep and goats that were pushed into the west-central sector of Tsavo West in the 1980s, resulting in serious overgrazing of several hundred square kilometres of natural pasturage. Fortunately the park is large enough and wild enough to tolerate these abuses in the short term. A great park indeed!

Above: *The Mzima Springs in Tsavo West, with their clear waters, allow one to view hippopotamuses* (Hippopotamus amphibius) *and crocodiles* (Crocodylus nilotica).

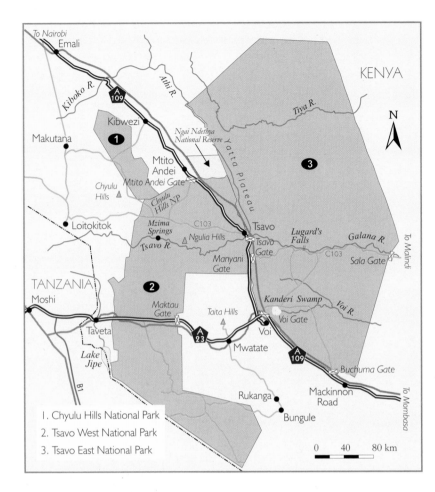

1. Chyulu Hills National Park
2. Tsavo West National Park
3. Tsavo East National Park

0   40   80 km

famed longbow-men who won the day for the English at such great battles as Agincourt and Crecy were amateurs by comparison. The Waata elephant bows had a draw-weight of up to 77 kg; no other bows are known to have equalled them. These supreme elephant hunters aimed their poisoned arrowheads at the lower abdomen of their quarry for rapid absorption. The target would crumple within minutes. Unlike the ivory poachers who had such an impact in the 1970s and 1980s, the Waata respected their elephant prey. It has been argued that the Waata contributed to the maintenance of the ecological balance by reducing pressure on the woodlands through the culling of several hundred elephants in any given year. The estimated elephant population was in the region of 12 000 to 15 000 animals and if the hunters were killing 600 to 750 individuals each year, the pachyderms would maintain their numbers at a level that did not destroy their habitat.

Geography

The Tsavo ecosystem extends over 43 280 km², with Tsavo East National Park covering 11 747 km² and Tsavo West some 9 065 km². Additional protected areas adjoining their boundaries are the Chyulu Hills National Park to the north-west, conserving 471 km², as well as two national reserves, South Kitui and Ngai Ndethya. The two Tsavo national parks, divided by the Mombasa-Nairobi road and railway, are managed as separate units and are very different in composition and character. Much of the east is flat country, with few major features other than the prominent flat-topped Yatta Plateau, with a few isolated hills in the north. The western park is relatively hilly with some impressive granitic ridges, a number of volcanic cinder-cones and evidence of numerous lava flows. Probably the most visited location in the park is the amazing Mzima Springs, whose abundant waters rise in the watershed of the Chyulu Hills, a relatively young range of volcanic origin. The high rainfall in the hills percolates through the porous volcanic rock and soil, forming underground streams where the water meets with the impervious bedrock. Many of these streams first bubble to the surface at Mzima

Above: *The prolific fruiting of the sycamore fig* (Ficus sycamorus) *attracts a host of fruit-eating birds and mammals, such as savanna baboons, vervet monkeys and elephants.*
Above right: *The green bush snake* (Philothamnus hoplogaster) *has a wide distribution and it is known to occur in Tsavo, being mainly found close to water.*

History

A number of tribes have occupied the Tsavo area and still live on its periphery: the Waata (Wata) sometimes referred to as the Waliangulu; the Taita which includes the Saghala, and the Kamba and Giriama. Although only limited archaeological investigation has been undertaken here, it is known they were preceded by inhabitants from the Stone Age and Iron Age. For thousands of years humans and elephants have shared the vast semi-arid plains of Tsavo and no tribal group has been more closely associated with the great pachyderms than the Waata. Up to the middle of the 20th century the vast tracts of bushland that now lie within Tsavo East National Park were the hunting and foraging grounds of these people.

The Waata are an Oromo-speaking group of hunters who ranged from southern Ethiopia to southern Kenya and were probably the greatest elephant hunters ever to evolve in Africa. Although the elephant was their principal prey, they also hunted black rhinos and buffaloes with the most powerful longbows ever produced by humans. Even the and these crystal-clear waters are so abundant that the coastal city of Mombasa draws much of its water needs from here.

Only two perennial rivers traverse the parks, the Tsavo and the Athi, but from their confluence the river is known as the Galana, sometimes called the Sabaki. The Tsavo rises in a series of springs on the north-eastern slopes of Mount Kilimanjaro in Tanzania, but collects much of its water from the Mzima Springs. The Athi rises in the highlands just to the south-west of Nairobi and in its southwards flow forms a natural boundary with the western boundary of Tsavo East. After the confluence of the Athi and Tsavo rivers the Galana flows due east, eventually reaching the Indian Ocean just north of Malindi.

Tsavo East receives a much lower rainfall than the west and this aridity is most pronounced to the north of the Galana River, where the vegetation is relatively sparse and dominated by low-growing, thorn-bedecked *Acacia* tree species. The vegetation that dominates the thickets, including numerous *Commiphora* species, is known locally as *nyika* and is found over much of eastern Kenya. Unlike other vegetation types, it is unsuitable for cattle grazing and cultivation. Much of the park consists of open grassland, low bush and scrub-scattered plains, with taller trees along the main watercourses, including great *Ficus* (fig) trees. Along the Galana River doum palms *Hyphaene compressa* are common.

With its higher precipitation Tsavo West is characterised by dense bush and thickets, particularly in the north, with more open grasslands in the south towards Lake Jipe on the Kenya-Tanzania border. There are extensive reedbeds at the lake and these are of considerable importance to the water-loving bird species that gather here. The grasslands in the south are called Serengeti Plains because of their similarity to that great Tanzanian national park, with its great game herds.

Elephant and rhino

Influenced by season and the abundance of food, elephant home ranges vary in size between the two Tsavos: in the drier east ranges as extensive as 3 120 km² have been recorded but in the better watered west ranges may be as small as 300 km². In general home ranges are at their smallest during the dry season because of the need to be close to water,

but in the wet season when water is more readily available the elephants can disperse to make use of greater areas.

In the not too distant past Tsavo was much more densely bush-covered than it is today and the change can be ascribed to the massive increase in elephant numbers that took place in the years leading up to the mid-1970s. By the early 1970s elephant numbers had soared to an unsustainable 36 000 animals. With their voracious eating habits they cleared vast tracts

Left: *The wood owl* (Strix woodfordii) *occurs in the more wooded areas and along the main river courses in the area of Tsavo.*
Below: *Tsavo in the 1960s and early 1970s had one of Africa's greatest concentrations of elephant but ivory poachers decimated their numbers. Gradually, however, numbers are starting to increase.*

Top: Superb starlings, found throughout Tsavo, with their multi-hued plumage certainly live up to their name.
Middle: *The secretive and seldom seen striped hyaena (Hyaena hyaena) is most at home in the drier eastern areas of Tsavo.*
Right: *The artificial waterhole on the plain below the Voi tourist lodge in Tsavo East attracts large numbers of buffalo and elephant.*

grazing and browsing areas were soon depleted. It is quite an eye-opener to realise that on average an elephant consumes 150 kg of plant food every day. At their peak of 36 000, these animals ate about 5 400 tons each day, which equalled almost two million tons of vegetation each year.

Droughts and elephant-induced vegetation changes had a catastrophic effect on what was one of Africa's greatest protected populations of black rhino. The number of rhinos occurring in Tsavo in the 1960s was believed to be at least 9 000; some estimates are double this figure! The 1961 drought resulted in high rhino mortality and as conditions worsened rhinos from a large catchment area concentrated around the few remaining water points. This resulted in disruption of the normal home-range networks and fighting, often severe, became frequent. A number of animals died as a result of their wounds. Large numbers of rhinos started to succumb to nutritional anaemia, disease and stress. The massive elephant concentrations along the rivers resulted in the destruction of the bush thickets on which the rhinos relied for food and cover.

It was during the drought of the early 1970s that poachers became active in the park, harvesting the ivory from elephants that died of starvation and stress. By the mid-1970s ivory and rhino horn prices were rising rapidly and active illegal hunting increased dramatically. In the space of just a few years the poachers, aided and abetted by corrupt politicians and officials, reduced the elephant population by more than 20 000 and killed an estimated 5 000 black rhinos – a loss from which the latter would not recover. With poaching spinning totally out of control, by 1973 it was estimated that 1 000 elephants were being killed each month in Kenya. Aerial surveys over the Tsavo parks revealed more dead than living elephants! By the time the "feast of the vultures" had passed and the poachers were crushed, Kenya's largest elephant herd had dwindled to an estimated 7 000, but this constituted probably more than 40% of the country's total population.

Although growth in elephant numbers after the slaughter was initially slow, the population has now stabilised. But the days of free-ranging black rhinos are gone and the survivors have been gathered in a special sanctuary in the Ngulia Hills in the north of Tsavo West where they live under intensive control.

of bushland. Grassland took its place. The situation was aggravated by elephants entering from areas surrounding the unfenced park, where human settlement and activities were rapidly increasing. Drought, a frequent phenomenon in this part of the world, struck in the years 1970 to 1972 and an estimated 6 000 elephants died of starvation and heat stress, as many of the trees that had provided shade in the past had been felled by them. Elephants must drink regularly, so the herds were forced to remain within easy walking distance of water. This means they were largely restricted to the Tsavo and Galana rivers, and adjacent

Other fauna

The massive impact that the elephants had on the vegetation, causing the loss of extensive areas of bush and scrubland, benefited the grazing species. Grasses became more readily available, but the browsers had to cope with a diminishing resource.

Apart from large herds of buffalo, Tsavo is home to some of East Africa's most significant antelope populations. Those species that are best adapted to semi-arid conditions and periodic droughts are particularly well represented in Tsavo and most occur in substantial numbers. By far the largest protected population of the elegant lesser kudu – some 4 000 to 8 000 – inhabit the thickets and acacia country, with the majority occurring to the north of the Galana River. That strange long-legged and long-necked antelope, the gerenuk, or giraffe-necked gazelle, is common, with more than 10 000 known to occur within the national parks. Almost 30 000 live in the Tsavo ecosystem, constituting more than a third of Africa's entire population. We have spent many hours observing the gerenuk in Tsavo and other East African parks and it never ceases to amaze us how they have evolved to browse at a level that reduces feeding competition with other species. Apart from their long limbs and elongated neck, they are able to stand perfectly erect on the hind legs to feed on newly sprouted leaves, shoots and flowers, principally from *Acacia* species. This height advantage has been taken one stage further as they use their front legs to pull down branches that are out of reach of the mouth. Only one other antelope has evolved to feed in this way, the rare dibatag which is restricted to the northern Horn of Africa.

The fringe-eared oryx, one of three races of the species *Oryx gazella*, may number as many as 15 000, although figures quoted vary widely. This race is only found in a small area of adjacent south-east Kenya and north-eastern Tanzania, and is characterised by long, black hair tufts on the tips of the ears. Unlike many other species in Tsavo, herds of oryx tend to

Above: *Gerenuk, or giraffe-necked antelope, with their long legs and elongated neck are able to easily reach tender shoots and leaves of their favoured food trees.*

Above: Female black-faced sand-grouse lack the distinctive facial markings of the male. This is one of three sandgrouse species occurring in the Tsavo region.
Below: Lions occur throughout Tsavo but they are most frequently heard and seen in the east.
Below right: Although outside their natural range, a number of Grevy's zebra (Equus grevyi) were introduced to the area north of the Galana River several years ago.
Bottom right: Large sycamore fig trees (Ficus sycamorus) are scattered throughout Tsavo where they are mainly associated with the watercourses.

keep their distance and are usually difficult to approach. North of the Galana there are large numbers of kongoni, or Coke's hartebeest, and the majority of the 10 000 Grant's gazelles are found in this area. There are also substantial numbers of impala, eland, waterbuck and the tiny, large-eyed Kirk's dik-dik.

One of Africa's most endangered antelope, the hirola or Hunter's hartebeest, whose natural range is far to the north of Tsavo, in a limited area close to the Somali border, has been translocated to the area north of the Galana River. In its natural range it has undergone catastrophic declines because of drought, hunting and competition for grazing with ever-increasing numbers of domestic livestock. In just 20 years the hirola population dropped from an estimated 14 000 animals to a tragic 350, and it was felt that the only way to save the species from extinction was to move some survivors into a national park with similar habitat, hence Tsavo. The first translocation took place in the 1960s. Monitoring at the release site was minimal, but it is believed that there may now be about 60 individuals. In 1996 14 hirolas were captured and translocated but a court action prevented the Kenya Wildlife Service from capturing more, so it is very possible that the survival of this unusual antelope will rest on the Tsavo population.

Because of Tsavo's arid nature hippos are found only in the perennial rivers, Lake Jipe and the amazing Mzima Springs, and in relatively low numbers because of the limitations of adequate grazing. In the crystal-clear pools

at the springs one is able to observe hippos underwater and a fascinating sight it is to sit on the bank and watch these barrel-bodied mammals strolling about on the pool bed. They are usually accompanied by a bevy of fish, in particular barbels, which feed on small animals disturbed by the large feet of the hippos, and by other species that relish their dung.

Although Mzima Springs, with good reason, attracts many tourists, many parts of the parks, particularly in the east, can be travelled for hours on end, day after day, with the only vehicle in sight being your own. As is our habit in dry, water-scarce conservation areas, we find a few picturesque locations and happily spend hours watching the daily parade. At the Kanderi Swamp, just a few kilometres from the Voi gate, large elephant herds are regular visitors, emerging onto the open grassed flats. Shall we ever forget the sight of a "macho" young bull charging at the swirling, synchronised swarming flocks of queleas coming to drink? Or sitting under a great spreading sycamore fig, with lions roaring far down the sandy bed of the Voi River, elephants breaking off branches and feeding just 100 m away, and the occasional youngster squealing in frustration?

It is not only the game animals that are the drawcards to Tsavo. There are more than 430 resident or migratory bird species in this fascinating corner of East Africa. A number of arid-area species reach their southernmost distributional limits here, saving the avid birder that impossible trip to Somalia.

TSAVO EAST AND TSAVO WEST NATIONAL PARKS

Travel and access: Lying astride the main Nairobi-Mombasa road, along which five of the nine park entrance gates are located, Tsavo is easily accessible. The main gate on the Nairobi side, Mtito Andei, is just over 230 km from that city, and gives entry to Tsavo West. The main access gate to Tsavo East is just outside the village of Voi, which lies a further 97 km from the Mtito gate. From Mombasa to Voi is about 150 km. This main trunk road is tarred but there are some badly potholed sections, and stretches where the shoulder drops as much as 40 cm below the road level; this is also a busy route with heavy lorry traffic. Nevertheless this is by far the best access road to the park. From Malindi the most direct access to Tsavo East is via the Sala gate (about 110 km) on the Galana River, but when we last travelled that route it was badly corrugated and potholed. However, we like this route, particularly towards the coast where you pass the northern fringe of the Arabuko-Sokoke Forest. The road (C103) linking Amboseli with Tsavo West is rough and at the time of writing it was advisable to enquire about the need for an armed policeman to accompany you – a result of some isolated incidents of banditry. Check the latest situation. The road that links the Maktau gate (TW) past the Taita Hills with Voi is shown as good tar on most maps; don't believe it!

Mobility: Although most guidebooks and brochures indicate that a saloon car is adequate to get around in, and minibuses with their high clearance are fairly plentiful in some sections of the parks, we feel that your mobility would be severely restricted in a standard vehicle. Quite a few of the internal tracks have high middle ridges, sand sections and bad corrugations. On our last visit, particularly on the Galana River road, several small bridges and culverts were in bad shape and a number of sections were washed out – and this was at the end of the dry season! Access to the area north of the Galana River is severely restricted but some safari companies are being allowed in on a strictly controlled basis. There are several airstrips, most associated with lodges and safari companies; the best course is to make enquiries at Kenya Wildlife Service HQ in Nairobi.

Accommodation: TSAVO EAST: Voi Safari Lodge (African Tours and Hotels); best to book through the Nairobi office; P.O. Voi; tel. 0147-2121. It is upmarket, 50 rooms, full catering, swimming pool, offers game drives, overlooks waterhole that attracts much game, particularly buffalo and elephant during dry season. Located a few kilometres from the Voi gate, and it sells petrol and diesel.

Aruba Lodge (booking through P.O. Box 14892, Nairobi; tel. 02-721382 – although usually not necessary) offers several run-down but clean and fully equipped cottages at reasonable rates. There is also a campsite and a shop selling basic food, beer and sodas.

The exclusive Tsavo Safari Camp (Kilimanjaro Safari Club, P.O. Box 30139, Nairobi; tel. 02-227136; fax 02-219982) is situated 25 km from Mtito Andei gate on east bank of Athi River; prior booking essential.

Just outside the Sala gate on the road to Malindi, the reasonably priced Crocodile Tented Camp (P.O. Box 500, Malindi; tel. 0123-20481) in a wooded location on the Galana River. Private camping is permitted outside the fence.

There are public campsites near the Voi gate, close to the Kanderi Swamp (Ndololo). This is our favourite, located on the usually dry Voi River under great spreading fig trees. Water is available (you pump it) and pit toilets. Baboons can be a nuisance. There are several semi-special campsites (for example Mukwaju in the south), so we suggest you enquire at park HQ about possibilities. There are also special campsites, for example Epiya Chapeya on the Galana, but safari companies seem to monopolise these; again enquire.

There are plans to allow selected operators a handful of comfortable double tents (en suite) and private mobile camps to offer drive or walk safaris north of the Galana River; contact Reachout Safaris (P.O. Box 48019, Nairobi; tel. 02-331191/220090; fax 02-216528), or consult your travel agent for any new options. East African Ornithological Safaris (P.O. Box 48019, Nairobi; tel. 02-331684/335935; fax 02-216528) operate a tented camp on the Tiva River and an itinerary can be adapted for clients' needs. North of Galana dry season only.

TSAVO WEST: Ngulia Lodge (AT & H, P.O. Box 30471, Nairobi; tel. 02-336858; fax 02-218109) is upmarket and has 52 en-suite rooms and conference facilities; excellent views and a waterhole that can be viewed from the bar and most rooms; offers game drives and swimming pool.

Kilaguni Lodge (same booking details as for Ngulia) has same facilities and also overlooks a well-frequented waterhole. On clear days views of Chyulu Hills to the north and Kilimanjaro to the west.

Kitani Lodge and Ngulia Safari Camp are two cheaper options, with a small number of cottages with bathrooms and equipped kitchens; both in nice settings. When we visited they were a bit rundown; we had heard variously that they were to be upgraded or closed down. We suggest you contact Let's Go Travel (P.O. Box 60342, Nairobi; tel. 02-340331/213033; fax 02-336890/214713) for the latest information.

The ultra upmarket Finch-Hatton's Safari Camp (P.O. Box 24423, Nairobi; tel. 02-882744) is located next to a clear spring-fed pool. Prior booking essential.

There are public campsites near camp HQ and at the Tsavo and Chyulu gates; they have pit toilets and water. It is usually possible to camp outside the other gates but there are no facilities. It is useful to check at the gate of entry where one may camp.

There are a few accommodation options outside the park, such as the Tsavo Inn in Mtito Andei (booking through Kilimanjaro Safari Club) and the Sagala View Lodge in Voi. Generally you should manage to find something in the park unless you arrive after sunset. Just outside the Voi gate, Lion Hill Camp (P.O. Box 298, Voi; tel. 0147-2647) has cottages and camping at reasonable rates.

Other facilities: There is an extensive network of roads and tracks (well over 2 000 km) but many are only suitable for 4x4 vehicles. Game drives can be arranged through the lodges; a short, escorted walking trail at Mzima Springs (no charge).

Climate: February-March and June-October are generally dry. Temperatures can be high but evenings may be cool.

Best times to visit: The dry season ensures greater concentration of game around permanent water; during wet months they tend to disperse. Wet season best for migrant birds but mobility greatly restricted on many roads and tracks, especially if you are not in a 4x4.

Main attractions: You may go for hours without seeing another vehicle, particularly in the east; great diversity of mammals and birds; ease of access; Mzima Springs with its crocodiles, hippos and fish (underwater viewing "tube"); Kenya's greatest elephant population.

Hazards: Potentially dangerous animals, particularly as campsites are not fenced; in the Ndololo campsite we had visits from elephant, buffalo, lion and leopard, with which we had no problems.

For further information: Contact the Kenya Wildlife Service HQ in Nairobi; for accommodation see the addresses given above.

①   *Mikumi National Park*
②   *Selous Game Reserve*
③   *Uzungwa Mountains National Park*

Chapter 14

THE GREAT SELOUS ECOSYSTEM

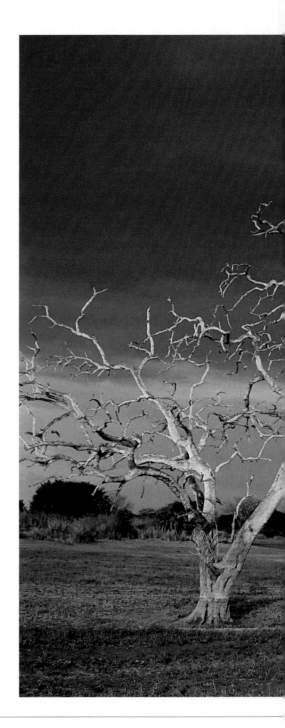

ARCADIAN VASTNESS

What would the world be, once bereft
Of wet and of wildness? Let them be left,
O let them be left, wildness and wet;
Long live the weeds and the wilderness yet.

Gerard Manley Hopkins, *Inversnaid*

The Rufiji is a river of legend and tales of daring, the grave of a gallant German battleship and the most important waterway passing through the Selous Game Reserve. It was here that Selous and Pretorius gunned down elephants for their ivory, where battles were fought in the War to End All Wars and where in the early decades of this century man-eating lions ruled supreme. As with many great rivers, one cannot help but wonder what this "old man river" has seen in its existence.

There are great groves of palm trees on the Rufiji floodplain, many with lost crowns – a stark reminder that all life is finite – and

cataracts and rapids in the waters that push their way to the mangrove-blanketed delta and eventually to the warm Indian Ocean. In the deeper pools of the river are giant pale pink vundu, sharp-toothed catfish, elephant-snout fish and their principal predator, the Nile crocodile.

Humans vacate the Selous as the rainy season draws close, the rivers overflow their banks and many game species withdraw to higher ground. At this time the reserve is at its best – without the disturbing influence of the naked ape! Nature takes its course when man flees the discomforts of the rains.

The Selous is a place of unequalled wildness in East Africa, its saviours being its great size and the tsetse fly. Perhaps the logo for the Worldwide Fund for Nature (WWF) within Africa should be the tsetse fly and not the giant panda? To many Selous is synonymous with the best wilderness area Africa has to offer, in large part thanks to its inaccessibility.

History

Little has been recorded about the area prior to 1900 but it is known that Arab slave and ivory traders passed through here, bringing

Above: *The* mikumi, *or borassus palm, is a common feature of the Selous ecosystem, particularly in association with the river courses.*
PHOTO: GETAWAY/D. BRISTOW

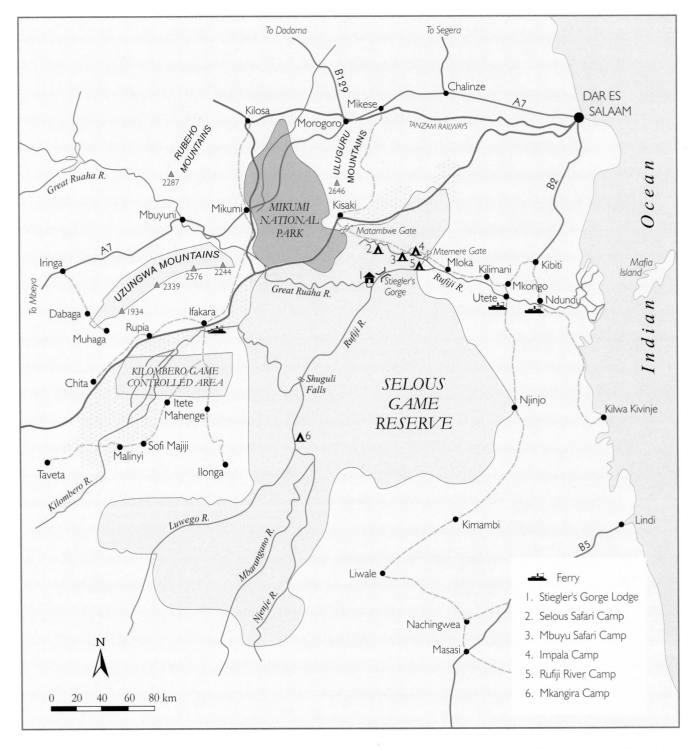

their goods from the interior to the then thriving port settlement of Kilwa. The village of Kisaki, lying close to the northern border of the Selous, was a transit station for the two major trading routes, and it is said that it was not unusual for more than 1 000 slaves, chained and yoked together and carrying ivory and other goods, to make up a single caravan. The movement of slaves and ivory was restricted to the dry season when rivers could be forded and seasonal swamps and pans were dry.

The earliest human records date back to between 1 500 and 2 000 years before present, with discoveries of steel-smelting kilns that had been operated by the ancestors of the Haya tribe. These people produced medium carbon steel in pre-heated, forced draught furnaces for weapon manufacture. This was far more advanced than anything achieved in Europe before the middle of the 19th century!

The first German interest in this part of Africa came when Carl Peters, founder of the Society for German Colonisation, arrived here in 1884, trading "protection treaties" with tribal chiefs for concessions to vast tracts of land. On 1 January 1891 Germany purchased from the Sultan of Zanzibar, for 200 000 British pounds, the entire coastline of Tanganyika. By 1914 the Germans controlled the entire territory we know today as Tanzania, from the Indian Ocean in the east to Lake Tanganyika in the west.

In 1905 the German colonial authorities started to demarcate wildlife reserves. In 1910 the German Kaiser gave part of what was to become the Selous to his wife as her hunting preserve on the occasion of her birthday, and it became known by the local people as *shamba la bibi* – "field of the woman". A large area, part of which was later to be incorporated into the Selous, in the vicinity of the Kibasira Swamp and between the Mgeta and Rufiji rivers, was proclaimed in 1912.

These good intentions were to exist only on paper, however: after the outbreak of the First World War wildlife conservation received no attention, as man shifted his energies to slaughtering his fellow man, and German East Africa was a grim place indeed at the end of this bloody conflict. The wildlife would have to wait! The man after whom the game reserve was named, Frederick Courteney Selous – skilled hunter and naturalist – was killed by a German sniper and was buried where he fell, close to the Beho Beho River in the north of this magnificent conservation area.

Under British colonial rule – to the victor the spoils – conflicts in the "paper parks" between wildlife and tribal agricultural interests grew as human populations expanded. It was left to an eccentric and most unusual Englishman to ensure the future of what was to become a greatly expanded game reserve. Constantine J. Phillip Ionides – referred to as *Iodine* by the colonials and *Bwana Nyoka* (Snake Man) by local peasants – was initially an officer in the King's African Rifles, then graduated to elephant poaching, followed by a spell as a safari guide. In September 1933 he was appointed as a game ranger whose primary responsibility was the shooting of man-eating lions and crop-raiding elephants. After the

Second World War he returned to the Selous area to hunt down lions that had been on a man-eating binge, with an estimated 1 000 men, women and children having been killed, and to bring under control severe ivory poaching. The poachers, with no one to hinder their activities during the war years, had gone on a slaughtering spree, but on the return of *Iodine* the tables were turned and it was the killers who were ruthlessly hunted down.

In 1945 Ionides started a campaign to have the authorities create a huge animal sanctuary that would ultimately increase the Selous to 20 times its original size. He was greatly aided in his endeavours by that tiny but highly effective conservationist, the tsetse fly, carrier of sleeping sickness, which caused a series of epidemics that prompted the authorities to institute the compulsory evacuation of all people from many thousands of square kilometres. This of course was not acceptable to the tribespeople, such as the Wangindo hunters and honey collectors and the Haya, who were to be removed from their traditional homeland, but they were given no choice. At the time of his retirement in 1955 Ionides, the "father" of the Selous, had by and large been able to see his conservation dream become a reality. After his death in 1968 his ashes were buried in a copper urn at the foot of Nandanga Mountain in the heart of the game reserve he worked so hard to create.

Geography

The Selous ecosystem comprises one of the world's largest conservation areas, and Africa's most extensive game reserve, encompassing

Below: Although heavily poached during the 1970s and 1980s, the elephant populations of the Selous are steadily increasing.

PHOTO: GETAWAY/D. BRISTOW

over 50 000 km²; Mikumi National Park on the reserve's northern fringe covers 3 230 km² and the recently gazetted 1 000 km² Uzungwa Mountains National Park adjoins it in the north-west. The total area of the ecosystem is more than 75 000 km² and incorporates the Kilombero Game Controlled Area on its western boundary.

The Selous is sometimes referred to as the place of sand rivers, at least in the dry season, although in the rains all streams pour their waters into the Rufiji, which in turn cuts its way to the Indian Ocean, exiting opposite Mafia Island. Larger rivers, such as the Rufiji and the Great Ruaha, flow throughout the year and provide daytime retreats for vast schools of hippos and one of Africa's largest crocodile populations. The Rufiji watershed is drained by a veritable lacework of rivers and streams: Beho Beho, Ulanga, Luhomberu, Madaba, Mawera, Lung'onyo, Namamba, Luwegu, Mbarangano and the Njenje, to name but a few. During the rainy season many of the rivers spill over their banks, turning vast tracts of the reserve into seasonal swamps and making movement by vehicle impossible. There are small lakes: Tagalala, Siwando, Manze, Nzerakera and Mzizima, which hold water throughout the year, and there are crystal-clear springs that continuously bubble from the earth, with some such as Maji Moto producing heated water.

Much of the Selous consists of flat to gently undulating terrain but in the south, lying along a fault line, are precipitous red cliffs flanking the Luwegu River. Within the ecosystem in the south-west are the Ukumu Hills, in the north the Uluguru Mountains and in the north-west the zoologically rich Uzungwa Mountains, these now being partially protected as a national park. Although within the Selous Game Reserve altitudes range only from 100 m to 1 200 m above sea-level, the Uzungwa Mountains rise to more than 2 800 m, with the highest peaks being Nyumbenito and Luhombero.

Flora

More than 60% of this magnificent wilderness is bedecked with miombo woodland, the vegetation type that extends in a broad and colourful cummerbund across central Africa, from the Atlantic in the west to the shores lapped by the Indian Ocean in the east. This woodland is dominated by *Brachystegia* and *Combretum* trees, and is characterised by deciduous and semi-deciduous trees. There are also areas of more open woodland and grassland, with *Terminalia spinosa* being the most abundant tree, riparian forest and great stands of *mikumi* or borassus palms.

In the Uzungwa Mountains there are extensive areas of montane forest but outside the national park they are in rapid retreat as a result of tree cutting by local people.

Fauna

The Selous ecosystem was once home to more than 130 000 elephants which undertook distinct dry and wet season movements. By 1986 they had been reduced to 55 000, and today that number has been slashed to around 30 000 – still a considerable number. Approximately 100 000 elephants were slaughtered for their tusks during the 1970s and 1980s when East Africa saw its pachyderms reduced by more than two thirds. The Selous has few usable roads and movement is virtually impossible during the rains, but during the "years of the killers" access was aided, unwittingly, by huge international companies, such as South African-based Anglo-American Corporation, which slashed networks of roads through the miombo while prospecting for oil and minerals.

While on the topic of elephants, this is one of our favourite quotes about this majestic beast, attributed to the explorer Baker, of Nile exploration fame:

> *Being charged by an elephant is a new sensation – very absorbing for the time – and would be an excellent relaxation once a week for over-worked men in high office.*

Unfortunately the elephant had no answer for, or defence against, the modern firearms wielded by the poachers supplying the international demand for the white gold. After the international ivory trading ban was put in place, elephant poaching virtually disappeared in the area of the Selous and the population has begun to grow steadily.

However, the state of the black rhino population is an unmitigated disaster. From an estimated 5 000 individuals (no accurate count was ever undertaken) in the 1970s within the ecosystem, today it is doubtful that more than

Above: It is believed that as many as 10 000 sable antelope live in the Selous, Africa's largest population.

20 survive and even that tends towards the optimistic. Within this vast wilderness area effective protection for the few remaining rhinos is almost impossible to provide and if left to their own devices the rhinos will disappear from this magnificent wilderness. It is generally believed that the only way to save East Africa's rhinos is to collect them in small, fenced sanctuaries that can be cost-effectively patrolled. This is already the trend in Kenya, with such highly guarded locations as Nakuru and Solio.

Poaching of other species has taken place, particularly in the north and east of the reserve, but on a much more limited scale. Many species occur in abundance, with an estimated 150 000 buffaloes, perhaps as many as 20 000 hippos, 10 000 common eland, 3 000 greater kudu, 5 000-12 000 common waterbuck, more than 1 000 bohor reedbuck and perhaps as many as 10 000 sable antelope, the largest single protected population. There are two races of wildebeest in the Selous, totalling some 80 000 animals: in the south the Nyasa or Johnston's with its characteristic white facial chevron and in the north the black-bearded form, in contrast to the white-bearded form found in northern Tanzania. The Selous has the largest population of Lichtenstein's hartebeest but there is some doubt as to the actual total as a result of poaching. It is possibly as high as 20 000, which is about one third of the entire population.

Apart from the impact that poaching may have had, there is the distinct possibility that organised safari hunting is having an effect on prime adult males of trophy species. The Selous, being a game reserve as opposed to a national park, has trophy hunting as its single most important source of revenue, as a lack of infrastructure precludes any major flow of tourists. Within the reserve there are 46 large hunting concessions and in at least some, large trophy heads are now said to be difficult to locate. The problem is to balance the game populations to prevent the removal of the best breeding animals while ensuring that high-paying foreign clients get what they come for – trophies.

The large numbers of game are of course well attended by an abundance of predators. The number of lions is substantial but uncounted; it could well be in the low thousands. Leopards occur throughout but cheetah are rare. There is growing evidence that the Selous ecosystem probably protects the largest remaining population of the threatened wild dog. One recent estimate of this superpredator's numbers within the Selous-Mikumi ecosystem puts the total at approximately 1 000; if this is correct between 20% and 50% of the entire wild dog population is found here. The reason for the differing percentages is that estimates of the entire population size range from 2 000 to 5 000 surviving individuals. That other great Tanzanian conservation area, the Serengeti, has lost almost its entire wild dog population to disease in recent years, so the Selous is the "painted dog's" last hope in that country.

Top: *Large numbers of hippo occur in the Rufiji River and its tributaries within the Selous Game Reserve.*
PHOTO: GETAWAY/D. BRISTOW

Above: *Buffalo occur throughout the Selous ecosystem and in parts form herds several hundred strong.*
PHOTO: GETAWAY/D. BRISTOW

S P E C I E S   T O   W A T C H   F O R

M A M M A L S

Elephant	*Loxodonta africana*	Wild dog	*Lycaon pictus*
Hippopotamus	*Hippopotamus amphibius*	Side-striped jackal	*Canis adustus*
Buffalo	*Syncerus caffer*	Spotted hyaena	*Crocuta crocuta*
Sable antelope	*Hippotragus niger*	White-tailed mongoose	*Ichneumia albicauda*
Johnston's wildebeest	*Connochaetes taurinus johnstoni*	Dwarf mongoose	*Helogale parvula*
Lichtenstein's hartebeest	*Sigmoceros (Alcelaphus) lichtensteini*	Sanje crested mangabey	*Cercocebus galeritus sanjei*
Bohor reedbuck	*Redunca redunca*	Iringa red colobus	*Procolobus gordonorum*
Suni	*Neotragus moschatus*	Giant elephant shrew	*Rhynchocyon cirnei*
Sharpe's grysbok	*Raphicerus sharpei*	Yellow-winged bat	*Lavia frons*
Lion	*Panthera leo*	Striped bush-squirrel	*Funisciurus flavivittis*
Leopard	*Panthera pardus*	Lord Derby's flying squirrel	*Anomalurus derbianus*

B I R D S

White-faced whistling duck	*Dendrocygna viduata*	Fiery-necked nightjar	*Caprimulgus pectoralis*
African black duck	*Anas sparsa*	White-eared barbet	*Stactolaema leucotis*
African marsh-harrier	*Circus ranivorus*	African broadbill	*Smithornis capensis*
Crowned eagle	*Stephanoaetus coronatus*	Eastern bearded scrub-robin	*Cercotrichas quadrivirgata*
Dickinson's kestrel	*Falco dickinsoni*	Swynnerton's robin	*Swynnertonia swynnertoni*
Udzungwa partridge	*Xenoperdix udzungwensis*	Moustached warbler	*Melocichla mentalis*
Crested guineafowl	*Guttera pucherani*	Common camaroptera	*Camaroptera brachyura*
White-headed lapwing	*Vanellus albiceps*	East coast batis	*Batis soror*
Blue-spotted wood dove	*Turtur afer*	White helmetshrike	*Prionops plumata*
Brown-necked parrot	*Poicephalus robustus*	Spectacled weaver	*Ploceus ocularis*
Green turaco	*Tauraco persa*	Orange-winged pytilia	*Pytilia afra*
Barred long-tailed cuckoo	*Cercococcyx montanus*	Yellow-fronted serin	*Serinus mozambicus*
Pel's fishing owl	*Scotopelia peli*		

Above: *Newly hatched Mozambique spitting cobras (Naja mossambica); this snake only occurs marginally in the southern part of the region.*

Mikumi National Park

For the ordinary visitor the most accessible part of the Selous ecosystem is the Mikumi National Park which lies at its northernmost point. Only a small section has been developed, the remainder being wilderness. The park comprises 3 230 km². It is dominated by the floodplain of the Mkata River and links with the Selous Game Reserve at the Great Ruaha River.

Mikumi is the Kiswahili name for the borassus palm *Borassus flabellifer* which is particularly abundant along the river courses throughout the ecosystem. Stanley, the journalist-explorer who seems to have cropped up all over East Africa during the 19ᵗʰ century, crossed the Mkata plain in 1872 and commented on its abundance of wildlife, and this remained true until 1951, when construction started on the Morogoro-Iringa road. This made access to the area much easier and by 1954 the wildlife of Mikumi had been greatly depleted. It was realised that to be saved the area had to be proclaimed as a national park, and this was done in 1964. Game numbers have increased steadily since that time.

Uzungwa Mountains National Park

The other national park within the ecosystem, Uzungwa Mountains, is difficult of access and mobility is restricted to walking. It is still poorly known botanically and zoologically, but nevertheless numerous species have been identified as endemic to its forests and montane grasslands. These include, amazingly, two monkeys, the Sanje crested mangabey *Cercocebus galeritus sanjei* – believed by many to be a full species – and the Iringa red colobus *Procolobus gordonorum*. The total population of the mangabey, only discovered in 1981, is estimated to be less than 3 000 strong and the colobus numbers no more than 500 individuals.

Within the Selous ecosystem almost 500 species of bird have been recorded but it is the forests of the Uzungwa that shelter most of its endemics, including the recently discovered rufous-winged sunbird *Nectarinia rufipennis* and the Uzungwa partridge *Xenoperdix udzungwensis*. There are also chameleons, frogs, butterflies, moths and beetles found nowhere else but in the Uzungwas.

SELOUS GAME RESERVE

Travel and access: Most visitors to the Selous, both tourists and sport hunters, are flown in light aircraft to the airstrips near the principal safari camps, where they are picked up by camp staff. Some visitors come by train on the Tanzam railway, alighting at Fuga – ensure that you have arranged a pick-up in advance. If you are coming overland a 4x4 vehicle is essential; expect generally bad roads; access and mobility during the rains is difficult to non-existent. There are only two road possibilities into the Selous: access into the far northern sector (some 350 km from Dar es Salaam to Matambwe gate) passes through the dramatic scenery of the Uluguru Mountains. Just before the town of Morogoro (to the east of Mikumi National Park), take the murram (dirt) road south-east to Msumbisi, then south to Matombo, Mvuha, Dutumi and Kisaki. You then cross the Tanzam railway line and it is a short distance to the gate. Before you undertake this journey we suggest you check the state of the long stretch of dirt road, particularly over the mountains. The alternative entrance route runs south from Dar es Salaam to Kibiti, according to some maps on good tar, but be assured you will encounter numerous potholes and corrugations, as well as the remnants of tarred stretches. The dirt stretch that runs to Mkongo and then along the north bank of the Rufiji River cannot be negotiated during the rainy season. Expect to spend 8–10 hours on this 250 km run!

Mobility: All tracks within the park require 4x4 vehicles and you must be totally self-sufficient. Entry during the rainy season should not even be considered! Walking safaris are arranged by several companies but always with an armed escort.

Accommodation: There are four upmarket luxury camps; most visitors arrive with prior bookings. Stieglers Safari Camp, located on the gorge of the same name on the Rufiji River, offers 10 double, self-contained chalets (about US $120 per person, full board if booked with safari). Stiegler's Safari Camp, P.O. Box 20066, Dar es Salaam; tel. 051-21849/29639/29631; fax 051-44783. For Beho Beho, Mbuyuni and Rufiji River camps book through the Oyster Bay Hotel, P.O. Box 2261, Dar es Salaam; tel. 051-68062; fax 051-68631.

Other facilities: Only those associated with the camps and safari companies; includes river rafting, boat trips, walking safaris, sport hunting (several companies have concessions here) and fishing.

Climate: The coolest months, between June and the end of October, are the most pleasant; January and February are very hot. Between February and the end of May, during peak rainy season, the camps are closed and in any case access and mobility are impossible.

Best times to visit: See under Climate.

Main attractions: Vast tracts of wilderness; great diversity of mammals, birds and reptiles; few visitors; small, personalised camps.

Hazards: No camp is fenced; potentially dangerous animals; tsetse flies; malaria.

For further information: See Useful addresses.

MIKUMI NATIONAL PARK

Travel and access: The main (tarred) Dar es Salaam-Morogoro-Iringa-Mbeya-Zambia road bisects the park between Morogoro and Iringa. This is 283 km from Dar. This road is generally in fair condition but heavy lorries have chewed up the tar in some highland sections; there are quite bad potholes and ridges from Iringa to the park.

Mobility: During the rainy months of November-December and March-May mobility can be severely limited, as the black-cotton soil turns rapidly into a quagmire. Although some tracks can be traversed by ordinary high-clearance vehicles during the dry season, others will require 4x4. If you intend to travel to the north of the park (Choga Wale) you must be accompanied by a ranger.

Accommodation: Mikumi Wildlife Lodge is located 3 km to the south of the public tarred road and the turn-off is clearly signposted. It has two suites and 50 double rooms, each en suite and air-conditioned; full dining facilities (Mikumi Wildlife Lodge, P.O. Box 14, Mikumi; tel. ask for Mikumi 27; otherwise Coastal Hotels, TTC Reservations Office, P.O. Box 2485, Dar es Salaam). The Mikumi Wildlife Camp has 13 self-contained bandas (huts); restaurant with bar; each banda can sleep 2-6 people.
    There are three public campsites (all close to park HQ), each with pit toilets, firewood but no water. Booking for accommodation and camping is not usually necessary.
    A basic hostel for large parties (up to 50 people), with toilet and kitchen facilities, is located at park HQ and should be booked through the warden.

Other facilities: There is no fuel available, the nearest source being Morogoro; basic repairs, such as fixing punctures, can be arranged at HQ; a small museum is located at the park entrance.

Climate: The short rains usually fall in November and December, with the longer rains extending from March to May. During the mid-year months be prepared for cool evenings, otherwise temperatures range from mild to hot.

Best times to visit: Mobility is greatly limited during the principal rainy months (March to May); game animals are most concentrated from about mid-August and into October when surface water is greatly reduced.

Main attractions: Easy access; abundance and diversity of game; many bird species present that do not occur in the northern parks.

Hazards: Camps are not fenced so be aware of the presence of potentially dangerous animals such as elephant, buffalo and lion. Malaria; tsetse flies in bushed areas can transmit sleeping sickness but incidence very low, although they do inflict a rather unpleasant bite.

For further information: See addresses under Accommodation above; Tanzania National Parks HQ, Arusha; The Warden, Mikumi National Park, P.O. Box 62, Mikumi.

①   *Ruaha National Park*
②   *Lake Rukwa and Uwanda Game Reserve*
③   *Katavi National Park*
④   *Ugalla Game Reserve*

Chapter 15

WESTERN TANZANIA

RUAHA ECOSYSTEM, THE KATAVI PLAINS, UWANDA AND UGALLA

Ex Africa semper aliquid novi
(There is always something new out of Africa)

Pliny the Elder

Towards the end of the dry season the old grass has burned and the first rains have provoked a flush of new green growth. It is here that the grazers are gathering, the reedbuck and topi, the resident groups of oribi, but they are skittish and do not allow a close approach. Ugalla, like most of Tanzania's game reserves, is divided into hunting concessions, and now at the end of the dry season the hunters have returned, but the game have not forgotten.

The trusting nature of the birds in this seasonal swampland leaves the biggest impression on us. Fish eagles perched above the last of the dry-season pools allow close approach and

continue their preening, open-billed storks, seemingly part of a dead tree, ignore our presence. A pair of saddle-billed storks continue their patient pursuit of frogs and other aquatic beasties, as if browsing the shelves and display cases of Harrod's or the delicatessen counters of Sainsbury's!

Mention the names Ruaha, Kisigo, Rungwa, Uwanda, Katavi, Ugalla, Moyowosi and Kigosi to almost anyone in the conservation fraternity and the chances are very good that nobody will have heard of their existence, let alone paid them a visit. These are some of East Africa's wildest and least known conserva-

tion areas and all are located in Tanzania's "wild west". We have visited four of these "far frontier" reserves; with the exception of the south-central entry to Ruaha and the Tunduma-Mpanda road that traverses Katavi National Park, access is extremely difficult. If one goes prepared for difficulty and hardship the travels are journeys into the "real Africa" that has sadly gone from most of the continent.

Because of the lack of comprehensive scientific knowledge or information on most of these conservation areas we will concentrate on the Ruaha ecosystem, the Katavi plains and the two that fascinate us most, Uwanda

Above: Large buffalo herd crossing the Ruaha River in Ruaha National Park. There are some 40 000 buffalo in the park.

PHOTO: GETAWAY/D. BRISTOW

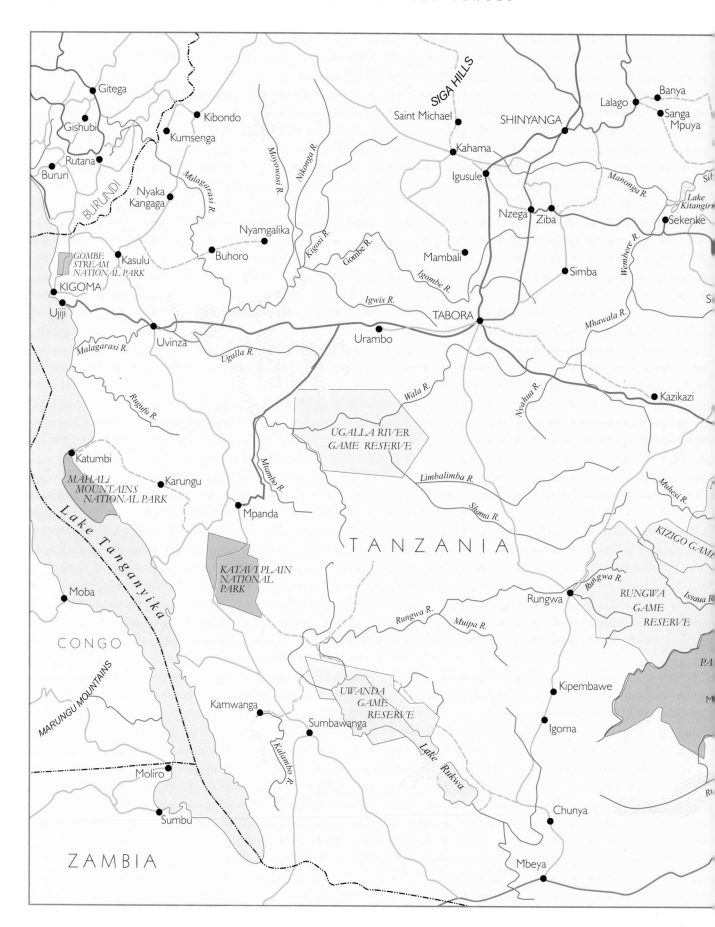

and Ugalla. In part the fascination lies in the fact that we succeeded in getting lost in both and movement is very difficult in the dry season and impossible in the wet! All owe their continued wildness to their remoteness, the fact that they are waterlogged for a large part of the year, roads are indifferent to non-existent (except on maps) and they are host to some of the highest densities of tsetse flies we have ever encountered. The flies follow a moving vehicle in clouds, attack exposed skin with relish and most importantly keep the cattle out. Anyone contemplating a trip to this region, with the exception of the tourist sector of Ruaha, must not take the journey lightly; this is very serious "going on safari" and the visitor must be able to handle every situation that may arise.

Throughout Tanzania the national parks, in theory, allow no natural resource harvesting but a variety of activities occur legally and illegally in the game reserves. There are sport hunting concessions in several of the western game reserves and honey-gatherers hang their hollowed log-section hives in trees in Ugalla. Although we heard of some illegal cattle grazing, there are few herds and these are concentrated in open grasslands away from major tsetse infestations. Cattle are only moved through the worst tsetse areas at night when these wonderful six-legged conservationists are not active. The boundaries of the game reserves are ill-defined and we encountered hardwood-cutters operating in Uwanda. We were amused at their attempts to sleep out of reach of prowling lions by constructing rickety platforms on stilts that certainly didn't give us the impression of being lion-proof. It reminded us of the story about the wolf and the three little pigs, and the house made from straw, "I'll huff and I'll puff and I'll blow your house down."

History

The prehistory of western Tanzania generally appears as a large blank in archaeological reports and texts, but it is hard for us to believe that the different Stone Ages at least are not represented here. We presume that because of the difficulty of access, distance from major centres and too much to document elsewhere (not to mention our friend the tsetse fly), most scientists and researchers have given the area a wide berth.

Above: *The umbrella-like mounds of this* Cubitermes *species serve to deflect the heavy rains from the core of the colony.* *Below:* *The grey heron (*Ardea cinerea) *is one of sixteen species of heron that are known to occur in western Tanzania.*

Today the human population, except in the vicinity of the few towns and villages, is at very low densities compared to many other parts of Africa and it seems likely that it was always so. The ancestors of the tribes of western Tanzania, referred to as Western Bantu, migrated from West Africa hundreds of years ago. In more recent years there have been periodic influxes of other tribal groupings, mainly from the Great Lakes region.

As far as is known the first "outsiders" to arrive in western Tanzania were Arab traders and slavers who penetrated the interior with their caravans at the beginning of the 19th century. The first Europeans to cross from the coast to Lake Tanganyika following the routes used by the slave caravans were Burton and Speke in 1858, in their search for the elusive source of the Nile River. Other early explorers to enter western Tanzania were David Livingstone from 1866, and then on several later occasions the American journalist Henry M. Stanley. By the end of the 19th century Germany had laid claim to German East Africa, the present-day Tanzania, and it was claimed as "victors' spoils" by the British at the end of the First World War.

The principal tribes in the region now are the Hehe, who are dominant in the south, the Nyamzwezi who live in the central area, and the Ha, who settled the swamps and woodlands between lakes Victoria and Tanganyika. Tanzania's most populous tribe, the Sukuma, live to the south of mighty Lake Victoria.

The Ruaha ecosystem

The Ruaha ecosystem extends over more than 25 600 km², incorporating the national park (12 950 km²) as well as the adjoining Rungwa, Kizigo and Muhesi game reserves. Most of the area consists of flat to undulating country that is interspersed with montane ridges, rocky outcroppings and two great river valleys that define the southern and northern boundaries of the national park. The Great Ruaha River, rising in the Poroto Mountains as the Mkoji and the Kimani, crosses the Usangu Flats and eventually winds through the south of the park, later to be joined by the northern Njombe River, and both contribute their flow to the Rufiji before it passes through the Selous. The Njombe rises in the Mbeya Highlands, with the Issaua River linking with it before it exits the park. The Rungwa River rises in the game reserve of the same name, eventually spilling its seasonal waters into Lake Rukwa to the west, encompassed in large part by the mysterious Uwanda Game Reserve. The name Ruaha is a corruption of the Hehe word for river, *luvaha*, with the local name of the river being *Lyambangari*. So the clever colonials, and Westerners today, used and use the name *Great River River* – a classic case of linguistic muddle!

Although the boundaries of Ruaha were only finalised in 1973, it has held national park status since 1964. Prior to this it was part of the Saba River Game Reserve, which was proclaimed in 1910 and became part of the Rungwa Game Reserve in 1946.

The great, gently undulating plain that dominates the park averages 1 000 m above sea-level, but rises to more than 1 700 m in the Datummbulwa Mountains in the south and to over 1 800 m in the Ikungu range to the west. Although this altitudinal difference is relatively small, it has a profound influence on rainfall, with more than 800 mm falling in the hills but only an average of 500 mm on the plains.

The "wild west" falls within that great swathe of woodland that bisects Africa and is known by the collective name of miombo, with *Brachystegia* trees dominating. Ruaha's (should we perhaps call it Lyambangari?) vegetation types can be broadly divided into two great blocs: in the east typical miombo and in the west *Commiphora*, "myrrh" tree and bush-dominated woodland, with areas of acacia trees and the delightfully named hairy drypetes *Drypetes gerrardii*. Of course this is an oversimplification, as there are expanses of treeless grassland, patches of evergreen and riparian forest, as well as reedbeds and grasses associated with the riverine floodplains. Some of the most obvious tree species are the

Below: A pair of mating grass frogs (Ptychadena sp.) – there are many suitable habitats for amphibians in western Tanzania and the diversity is great, although poorly known by the scientific world.
Bottom: Several species of freshwater terrapin occur in the rivers, marshes and lakes of western Tanzania, all in the genus Pelusios, and commonly called hinged terrapins because of the flap in the plastron that can be closed to protect the front legs and the head.

baobab, ana, *Combretum*, candelabra *Euphorbia candelabrum* and the distinctive sausage tree.

In 1973 it was estimated that some 60 000 elephants roamed the unfenced Ruaha ecosystem, but the uncontrolled ivory poaching that spread like a cancer during the 1970s and 1980s reduced this number to perhaps a tenth of its former strength. However, the latest estimate indicates that there are now probably 20 000 grey giants roaming the woodland, grassland and floodplains of Ruaha. Sadly, as in virtually all Tanzanian parks and reserves, the black rhino is but a memory; it is now believed unlikely that any survive in the western parks and reserves. The last confirmed sighting in Ruaha was in 1982.

Wildlife monitoring and counting are undertaken regularly only in the Ruaha ecosystem, but not even this vast area is a closed system and there is much movement out of it, particularly to the north-west. There are substantial numbers of buffalo (40 000), giraffe (more than 8 000), impala (about 18 000), common eland (over 6 000) and plains zebra (more than 30 000). Two ungulates reach the southern limits of their range here: the elegant Grant's gazelle and the thorn-thicket-loving lesser kudu. Both *Tandala mkubwa*, the greater kudu, and *Tandala ndogo*, the lesser kudu, occur here in the same habitat, and both are strong contenders for the title of Africa's most handsome spiral-horned antelope.

One of the antelope species most frequently sighted in the miombo woodlands is the Lichtenstein's hartebeest, with this area and the Selous ecosystem in the south-east of the country being this species' continental stronghold. Although numbers are fairly low in Ruaha, there are more than 10 000 Lichtenstein's hartebeest around the Uwanda-Lake Rukwa complex and several thousand in the vicinity of Katavi and Ugalla.

Other species that occur widely and commonly in the region include bushbuck, common duiker, defassa waterbuck, bohor reedbuck, southern reedbuck, roan, sable, oribi and *swala pala* or impala.

Topi occur here in substantial numbers, with several thousand around Lake Rukwa (Uwanda), Katavi and Ugalla, reaching their southernmost distributional range at Rukwa. Human encroachment and meat poaching are a problem in some areas, but around Lake Rukwa it is the level of the lake's waters that

strongly affects the strength of the topi population. When the water is high the most suitable topi habitat is inundated and may remain so for several years, forcing major declines – it is nice to know that not all negative impacts have to be placed at man's dirty doormat!

Uwanda Game Reserve

Uwanda Game Reserve, dominated by Lake Rukwa and the Mbizi Mountains in the west, is a difficult place to find and to get into! Most of the through roads marked boldly on maps either existed only in the past or the cartographer felt that without adding a few it would make his work incomplete, so to hell with the fact that they were not there! Tracks ended in dense reedbeds and marsh on Lake Rukwa's western shore, or faltered at the edge of sheer cliffs, and one becomes suspicious when one crosses the river at exactly the same spot three times in the space of a couple of hours. But the frustration and the tsetse flies were well worth the effort of getting there.

Although at the time of our visit Lake Rukwa was very full, with large tracts of floodplain under water, there have been times when it dried up completely, most notably in 1949 when large numbers of hippos, crocodiles and fish reportedly perished, with remnants surviving in adjoining

Above: Although nowhere common, roan antelope occur throughout the tsetse fly-infested miombo woodland of western Tanzania.
Below: Unusual neighbours at rest, a hamerkop (Scopus umbretta) and a terrapin (Pelusios sp.).

Above: *On our visit to the Ugalla Game Reserve we found a pair of fish eagles* (Haliaeetus vocifer) *at almost every reasonably sized pool.*

swamps and in pools along the Rungwa River. Lake Rukwa consists of a large northern section that is joined by a narrow channel and densely reeded swamp to a much smaller body of water in the south-east. Apart from extensive areas of short, seasonally flooded grassland, there are also considerable expanses of medium and long grassland, but *Brachystegia*-dominated miombo woodlands cover most of the area.

Unlike in Ruaha and Katavi the game animals here are skittish, in part because several hunting concessions operate here. Still, there are fair numbers of puku on the floodplains, and we saw sable, Lichtenstein's hartebeest and buffalo. Sitting in camp, after the tsetse flies have gone to rest up for the next day's assaults, with the sun shedding its final colours on the multi-hued leaves of the *Brachystegia* trees, lions and hyaenas calling – this is the Africa of old. It has been lost forever in the mass-tourism parks of Kenya, northern Tanzania and South Africa. Because of its lack of roads and tracks, and absolutely no tourist infrastructure, the only way to explore this area is on foot – but only if you are experienced in the ways of the wild, or take on a local guide.

SPECIES TO WATCH FOR

MAMMALS

Elephant	*Loxodonta africana*	Lion	*Panthera leo*
Buffalo	*Syncerus caffer*	Leopard	*Panthera pardus*
Giraffe	*Giraffa camelopardalis tippelkirchi*	Side-striped jackal	*Canis adustus*
Sable antelope	*Hippotragus niger*	African civet	*Civettictis civetta*
Roan antelope	*Hippotragus equinus*	Water mongoose	*Atilax paludinosus*
Topi	*Damaliscus lunatus jimela*	Warthog	*Phacochoerus africanus*
Lichtenstein's hartebeest	*Sigmoceros (Alcelaphus) lichtensteini*	Giant elephant shrew	*Rhynchocyon cirnei*
Defassa waterbuck	*Kobus ellipsiprymnus defassa*	Four-toed elephant shrew	*Petrodromus tetradactylus*
Puku	*Kobus vardoni*	Spectacled elephant shrew	*Elephantulus rufescens*
Bohor reedbuck	*Redunca redunca*	Yellow-winged bat	*Lavia frons*
Southern reedbuck	*Redunca arundinum*	Giant rat	*Cricetomys gambianus*
Greater kudu	*Tragelaphus strepsiceros*		

BIRDS

Dickinson's kestrel	*Falco dickinsoni*	Fischer's greenbul	*Phyllastrephus fischeri*
Long-crested eagle	*Lophaetus occipitalis*	White-tailed crested monarch	*Elminia albiventris*
Lizard buzzard	*Kaupifalco monogrammicus*	Grey-rumped swallow	*Pseudhirundo griseopyga*
Hildebrandt's francolin	*Francolinus hildebrandti*	Retz's helmetshrike	*Prionops retzii*
African skimmer	*Rhynchops flavirostris*	Sulphur-breasted bush-shrike	*Malaconotus sulfureopectus*
Black coucal	*Centropus grillii*	Rufous-bellied tit	*Parus rufiventris*
Bare-faced turaco	*Corythaixoides personata*	Scarlet-chested sunbird	*Nectarinia senegalensis*
Yellow-collared lovebird	*Agapornis personata*	Eastern golden weaver	*Ploceus subaureus*
Racket-tailed roller	*Coracias spatulata*	Bertram's weaver	*Ploceus bertrandi*
Pale-billed hornbill	*Tockus pallidirostris*	Pied mannikin	*Lonchura fringilloides*
Whyte's barbet	*Stactolaema whytii*	Variable indigobird	*Vidua funerea*

Katavi National Park

Just to the north of Lake Rukwa is the Katavi National Park, accorded this conservation status in 1974. Although its unfenced boundaries encompass some 2 250 km², the game herds and their predators move freely in and out, particularly to the densely wooded Mlala Hills to the east. The park is flat to gently undulating, with extensive areas covered by miombo and acacia woodlands. There are small lakes and marshlands fringed by reedbeds, and open grasslands on the floodplains of the Mfulsi and Katuma rivers.

Katavi is well known for its large buffalo herds and it is a memorable sight to see more than 500 of these great black wild cattle grazing on the Mfulsi floodplain, with small groups of elephant feeding on its fringes. Later a great dust- and smoke-enshrouded sun bids farewell to the day and the chirruping of the scops owls greets the night.

Until the mid-1970s many thousands of elephants ranged through the Rukwa corridor but today there are probably no more than 1 000 and their nasty experiences have made them timid and difficult to approach.

The Rukwa corridor, which encompasses Uwanda and Katavi, is known for two twists of nature: albino giraffes and unusually patterned plains zebras. These genetic variants were first recorded several decades ago and although they form only a small percentage of the overall populations there is no doubt that they stand out in a crowd.

Ugalla Game Reserve

By far our favourite of the "wild west" selection is Ugalla. It covers almost 5 000 km², with no recognised access roads; you simply have to find a way for yourself. Miombo woodland dominates but there are extensive grasslands, particularly along the floodplains of the Ugalla, Katum biki and Msima rivers and around the numerous natural waterholes. The reserve is surrounded by woodland and to the north-west by the Sagara Swamp, into which game moves freely, but again courtesy of the tsetse fly the cattle do not.

There are estimated to be more than 1 500 elephants but they are timid and it is obvious that poachers have been active here in the recent past, although we had the impression

Top: Crocodiles are relatively common in the rivers and lakes of the "wild west" of Tanzania.
PHOTO: GETAWAY/D. BRISTOW

Above: *In the miombo woodlands of western Tanzania there are many species of termite, including a number that construct their "castles of clay" in trees.*

Above: For us one of the most fascinating features of Tanzania's western woodlands is the extensive "termite cities".

with them, with their elongated, ever-twitching snouts, matchstick thin legs, tissue-thin ears and nocturnal activity (they are generally held to be diurnal in the handful of places they have been studied), were we not saddled with vehicle problems.

The most lasting impression we came away with, apart from the wonder of finding a genuinely wild area, was the high densities of fish eagles and open-billed storks and their lack of fear of us. In fact the bird life throughout the west is unsurpassed in Tanzania, with the meeting of bird faunas from the Congo Basin, the north-east, miombo and southern Africa. Checklists for many areas are incomplete, but we estimate that well over 600 species occur, either as residents or regular migrants. The problem is to gain access during the rains (nigh impossible) to observe the numerous species that arrive at this time.

The western Tanzanian conservation areas probably have a better chance of long-term survival than many other African parks, reserves and wild areas, in the main because of the tsetse flies, the large areas that are inundated during the rainy season and their distance from any major centre or tourist access point. For us this is truly wild Africa, although with a few exceptions such as buffalo there are no great game herds.

Not much has changed here since the Arab slave traders, Burton and Speke, Livingstone and Stanley made their way through this part of the Dark Continent. And long may it remain so!

that elephants were not uncommon between Ugalla and the road to the provincial town of Tabora to the north-east. After shearing a spring-shackle on a hidden tree stump in Ugalla, binding it with wire and swearing at the persistent tsetse flies, we drove through the night towards the town and numerous herds of elephant crossed the road in front of us.

Although it was good to see so many signs of elephant, it was their namesakes, the abundant four-toed elephant shrews, that sparked our imagination. We would have spent time

KATAVI NATIONAL PARK

Travel and access: The main road (fair dirt, tarred in a few sections but some areas badly potholed and corrugated) from Tunduma (near Zambian border) to Bukoba on Lake Victoria bisects the park. Sections of this road could become badly waterlogged during the rains and in any case you will not get into other conservation areas at this time; plan to explore only in the dry season. You pay no park entrance fees if you stick to the main road, and a lot of game can be seen in this way; should you wish to explore, however, you must first go to park HQ (close to the village of Mpanda).

Mobility: A 4x4 vehicle is essential off the main road; extensive areas of black-cotton soil indicate that mobility will be severely restricted during the rains. A guide can be hired from HQ if you prefer to be accompanied.

Accommodation: Nothing in the park but some basic lodgings in

Mpanda. There is a campsite with pit toilets but no water (obtain at HQ); at the time of writing one can also camp anywhere in the park.

Other facilities: Guides can be hired if required but this is not obligatory; network of rough tracks.

Climate: Distinct wet and dry seasons; July to October dry.

Best times to visit: Dry season only.

Main attractions: Well off the tourist circuit; large numbers of game animals; you are free to select your own campsite.

Hazards: Potentially dangerous animals; tsetse flies; malaria.

For further information: Tanzania National Parks HQ, Arusha.

RUAHA NATIONAL PARK

Travel and access: Ruaha lies 112 km from the town of Iringa (this is on the main tarred road – some potholes and rough sections – between Dar es Salaam and the Zambian border). The dirt road (forget about using it during the rainy season) runs due west from Iringa to Msembe park headquarters. You should allow about three hours for this journey.

Some people make prior arrangements for transport and fly in to Msembe, either through a safari company or the park authority.

Mobility: A 4x4 vehicle is required for full mobility but access and movement are very restricted during the rainy season. Walking safaris are conducted in the adjacent Rungwa Game Reserve for about 8 days (Mzombe River Wilderness Trek, Dorobo Tours and Safaris, P.O. Box 2534, Arusha; tel. Arusha 057-2300; fax 057-8336); about US $3 200.

Accommodation: Ruaha River Camp has small bandas (huts) and safari tents, open throughout the year (owned by Foxtrots Ltd); can be pre-booked but unlikely to be full. The same company has two satellite tented camps, Jongomeru junction and the Mwagusi Sand River. These two camps are open between July and December and must be booked in advance. For these three camps contact Valji and Alibhai Ltd, P.O. Box 786, Dar es Salaam; tel. 051-20522/26537 /37561; fax 051-37561.

Bandas (huts), 7 accommodating two people and 2 accommodating four or five people, are available near Msembe, inclusive of bed-ding, kitchen utensils and firewood; there is a dining area, toilets and showers. Also in the vicinity are campsites with pit toilets, but no water. A basic hostel at HQ, which can accommodate 32 people, can be booked for large groups; mattresses, kitchen facilities and water are provided. A public campsite with pit toilets (no water) is located near HQ. Special campsites, exclusive to a booking party, are available by prior arrangement with the warden.

Other facilities: Basic repairs, such as punctures, at HQ; the nearest fuel is available at Iringa. Dorobo Tours and Safaris (P.O. Box 2534, Arusha; tel. 057-2300; fax 057-8336) offer "portered" walking safaris in the Rungwa Game Reserve. We have not used them but we have heard favourable reports.

Climate: Principal rainfall months are December to April.

Best times to visit: Dry season, otherwise mobility very limited.

Main attractions: Wilderness atmosphere; good game numbers; few visitors; walking safaris in adjacent areas.

Hazards: Potentially dangerous animals; tsetse flies; malaria.

For further information: Other than those given above, Tanzania National Parks HQ, Arusha; Chief Park Warden, Ruaha National Park, P.O. Box 369, Iringa.

UGALLA GAME RESERVE

Travel and access: Getting into the reserve is not easy and calls for determination. A rough dirt road runs east from Mpanda (near Katavi), then north-east to Isimbira. There are numerous unsignposted turn-offs, so the best we can advise is to ask for the Isimbira road after travelling about 100 km from Mpanda. You will pass through the Nyanga controlled area. If you intend exploring the area we would suggest that you try to hire a local who knows the area well (there are a number of honey-gatherers), but you will have to have some knowledge of Swahili. There is another track that enters Ugalla from the north; travel south from Usoke (64 km west of Tabora) for about 70 km. We have not used this track and we know no one who has; ask locally.

Facilities: There are none. If you want real adventure this is it, but you must be fully equipped and be able to fix your vehicle should you have problems.

★ See entry on Ruaha National Park for information on climate, best time to visit and hazards.

UWANDA GAME RESERVE AND LAKE RUKWA

Travel and access: The area towards the eastern shore is crisscrossed with logging and hunting tracks (deep sand and mud in parts, numerous stream crossings) and you will need a compass, or preferably a GPS. A scenically magnificent road (the steep section recently tarred) drops to the northern marshes.

Access from Tunduma (near border crossing into Zambia) involves taking the fair gravel road (said to be all-weather) north-west to Sumbawanga (some sections were being tarred at the time of our visit). After about 20 km you come to the tiny settlement of Nkundi; turn right (road very rough to the pass) to the fishing village of Muse. You will have to enquire here about hiring someone to guide you (on foot), or persuade a fisherman to take you into the marshes by canoe.

Facilities: There are no facilities at all but this is really wild Africa at its best. There are large numbers of tsetse flies, particularly on the eastern shores. Make sure you have a good stock of fuel (closest Mbeya, Tunduma and Mpanda, be aware that they sometimes run out) and everything else you need, although you will be able to purchase some fruit and vegetables, as well as fresh fish.

★ See entry on Ruaha National Park for information on climate, best time to visit and hazards.

USEFUL ADDRESSES

SOUTH AFRICA
National Parks Board
PO Box 787, Pretoria 0001
Tel: (012) 343-1991 • Fax: (012) 343-0905

PO Box 2400, Roggebaai 8012
Tel: (021) 419-5365 • Fax: (021) 24-6211

KwaZulu-Natal
KwaZulu-Natal Conservation Service
PO Box 662, Pietermaritzburg 3200

Central Reservations Office
PO Box 1750, Pietermaritzburg 3200
Tel: (0331) 47-1981 • Fax: (0331) 47-1980

General information: Tel: (0331) 47-1961

Northern Cape
Northern Cape Province Nature Conservation Service
Private Bag X6102, Kimberley 8300
Tel: (0531) 2-2143 • Fax: (0531) 81-3530

NAMIBIA
Director of Tourism
Reservations
Private Bag X13267
Windhoek, Namibia
Tel: (061) 3-6975/3-3875/22-0241
Fax: (061) 22-9936

BOTSWANA
The Department of Wildlife and National Parks
PO Box 131, Gaborone, Botswana
Tel: 37-1405

PO Box 17, Kasane, Botswana
Tel: 65-0235

PO Box 11, Maun, Botswana
Tel: 66-0368

ZAMBIA
The National Parks and Wildlife Service
Post Bag 1, Chilanga, Zambia • Tel: 27-8366

The Zambia National Tourist Board
PO Box 30017, Lusaka, Zambia
Tel: 22-9087

ZIMBABWE
National Parks Central Booking Office
The Department of National Parks and Wildlife Management
PO Box 8151, Causeway, Harare, Zimbabwe
Tel: 70-6077

GOVERNMENT AND NON-GOVERNMENT ORGANISATIONS
Kenya
Association of Tour Operators Kenya (KATO)
PO Box 48461, Nairobi, Kenya
Fax: 254-2-218402

East African Wildlife Society Kenya
PO Box 20110, Hilton Hotel, Nairobi, Kenya

Survey of Kenya
PO Box 30046, Nairobi, Kenya
(Detailed maps of most of the National Parks and Reserves of Kenya are available here.)

Tourism Kenya
PO Box 54666, Nairobi, Kenya
Tel: 254-2-331030

Tanzania
National Parks Tanzania (TANAPA)
PO Box 3134, Arusha, Tanzania
Tel: 255-57-3181 ext 1386

Ngorongoro Conservation Area Authority Tanzania
PO Box 776, Arusha, Tanzania
Tel: 255-57-3339

Tourist Board Tanzania
PO Box 2485, Dar es Salaam, Tanzania
Tel: 255-51-46573/4 • Fax: 255-51-46780

Tourist Corporation Tanzania
PO Box 2485, Dar es Salaam, Tanzania
Tel: 255-51-27671/2/3

Wildlife Corporation Tanzania
PO Box 1144, Arusha, Tanzania
Tel: 255-57-3501/2 • Fax: 255-57-2828

Wildlife Division Tanzania
(all game reserves and controlled areas)
PO Box 1994, Dar es Salaam, Tanzania
Tel: 255-51-27271

Uganda
Department of Lands and Surveys
Entebbe
(Here you can try to buy detailed topographical maps of the country. The staff is very helpful but the stocks of available maps are very limited.)

East African Wildlife Society Uganda
PO Box 7422, Kampala, Uganda
Tel: 256-41-233061

Ministry of Tourism, Wildlife and Antiquities Uganda
PO Box 4241, Kampala, Uganda
Tel: 256-41-232971 • Fax: 256-41-241247

Mountain Clubs of Uganda
PO Box 4692, Kampala, Uganda

National Parks Uganda
PO Box 3530, Kampala, Uganda
Tel: 256-41-530158 • Fax: 256-41-530159

Tourist Board Uganda
PO Box 7211, Kampala, Uganda
Tel: 256-41-232971/2 • Fax: 256-41-241247

INDEX

*Page numbers in **bold** refer to main sections; page numbers in italics refer to information boxes.*